Romance Revisited

Romance Revisited

Edited by

Lynne Pearce and
Jackie Stacey

NEW YORK UNIVERSITY PRESS
New York and London

NEW YORK UNIVERSITY PRESS
Washington Square, New York

Library of Congress Cataloging-in-Publication Data
Romance revisited / edited by Lynne Pearce and Jackie Stacey.
p. cm.
Includes bibliographical references.
ISBN 0-8147-6630-7 (cloth : alk. paper). — ISBN 0-8147-6631-5 (pbk. : alk. paper)
1. Love stories, English — History and criticism. 2. Feminism and literature — Great Britain. 3. Man-woman relationships in literature. 4. Women and literature — Great Britain. 5. Lesbians in literature. I. Pearce, Lynne. II. Stacey, Jackie.
PR830.L69R66 1995
823'.08509 — dc20 95-18509
CIP

New York University Press books are printed on acid-free paper, and their binding materials are chosen for strength and durability.

Manufactured in the United States of America

10 9 8 7 6 5 4 3 2 1

For all those whose labours of love
contributed to the success of the conference
(the 'Romance Team') and, in particular,
for Liz Wilkinson.

Acknowledgements

We would like to take this opportunity to thank all the staff and students connected with Lancaster Women's Studies Centre who were involved with the *Romance Revisited* conference and to whom this book is dedicated. Special thanks are due to our Women's Studies secretary, Janet Hartley, who put in many hours of stressful work in the months leading up to the conference, and to Alison Pryce who helped hold the operation together during the last week. Without wishing to single out other members of our wonderfully committed 'team' of helpers whose hard work and exuberant visibility on the day undoubtedly contributed to the conference's success, we feel we must give special thanks to Josie Dolan whose struggle to organize a creche was a quest worthy of the most gruelling romance.

We would also like to thank Sally Davison at Lawrence and Wishart for her editorial guidance and all the contributors for their speed, efficiency and hard work. We are also deeply grateful to Hilary Hinds and Rowena Murray for their transformative influences. In particular we are indebted to Hilary for eagle-eyed scrutiny of the final stages of this manuscript. And finally, we would like to offer our heartfelt thanks to each other for making this particular 'working relationship' so enjoyable: here, at least, is one textual romance which has arrived at a satisfactory closure (publication).

Contents

NEGOTIATIONS: LOVE ACROSS THE TRACKS – INTERRACIAL ROMANCE

REFUSALS: RESISTING ROMANCE

Preface

This book has its origins in the *Romance Revisited* conference which was hosted by the Centre for Women's Studies at Lancaster University in March 1993, and was inspired by our shared conviction that it was time to put romance back on the feminist agenda. An interdisciplinary conference, we believed, would provide the ideal forum in which to re-evaluate feminism's relationship to an institution which, however problematic, still has a major impact on everyone's lives (feminists included!).

Our hunch that this was, indeed, the moment to reopen the debates around feminism and romance was proven right. Both the feminist academic community and the media (national and international) responded with overwhelming enthusiasm. While the interest of the feminist academic community demonstrated just how much recent work has been, either overtly or covertly, concerned with romantic discourse, the concomitant explosion of press interest took us somewhat by surprise. In the week preceding the conference we were besieged by newspaper, radio and television reporters all wanting to know where romance fitted into contemporary feminist debates (as signalled by the *Independent*'s headline, 'Feminists: Their True Story'). On this last point it is significant that, even after interviews in which we carefully stated our position as one of 'critical and sympathetic enquiry', the media remained on the whole stubbornly insistent upon a positive or negative feminist verdict on the subject of romance. We were thus simultaneously billed as part of the 'backlash against feminism' (women wanting to allow romance back into their lives after two decades of feminist disapproval) and as 'radical killjoys' out to rob women of their most basic pleasures! The reporter from the *Sunday Express*, for example, was utterly convinced that the whole point of the event was to *deplore* the fact that 'women still turned in their thousands to the suave, horse-riding heroes of paperbacks' (Kermode, 21.4.93).

Looking back, we see this media 'hysteria' as itself symptomatic of the combined fascination and anxiety with which romantic love is regarded by the public at large. While the explicit discussion of sex and sexual desire has become more and more audible in the past thirty years, (romantic) 'love' has somewhat disappeared from the discursive arena (or, at least, has not been redefined in line with the major changes taking place in sexual behaviour). In a year, then, which had just witnessed the official end of the nation's best-loved 'fairy-tale romance' (in the separation of Charles and Diana), the media looked to us to offer some explanation of what 'love' in the 1990s means: most importantly, whether or not it still exists.

While the nineteen chapters which comprise this volume are a clear testimony to the fact that, for feminists as well as for everyone else, romance most certainly still *does* exist, they also offer fresh insight into the questions of what love is and how, in contemporary culture, its 'scripts' are being radically challenged, fractured and transformed.

The Heart of the Matter: Feminists Revisit Romance

Jackie Stacey and Lynne Pearce

Despite the fact that the late twentieth-century has offered us many new possibilities for how we may conduct our interpersonal relationships, romance itself seems indestructible. While studies like Shere Hite's (Hite, 1987) reveal a dramatic increase in divorce, non-monogamy, couples living together outside of marriage, and other 'non-standard' relationships (including a noticeable increase in the number of gay and lesbian relationships), the trappings of 'classic romance' (love songs, white weddings, Valentine's day and so on) remain as commercially viable as ever. In terms of its cultural representation, too, the popularity of romance appears undiminished. In popular fiction, Hollywood cinema, television soap-opera, and the media in general, the appetite for romance is as gargantuan as ever. As Jeanette Winterson writes in *Oranges Are Not The Only Fruit* (1985): 'Romantic love has been diluted into paperback form and has sold thousands and millions of copies' (p. 170), the point being that its dilution and mass production has *not* brought about its destruction. Against all the odds (social, political, intellectual) the *desire* for romance has survived.

Feminism is, of course, one of the contemporary political and intellectual movements that might have been expected to bring about the end of romance, or at least radically to undermine its power. The fact that this has not happened, despite the opprobrium of earlier feminist writers like Simone de Beauvoir (1949), Kate Millett (1969),

Shulamith Firestone (1970), and Germaine Greer (1971), is one of the reasons that we have chosen to 'revisit' it here. Both the nineteen chapters which make up this book, and the conference from which they are derived, represent an enquiry into *why* romance retains such a hold in the postmodern world. Neither intellectual nor political scepticism seems to save anyone – feminists included – from succumbing to its snares. We may (as individuals, as communities, as nations) no longer *believe* in love, but we still fall for it.

Romance Revisited, we believe, goes some way to explaining why romance is unlikely to go away, at the same time confirming that this is a timely moment to move it back to the centre of the feminist agenda. For what this collection of essays reveals above all else is that romantic love, for all its persistence, *is changing*: indeed, that the continued success of romance as a cultural institution might be seen to depend, in large part, on its *ability to change*. To invoke the metaphor of the virus, it is its capacity for mutation which has enabled romance to survive.

So, how *does* romantic love, an emotional configuration that most of us experience in a hot confusion of sickness and delight, continue to do so well? The answer, and the one upon which the majority of the chapters which comprise this book seem to be predicated (despite their different disciplinary backgrounds), is that romance survives because of its *narrativity*. In the same way that romantic love may be thought of as a phenomenon which (as **Sue Vice** observes in her chapter) is 'always already written', so it is liable to perpetual *re-writing*; and it is its capacity for 're-scripting' that has enabled it to flourish at the same time that it has been transformed.

For feminist theorists like Stevi Jackson (see Chapter 1) it is, indeed, the fact that romantic love is a *discourse* that is the heart of the matter. Unconvinced by the attempts of scientists to explain love as either a biological or a psychological 'fact of life', she argues that its success depends precisely upon the fact that it is one of the most compelling discourses by which any one of us is inscribed; throughout the world there are cultures in which individuals are educated in the 'narratives of romance' from such an early age that there is little hope of immunity. While resisting the notion that this renders all of us the dupes of 'false consciousness' (several of the chapters in this collection detail the way in which individuals can, and have, gained a critical perspective on their conditioning), Jackson uses this thesis to explain our enduring fascination with (and enthralment by) romantic love.

Jackson's emphasis on the *textuality* of romantic love also relates to the work of feminist critics like Tania Modleski (1982) and Janice Radway (1984) who have attempted to show why popular romance – from Harlequin and Mills and Boon novels to television soap operas – continues to be so massively popular with women readers and viewers, and why it is consequently impossible to dismiss such activity as either inconsequential or morally and politically indefensible. Romance, these writers argue, offers women a place in which to explore their own gendered identities, social and emotional desires, and life-expectations. Radway, for example, argues that part of the function of romance reading is to secure an independent time/space for themselves from which to say 'no' to insistent family demands. Furthermore, she suggests that the fantasies of fulfilling relationships contained in romance fiction tell us important things about the construction of gender identity in patriarchal culture. As so many books and films have shown, desire for 'another' (taller, richer, braver, more experienced than ourselves – and not necessarily a man!) is often symptomatic of discontent with ourselves and our way of life, and a recognition of this can sometimes provide the catalyst for transformation and change. An engagement with the narratives of romance, in other words, facilitates the re-scripting of other areas of life.

In terms of feminist attempts to theorize romance, then, the work of Modleski and Radway in the 1980s signalled a radical departure from the earlier feminists (de Beauvoir, Millett, Firestone, Greer et al) who perceived it to be a monolithically pernicious and disabling ideology. These writers saw romantic love as a species of 'false-consciousness' which could, and should, be resisted: 'romanticism is a cultural tool of male power to keep women from knowing their ['real'] conditions' (Firestone, 1971: 139). While such exhortations disclaimed the material 'reality' of love (it was, like all ideologies, an expression of the 'imaginary relationship' between individuals and the world in which they live), however, they seriously underestimated the strength of its 'fiction'. And even whilst the vehemence of their challenge was matched by their optimistic enthusiasm for the possibility of moving beyond the possessive individualism of patriarchal romance, it was followed by something of a silence from those whose attempts at such 'alternative relationships' failed. Breaking this silence, what the work of Modleski and Radway revealed, and what Jackson and others have gone on to develop, is the extraordinary power and seduction of romantic discourse. This is not to say that it is a narrative that we cannot challenge or transform, but that attempts at wholesale rejection or refusal are unlikely to succeed. On top of this, as we shall see, cultural representations of romance can be figured as a more positive aspect of women's self-development and need not always be viewed so sceptically.

A new and more creative approach to the 'fictionality of romance' may therefore be seen as central to its appraisal in the feminist arena. It is significant that, after the many years of silence on the subject, our conference saw the majority of speakers – empirical researchers as well as textual critics – starting from this premise. What was striking, however, and what we feel will be one of the major contributions of this book, was the extent to which the traditional narratives of love are being re-written. As we go on to detail in the next section, romance today is clearly an institution under severe stress: a stress that is evident both in society itself as a consequence of the radical changes that have been taking place within interpersonal relations (see Hite, 1987), *and* in the feminist and post-structuralist theorizings that are causing cultural representations of romance (both contemporary and historical) to be re-read and re-figured. Attention to factors such as class, race and sexuality, for example, reveals not only how the structures of 'classic romance' are being radically transformed in the present, but also how they were present (but *unseen*) in the past.

This emphasis on the pervasive textuality of romance, its 'always already' written character, of course begs the question of whether the 'classic romance' – from which all the re-writings represented in this volume may be seen to deviate – ever existed. This is a moot point, and one that we address directly in the next section, but basically we believe that (in western cultures) romance is a discourse with a structural(ist) 'heart': it is known to us through a set of conventions, the re-writing of which has given rise to the transformations now taking place.

We should note at this point, too, that the 'textualization of romance' we have been describing here has impacted *across the disciplines* and is as much a feature of ethnographic studies of love relationships as of the representational analyses of romantic fiction. Indeed, it has been the pervasive emphasis on the narrativity/performance of romance that has enabled us to group the work of our contributors in a fully interdisclipinary manner, thus avoiding a rather uncreative carve-up of material according to disciplinary boundaries. This having been said, it is also the wide representation of disciplines contained in this volume that has enabled us to hypothesize the changing status of romance at the present time.

This introduction now proceeds with a section in which we detail the 'Narratives of Romance' in more detail, beginning with the hypothetical ingredients of 'classic romance', and moving on to a discussion of the different ways in which this script has been challenged and re-written in the following chapters across a range of cultural representations. This is followed by an account of some of the theories (such as structuralism and psychoanalysis) which have been employed by feminist theorists to explain both romantic love itself and its cultural representation. We conclude with a brief description of the chapters which follow and how they have been grouped. Readers should note, however, that we draw extensively upon the work of our contributors *throughout* this introduction and that they are identified in our bracketed references by the use of **bold type**.

The Narratives of Romance

The dictionary definition of romance as a 'love affair viewed as resembling ... a tale of romance' (see **Helen (charles)**) confirms that, in life as well as art, it is first and foremost a *narrative*. As has already been indicated, it is the narrativity of romance which crosses the common-sense boundaries of 'fact and fiction', 'representations and lived experience', and 'fantasy and reality'. In our relationships, as well as in our reading or viewing, romantic scenarios accord to cultural codes and conventions, whose changing (and enduring) patterns are explored throughout this volume. The typical trajectories outlined below extend beyond the Hollywood screen or the supermarket paperback and into the stories we tell ourselves (however much reformulated) about our past, present and future romantic relationships, or lack of them. As we noted at the beginning of this introduction, feminist analyses of romance have taken issue with the ways in which the classic romance narrative has constituted gender, power and sexual desire; but first we want to address the question: what characterises this classic romance narrative which has received such critical disclaim?

Typically, the story offers the potential of a heterosexual love union whose fulfilment is threatened by a series of barriers or problems. At the most general level, then, romance might be described as a *quest* for love; a quest for another about whom the subject has very definite fantasies, investments and beliefs. This quest involves a staging of desire whose fulfilment may be realised with attainment, or, just as likely, with its loss. To whichever closure the narrative tends, however, like all quests its structure requires the overcoming of obstacles: in the case of romance this means the conquest of barriers in the name of love, and perhaps, by extension, also in the name of truth, knowledge, justice or freedom.

In its fictional forms, which have produced such a never-ending source of romantic narratives, the classic trajectory might be typified in the following way (see Stacey, 1990). A 'first sighting' ignites the necessary 'chemistry' between two protagonists. A series of obstacles usually function as a barrier to their union: for example, geographical distance as in the films *Out of Africa* (1985) and *Sleepless in Seattle* (1993); class, national or racial difference, deeming the relationship unsuitable as in Charlotte Bronte's *Jane Eyre* (1847) or, more recently, the film *Mississippi Masala* (1991); inhibition or stubbornness of temperament as in Jane Austen's *Persuasion* (1818); a murky past as in du Maurier's *Rebecca* (1938, film adaptation 1940); the existence of another lover or spouse, as in David Lean's celebrated *Brief Encounter* (1945). Alternatively, an initial clash of personalities may itself be the narrative problem; indeed, mutual dislike with sufficient spark often prefigures the inevitable union of the couple, despite, or rather because of, protestations along the way. One standard Mills and Boon formula, for example, is precisely the taming of the male 'boor' and the heroine's eventual love for the civilised beast (Radway, 1984:134). The 'romantic comedies' of Hollywood have repeatedly reused the power of antipathy as a foil for the power of love: Doris Day and Rock Hudson's battle of the sexes in *Pillow Talk* (1959), for example, ends with recognition of their mutual attraction, as does Kenneth Branagh's adaptation of Shakespeare's *Much Ado About Nothing* (1993).

Whatever the barrier to the romantic union, the narrative question is 'will they or won't they', or, rather, *how* will they (see **Rosalynn Voaden**)? Pleasure in the 'progress of romance' lies in the solution to the narrative problems, and the affirmation of the desire to see 'love conquering all', thus confirming its transcendental power. In popular romantic fiction the underlying pattern, despite more superficial variations, very often moves from the heroine's initial loss of social identity (through force of external necessity) and an initial unpleasant encounter with an aristocratic or otherwise powerful man (whose behaviour is misunderstood) through a series of stages including 'hostility' and 'separation' towards 'reconciliation', and the transformation of the man into an emotional being with a heart who declares his love for the heroine, whose new social identity is in turn restored (Radway, 1984: 134).

One final favourite variant of the classic formula worth mentioning is the tragic one in which illness or death threatens the loss of the loved one, and in so doing intensifies the desire. From *Romeo and Juliet* (1594) to *Love Story* (1970) and *Shadowlands* (1994), love's connection to loss and death has a long history. In these tragic scenarios, the pleasure lies in the heightened value of love in the light of its loss. Indeed many classic romances (for example, *Wuthering Heights* (1847) and Puccini's opera *La Bohème* (1895)) tell the story of lost loves: of sacrifice and of suffering.

This raises the interesting question of whether 'true romance' is most often affiliated with comedy (in the generic sense of a narrative with a 'happy ending') or tragedy (see **Gabriele Griffin**, this volume). The fate of romantic heroes and heroines has been of particular interest to feminists who have baulked at the frequent sacrifice of the heroines for the benefit of the heroic status of male characters (as in *Love Story, Rebecca, La Bohème*). Indeed, this 'sexual division of suffering' is investigated in Sally Potter's experimental film *Thriller* (1979) in which the heroine of *La Bohème* returns to life and asks: why is it that the romantic heroines must suffer, if not die, for the tragic heroes to achieve their aspirations to universal transcendence? Furthermore, in many representations, it is taboo for women to try to usurp such heroic status: the majority of heroines in 'non-standard' sexual relationships (i.e. not white or heterosexual) have been similarly doomed. In the majority of lesbian romances in Hollywood cinema, for example, the heroines end up dead, depressed, or lonely and rejected: whatever their punishment, it is usually connected to their 'deviant desires'.

The attainment of 'heroic status' on the part of the male characters relates to another key ingredient common to all these romantic trajectories: that is their power of *transformation* vis-à-vis both male *and* female characters. This process of transformation may take several forms: the bringing to light of something already present (Rochester's love and tenderness for Jane in *Jane Eyre*, for example); the emergence of something entirely new (*Calamity Jane* (1953) in which the protagonist becomes a lady instead of a tomboy); or the taking on of a characteristic of the new partner (as in *Strictly Ballroom* (1992)). The possibility of becoming 'someone else' through a romantic relationship is most certainly one of the most interesting and positive aspects of the process, and a powerful ingredient in its appeal. This transformative promise holds out possibilities of change, progress and escape, which the romance facilitates through its power to make anything seem possible and to enable us to feel we can overcome all adversities. Such possibilities are often figured through both a literal and a metaphorical journey (to a new self); hence travel, relocation and movement have been central to such romantic trajectories: in the film *Now Voyager* (1942), for example, Charlotte's journey has this dual function, and furthermore, locates the 'union' of the couple in 'another culture' (in this case, Brazil), typically one which is associated with a more 'passionate' temperament. Similarly, in E.M. Forster's 'Italian novels', the protagonists' journey to the exotic 'South' initiates a romantic and sexual awakening. In this way, romance offers its subjects the possibility of a new 'becoming': through the encounter/fusion of self and other, a new self might be imagined.

So, what of resolution in these romantic scenarios? What counts as the classic satisfactory closure to a romance narrative? If romance is a quest for love, does it end once it has been found, once it has been secured, or once it has been lost or destroyed (see **Rosalyn Voaden**)? Thus, we might ask: is romance a prelude to a first meeting, to a sexual encounter, to a relationship, to marriage (or an equivalent commitment) or, indeed, to divorce (or separation)? The fact that even within classic romance texts there is considerable variation on this point links backs to the question of whether romance is essentially a 'comic' or a 'tragic' genre: is a happy ending a required or expected component?

One of the things that has struck us most powerfully in editing the chapters which comprise this volume is this variation in the *duration* of, and boundaries around, romance. Neither for those working with more empirical data nor those working with textual representations was there any consensus on what constituted the 'life-cycle' of romance. While Stevi Jackson makes the persuasive point that what we generally understand by 'romantic love' is very different to the 'love' associated with long term relationships (i.e. it is centred on the moment of Barthes's 'ravissement' or 'falling in love' rather than the 'sequel'), other contributors have researched romance within the context of long-term relationships (see **Jean Duncombe and Dennis Marsden; Judy Giles; Wendy Langford**); while for others again 'romance' may mean a one-night stand in which sexual gratification (the protracted climax of 'classic romance') is simultaneous with the moment of 'ravissement' (see **Inge Blackman; Helen (charles); Gabriele Griffin**).

Vis-à-vis this last point, it is interesting to observe recent changes in romantic trajectories (even within the formulaic world of popular fiction and film), where the obstacles traditionally associated with the 'quest' for resolution now often occur *after* the relationship has been consummated. In these narratives, the quest is to *secure* or win back what has already been achieved.

This recognition of variations and 'deviations', even *within* the narratives of 'classic romance', leads us on to a consideration of the many and various ways in which the typical trajectory is challenged by the contributors to this volume. For these chapters demonstrate not only that the meaning of romance is culturally and historically specific (see **Stevi Jackson**), but also that its formation varies enormously *within* one culture, and *within* one historical moment. Ultimately, of course, such variations work to undermine the stability of the category of romance itself. Indeed, we might find ourselves asking: is romance a discrete category at all? Does it contain the same characteristics when it shapes scientific trajectories of enquiry (see **Sarah Franklin**) as when it produces stories of imagined aristocratic heritage (see **Steph Lawler**)? What is it that unites such diverse investigations as Valentine's Day messages in *The Guardian* (**Wendy Langford**), science fiction (**Jenny Wolmark**) and feelings about a city (**Felly Nkweto Simmonds**)? Is the principle of narrativization which connects these articulations of romantic discourse resilient enough to embrace such diversity, or should we acknowledge that there is no shared principle? In an attempt to address these questions we will now suggest some of the different ways in which the following chapters challenge the classic trajectories of romance.

Despite the fact that classic romances are centred on heterosexual relationships in which the male and female partners enact very clearly delineated roles, Western culture continues to naturalise and essentialize such conventions and thus make invisible the *gendering* of those roles and the power dynamics involved. Stevi Jackson makes the point that romance is experienced very differently by men and by women, and this is confirmed in the ethnographic research conducted by Jean Duncombe and Dennis Marsden into long-term love relationships. Interviews with these couples confirm that 'romantic discourse' is 'accessed' differently by men and women, and that consequently they are liable to produce/enact different (and often incompatible) narrative scripts. Extending Sharon Thompson's (1989) contrasting of the masculine 'sexual event' with the feminine 'romantic trajectory', this research suggests, for example, that men are less likely to participate in the 'staging' of romance (predicated on narratives of courtship), despite the fact that 'active pursuit' is ascribed to them in classic romance (see **Joan Forbes** and **Rosalynn Voaden**); and that for the majority of men *all* romantic behaviour (characterized variously as passion, affection, intimacy) ends with sexual conquest and/or marriage.

In contrast (and although few of them secure it!), most women believe that the 'sequel' (Barthes, 1977) should be part of an ongoing (romantic) story. A similar message is emerging in Wendy Langford's work on heterosexual love relationships, and is also implicit in her analysis of the role of 'alter-personalities' in her chapter in this collection. As exemplified in Valentine's Day messages, couples often adopt cute, asexual, non-human identities for themselves (such as 'Snuglet Puglet') as a way of sustaining an intimate relationship once the romance narrative has had its day and the couple enter a long-term relationship. Langford's research also reveals the way in which the narratives of romance frequently conceal/detract from the unequal power-relations which exist between men and women in the public sphere and how, after courtship is over, the prevailing status quo will frequently reassert itself (Langford, forthcoming).

The gendering of romance raises important questions about the specificity of 'the romantic quest': to what extent is it a feminine form, and how does it overlap, or get refigured, within the more traditionally masculine genres? Two chapters in this collection address these questions in relation to the discourses of science and science fiction: Sarah Franklin relocates the debates about the gendered conventions of romance within an analysis of the new forms of pursuit of knowledge and scientific discovery. Similarly, Jenny Wolmark offers an investigation of the postmodern romances of science fiction writing. Both chapters, though in very different ways, highlight the limits of simple ascriptions of a gender dichotomy to the meanings of romance, as well as illustrating the pervasiveness of romantic codes beyond their usual generic associations.

Most readers will doubtless already have reflected on the heterosexism of 'classic romance'. Within lesbian criticism and artistic production (contemporary film and literature in particular), this prejudice has given rise to some inspired attempts to 're-write' the romance narrative. Some feminist critics, however, have argued that many writers and directors have not gone far enough in liberating their (lesbian) heroines from heterosexual plots, and that tragic endings (relationships curtailed by separation or death) have been all too prevalent: such fates are not only characteristic of classic films such as *The Children's Hour* (1961), but also of those more recent lesbian films such as *Another Way* (1982), *Lianna* (1982) or *Personal Best* (1982) (see Stacey, 1995, forthcoming). We are fortunate, in this book, however, to have a reading of a recent feminist film which challenges the trajectory of the heterosexual romance (and the inevitable oedipality of the Freudian formulation) in a complex range of ways. Lizzie Thynne's analysis of *Anne Trister* employs Irigaray's work on mother-daughter relationships to explore the ways in which the film reworks the classic Freudian narrative trajectory to offer a positive treatment of a lesbian love-story, resisting tragic closure (indeed, resisting closure altogether). Similarly, Diana Collecott's chapter on the romance between H.D. and Bryher shows how the kiss, with which Bryher's *Two Selves* ends, replaces the usual conventions of narrative closure with an explosive 'threshold' moment.

The way in which different sexual practices put pressure on the traditional romance plot is also explored in Gabriele Griffin's chapter on 'lesbian erotica'. Griffin offers an analysis of the way in which safer-sex discourse is (or is not) 're-scripting' erotic writing and offering a profound challenge to the conventional narratives of romance. Griffin's chapter, like those of Inge Blackman and Helen (charles), also confounds the more conventional romance narratives by focusing on romantic scenarios in which romance and the 'erotic' (traditionally separated into feminine and masculine preserves respectively – men are concerned with sex, women with romance) becomes a single discourse. In classic romance, as we have already seen, sex is either made invisible within the discourse of romance (i.e. part of the purpose of romance is to conceal/sublimate sexual desire by invoking elaborate courtship rituals: see chapters by **Joan Forbes** and **Rosalynn Voaden**), or the two are separated from one another by making sex the (legitimate but 'unspoken') goal of romance. In many of Inge Blackman's interviews with inter-racial lesbian couples, however, there is no clear distinction between the erotic and the romantic script. 'Falling in love' does not signal the start of a long and protracted quest, but an immediate decision on whether or not to enter into a sexual contract in which the 'obstacles' are very explicitly political, and which will be a permanent consequence of the union rather than something the union can resolve (see also chapters by **Kathryn Perry** and **Felly Nkweto Simmonds**).

As in other areas of feminist work, white agendas have dominated discussions of love and romance. Despite the centrality of colonial and postcolonial 'others' (countries, cultures, religions, races, ethnicities and skin colours) to romantic discourses, there has been a stunning silence about such issues within standard feminist debates about romance. Much of the earlier feminist critiques of romantic love, for example, ignored the factors of race, ethnicity and cultural difference in the construction of romance (with the exception of work such as Taylor, 1989). This lacuna could be said to have reinforced the universalising power of romantic discourse which would have us believe that romantic love is an inevitable product of the 'biological fact' of sexual difference.

So how might we begin to make the 'whiteness' of romantic narratives visible? In particular, how are the conventional constructions of love, desire and sexuality connected to white fantasies of 'racial others'? How does power mediate and/or reproduce desire in a racist culture? These are amongst the questions which have recently begun to be addressed in debates about 'race', 'ethnicity' and romance which, we hope, will help reshape the feminist agenda on romance. The four chapters which comprise the 'Negotiations: Love Across the Tracks' section of this book form a crucial and long-overdue contribution to ongoing debates and dialogues on romance. They all address what is perhaps the most explosive of all taboos in this context: 'the interracial relationship' – that classic sign of fear and fascination in contemporary Western culture. This subject is discussed in each of these chapters in very different ways, offering some fraught, yet highly suggestive, insights into *both* the place of 'racial difference' in classic romantic scenarios (as in **Kathryn Perry**'s exploration of the whiteness of romantic desire) *and* into what it means to re-write the narrative of romance 'across the tracks' and produce alternative outcomes (as explored in the chapters by **Inge Blackman, Helen (charles)** and **Felly Nkweto Simmonds**). The specificities of interracial relationships between women (see **Inge Blackman**'s chapter, in particular) further problematise the taken-for-grantedness of the centrality of sexual difference to the meanings of desire and love in classic romantic trajectories and the usual theoretical interpretations of them. Finally, the limits (as well as the possibilities) for Black authors/speakers to rewrite the narrative of romance in the predominantly white context of academia (and indeed, of Women's Studies) is questioned by Helen (charles); she draws attention to the existing inscriptions of Black women as objects of voyeuristic fascination in the white imagination and tests the boundaries of transforming such connotations within feminist practices.

Since the fairy-tale sublimation of class differences has been a staple ingredient of romantic fiction for many centuries (see Light, 1984), it is significant to observe the challenge represented to this fictive narrative by the working-class British women interviewed in Judy Giles's study. Giles's interviewees reveal a profound alienation from the narratives of romance. In a society in which the emotional economy was securely wedded to the economic one, all the women's creative energies were centred on making a 'good marriage', a sensible choice. 'Romance', of the hearts and flowers variety, was regarded as 'silliness': a middle-class indulgence. Giles's study further reveals that this anti-romantic sentiment was represented in the popular literature of the day (she cites a number of women's magazine stories), which makes an interesting point of connection with the 'strategies of resistance' revealed by Joan Forbes in her study of eighteenth-century literature. One final point that should perhaps be made about these findings is that women can be just as critical of romantic discourse as men. While the research of Wendy Langford and Jean Duncombe and Dennis Marsden may suggest that it is primarily women who favour romance (as an expression of intimacy and relatedness), Judy Giles's historical sample, and Joan Forbes's textual one, refuse to see the attraction. Steph Lawler's chapter also interrogates the meanings of romance in terms of class difference through her analysis of Freud's family romance, which she reworks to investigate the significance of forms of envy and desire in mother-daughter relationships.

One final, and fascinating, example of how the romance script has been rewritten is Celia Lury's examination of the role of the public in the romance of Charles and Diana. Playing with concept of the 'public romance', Lury argues that the British public (through the mediation of the press) was instrumental in writing the narrative of the royal romance (and its demise). At the same time, the particular scripts chosen can be seen to 'reveal the public': their desires are a projection of the (confused and contradictory) status of romance in late twentieth-century Britain.

In conclusion, what all these deviations from the narratives of classic romance would seem to reveal is that romance is a category 'in crisis'. When we refer to romance today, either with respect to a book or film, or with recourse to our so-called private lives, we cannot be sure that we are dealing with a common meaning or set of values. Romance is under pressure, and it is also 'in process'. This seems to us most noticeable in the chapters dealing with ethnicity and lesbianism where particular communities and cultures have re-written the narratives of romance so effectively that the model outlined at the beginning of this section (meeting–quest–resolution) has all but disappeared. For individuals involved in lesbian and/or inter-racial relationships, indeed, obstacles are shown to be *integral* to romance: they are not something to be magically 'disappeared' through consummation/resolution. At the same time there *are* many cultural representations of romance which achieve their effect/critique through a very visible re-working of classic romance (i.e. the typical trajectory is always kept in view even as it is reworked – as in the 'Hollywood' lesbian romance *Desert Hearts* (1985)). These two rather different interventions into romantic discourse may, perhaps, be characterized as *revision* and *rewriting*, and perhaps represent the divided legacy of the 1970s and 1980s in which feminists have been split on whether romance should be assimilated or reconstructed. None of this is to dispute Stevi Jackson's claim that romantic love has pursued feminists into the 1990s, but to suggest that it is now a *fractured* discourse that addresses some of us very differently from others. So when someone tells you that they love you, beware: their story might have a different beginning, middle and end from your own.

Theories of Romance

In this section we move from a discussion of the construction of romance as a narrative to a consideration of some of the other theories that can, and have, been employed to explain both the emotion itself (i.e. 'romantic love') and its cultural representation, 'romance'. The section opens, however, with a brief explication of the structuralist principles which underlie all the 'narratives of romance' discussed in the last section.

The Structure of Romance

Structuralist analysis, which emphasizes 'the systematic interrelationships among the elements of any human activity' (Baldick, 1990: 213), looks for the system or pattern underlying a particular sign system or cultural practice (such as 'romance') and reveals its pervasiveness across a range of texts or social situations. As we have seen through the narratives of our own chapters, *difference* is established through deviation from a standard model or 'structure' which has become 'the dominant' within a particular textual/cultural practice.[1]

Central amongst the theorists who have popularized a structuralist reading of romance/romantic love are Roland Barthes, the French semiotician, and feminist literary critics Tania Modleski (1982) and Janice Radway (1984). Barthes's *A Lover's Discourse* (1977) is a text which presents the 'classic' love affair as a series of discrete '*figures*' (e.g. 'absence', 'waiting', 'declaration', 'jealousy', 'fade-out', 'union'). These figures cluster around the climactic moment of 'ravissement' (or 'falling in love'), but Barthes distinguishes another seventy-nine nuances of emotional ecstasy and pain which together make up the full repertoire of 'the lover's discourse'. Unlike other structuralist theories of romance (see Radway below, for example), Barthes's model contests the idea that these 'figures' occur in any particular order by presenting them alphabetically ('To let it be understood that there was no question here of a love story (or of the history of a love)' Barthes, 1977: 8). This attempt to deny the temporal trajectory of romance is, however, somewhat contradicted by the fact that the majority of Barthes's figures appear to belong to a period either before or after 'ravissement': either to the period of 'preparation' designated 'twilight' or to the 'sequel' (Barthes, 1977: 188–94). Indeed, under the entry 'rencontre' (encounter) he distinguishes three discrete 'movements' to the typical love-affair:

> First comes the instantaneous capture (I am ravished by an image); then a series of encounters (dates, telephone calls, letters, brief trips), during which I ecstatically 'explore' the perfection of the loved being ... This happy period acquires its identity (its limits) from its opposition (at least in memory) to 'the sequel': the 'sequel' is the long train of sufferings, wounds, anxieties, distresses, resentments, despairs, embarrassments and deceptions to which I fall prey ... (Barthes, 1977: 197–8)

Barthes attempts to mediate the contradiction between the various figures of the lover's discourse being experienced both arbitrarily *and* historically by suggesting that the historicization is part of the subject's ('hallucinatory') tendency to make his/her love 'into a romance, an adventure' (Barthes, 1977: 197). The fact that such historicization is endemic to *all* romantic encounters ('I believe (along with everyone else) that the amorous phenomenon is an "episode" endowed with a beginning ... and an end' (Barthes, 1977: 193)) would seem to suggest, however, that the ordering of the figures is *never* arbitrary.

Barthes's construction of the 'typical' lover's discourse is culled from a range of literary, psychological and philosophical texts (e.g. Goethe's *The Sorrows Of Werther*, Freud, Lacan, Sartre), and the citation of these sources in the margins of *A Lover's Discourse* makes a graphic point about the 'always already' textual nature of romance (see **Sue Vice**). Modleski and Radway, meanwhile, unearthed the more popular origins of romantic discourse through their studies of Harlequin romances (the US equivalent of Mills and Boon), Gothic novels, and television soap-operas. While the political objective of both writers may have been to rescue popular romance and its readership from trivialization and contempt (see above), their theoretical contribution was a structural analysis of the 'typical' plots and characters associated with the various sub-genres. In her chapter on 'The Ideal Romance', for example, Radway draws on Vladimir Propp's classic structuralist analysis of fairy tales (Radway, 1984: 120) to construct her model of the ideal narrative structure (paraphrased in the previous section), and proceeds to show how closely the most successful/popular romances abide by it. Propp's revelations about the structural homogeneity of one particular literary genre, subsequently revised and adapted by other theorists such as Greimas and Levi-Strauss (see Hawkes, 1977), proposed that all fairy tales comprise thirty-one *functions* (events) and seven *spheres of action* (roles: such as 'hero', 'villain', 'donor'). What readers usually discover when testing this model on texts other than the fairy-tale is that while many of the functions are still recognisable, their order may vary and, most significantly, that the 'spheres of action' become difficult to ascribe to the characters should the text exceed a certain degree of moral/psychological/political complexity. This deviation is especially notable in texts which espouse even a small element of feminist consciousness (see **Bridget Fowler**) since the correlation between 'spheres of action' and traditional gender roles is dislocated. It becomes quite common, for example, for the principal female character to occupy the sphere of action usually ascribed to the *hero* (this may even be the case in a classic romance like Charlotte Brontë's *Jane Eyre*) rather than that of the *princess* (or 'sought-for-object'). Thus while within the realms of the most traditional popular romance the formula may hold, it is, as Bridget Fowler's analysis of contemporary 'middle-brow' fiction reveals, frequently liable to politically-charged variation.

Structuralist analyses of romantic love have therefore provided us with crucial insights into the 'typicality' of the emotion and its narrative construction, but they have often failed to point out that typicality is *not* universality (Barthes's 'lover's discourse' is, for example, typical only for certain communities within bourgeois Western culture), and that the exception often disproves the rule.

The Discourse of Romance

Closely connected to the structuralist theories of romance and romantic love are the cultural theories which regard it as a *discourse* or *ideology*. While structuralism is concerned with identifying the codes, conventions and narrative patterns common to a particular genre/cultural event, discourse theorists examine the way in which particular discourses (i.e. 'ways of thinking' associated with a particular historical moment and legitimated by its ruling institutions) wield power over society and individuals. In recent years, following in the footsteps of Michel Foucault, a good deal of work has been done, for example, on the discourses of nineteenth-century sexuality (see for example Nead, 1988). The big difference between using structuralist and discourse theory to explain the mechanism of romantic love is that while the former attempts to explain all romance according to a single (typical) model, the latter allows for plurality and contradiction within the construction. This is to say that the discourse of romantic love might be informed by many (competing) textual and cultural sources, and, indeed, that the discourse itself might be plural: throughout history, and within different cultures, there have been multiple discourses of romantic love. While the structuralist seeks a common skeleton within all representations/articulations of romantic love, the discourse theorist sees it as an organism predicated upon complex power/knowledge relations of which 'romance' is the sum total.

For feminists attempting to theorise romance, the prime advantage of the discourse model is that it is conceived as historically and culturally specific (different women, in different historical periods, and in different cultures will have experienced it differently), and that it is dynamic: liable to change and transformation (see **Stevi Jackson, Joan Forbes, Judy Giles** and **Celia Lury**). Celia Lury's work on the 'royal romance' is an excellent example of how the discourse of romantic love in late twentieth-century Britain has been transformed by the public's 'scripting' of events. As we saw in the last section, moreover, the re-narrativization of romance according to specificities of race, sexuality, and class is also impacting on the discourse of romance to such an extent that (in some instances) it is barely recognisable in Barthes's description.

One final word on romance as 'ideology'. While most of the contributors to this volume have preferred to refer to romance as a discourse, ten years ago they might as easily have chosen 'ideology'. Although theorists (see Terry Eagleton's *Ideology* (1992) and **Stevi Jackson**) have made serious claims for retaining a distinction between the two terms, it would be fair to say that for most of us the choice is simply indicative of our present theoretical affiliation: Marxist or Foucauldian. The most significant connotative difference between the two terms would seem to be that 'ideology' (favoured by Millett, Greer, Firestone and the earlier feminist critics) has a pejorative inference absent in 'discourse', and that it signals the existence (somewhere) of a world uncontaminated by ideological *mis*representation. Despite the revisions of the post-Althusserians, 'ideology' still carries with it the sense of 'false consciousness' (a way of thinking to be destroyed/rejected), while in a poststructuralist/Foucauldian universe we seem more able to accept the problematic nature of our social and cultural construction, together with an acknowledgement that there is no life 'outside' of discourse (see Althusser (1971) and Weedon (1987)).

Discourse theory, then, as Stevi Jackson shows in her chapter, provides feminist theorists with a means of understanding the complex and contradictory nature of romantic love. Foucault's work on power also enables us to conceive of romance as a(re)productive rather than a repressive discourse, and one that is constantly in the process of being remade and reconstituted (see Weedon, 1987: 113–7).

The Subject of Romance

Given the overlapping concerns of psychoanalysis and feminism with the formations of sexual and gender identities (despite their very different motives for such an interest), some feminists have turned to psychoanalysis to find explanations for the enduring appeal of romantic love (see especially Modleski, (1982); Radway, (1984)). Although Freudian, Lacanian and object relations theory all vary enormously in their accounts, all three are nevertheless concerned with the relationship between the self and the ideal, with the role of fantasy in the development of sexuality, and with the importance of early childhood experiences in the formations of adult desires (see **Stevi Jackson**).

> An obstacle is required in order to heighten libido; and where natural resistances to satisfaction have not been sufficient, men [sic] have at all times erected conventional ones so as to be able to enjoy love. (Freud, 1912: 256–7)

Freud's description of the cultural production of romantic love thus stresses the necessity of its narrativity to the function of libido: the pleasure of love depends upon the satisfaction of overcoming the barriers to it; in their absence, a story invents them. This process of 'erecting' obstacles (to ensure delayed gratification) makes the other person special, unattainable, or 'ideal', in so far as their status grows proportionally to the difficulty of attainment. A central characteristic of romantic love, then, is *idealisation*: the overvaluation of the 'love object' (as in the phrase 'love blinds'). According to Freud, the patterns of adult love (such as the over-investment in another person) can be explained by early psychosexual development (see Mitchell, (1975)). The oedipal attachments to parent figures involve many of the key ingredients of romantic love in later life, Freud argues; these include both the initial idealisation or obsession and the accompanying rivalry and jealousy (in which the child believes the parent to be the source of all knowledge, the solution to all problems and the 'meeter' of all needs), as well as the gradual disillusionment, resentment or hatred (as the child separates from the parents and eventually rejects them).

Despite the cultural association of romance with 'femininity', both generically (in terms of women's consumption of popular romantic forms), and formationally (in terms of the pleasures of merging or loss of the self in an other), Freudian psychoanalysis highlights the tendency for *men* to idealise their love objects. It is men, Freud argues, who overvalue their romantic ideals and endow them with impossible perfections. Unable to acknowledge their first love objects (their mothers) as sexual (and thus to concede the privileged position of the father in the mother's affection), some men maintain the division between 'the affectionate and the sensual currents' (Freud, 1912: 250) in later love and continue to see women as either virgins or whores, either 'sacred or profane' (Freud, 1912: 250). In extreme cases, this produces the following (familiar) dichotomy in men: 'where they love they do not desire and where they desire they cannot love' (Freud, 1912: 251).

For Freud, it is not only the parental echo, however, that determines the inevitable 'fall' of the romantic idol, almost guaranteeing disillusionment, but rather 'something in the nature of the sexual instinct itself is unfavourable to the realization of complete satisfaction' (Freud, 1912: 258). This can be traced back to the initial loss of the 'original object of a wishful impulse' through repression, which is subsequently 'represented by an endless series of substitute objects none of which, however, brings full satisfaction' (Freud, 1912: 258). He suggests that this might account for 'the inconsistency in object choice, the "craving for satisfaction" which is so often a feature of the love of adults' (Freud, 1912: 258). In other words, our desire to repeat romantic trajectories, to keep falling in love, or to keep reading about or watching others fall in love, could be seen to result from the 'incapacity of sexual instinct to yield complete satisfaction' (Freud, 1912: 259).

Similarly, Lacan argues that desire is ultimately beyond satisfaction. Extending Freud's insights on loss into an analysis of the constitution of the subject in language, Lacan investigates the 'division and precariousness of human subjectivity itself' (Rose, 1986: 52). In Lacanian terms, the obsessive repetition of romantic scenarios might be explained in terms of the fundamentally narcissistic character of the subject whose love affair with an idealised image begins with the 'mirror stage' and the original constitution of the ego through a fundamental division (for a full explanation of the 'mirror stage' see Lacan, 1977 and Moi, 1985: 99–100). For Lacan, the original lost object is symbolised by woman, who can never be represented in patriarchal language as anything other than 'lack': 'what man relates to is this object and the "whole of his realisation in the sexual relation comes down to fantasy". As the place onto which lack is projected, and through which it is simultaneously disavowed, woman is a "symptom" for the man' (Rose, 1986: 72). Consequently, Lacan sees 'courtly love' as 'the elevation of the woman into the place where her absence or inaccessibility stands in for male lack' (Rose, 1986: 72). Thus, the impossibility of fulfilment lies in an endless deferral of meaning onto the new symbolic object in a futile attempt to recapture the original lost object. As Sue Vice's chapter in this collection suggests, 'addiction to love' should consequently not be seen as an 'aberration', but rather as an extension of the conventions of romantic love in a culture where desire and 'lack' have become inextricably bound up.

What is particularly significant about psychoanalytic theory is that it does offer an account of how our needs and desires for intimacy with others are gendered. However, feminists have criticised the ways in which the Freudian and Lacanian frameworks tend to privilege and prioritise the masculine model. Several contributions to this collection interrogate the exclusion of the mother from these accounts of romance. Steph Lawler, for example, challenges the absence of the mother, and indeed, the daughter, in Freud's 1909 essay 'Family Romances' in which he describes the process by which children come to fantasise that their true origins lie in a nobler family. Her account, whilst drawing on the central Freudian insights about the parental focus of envy, extends the implication of such oedipal rejections in the specific context of working-class women's aspirations.

Similarly, Lizzie Thynne highlights the limits of psychoanalytic theory in her consideration of the lesbian romance film *Anne Trister* (1986, Leah Pool) which represents a radical departure from the usual oedipal trajectory and explores 'some of the other emotional dimensions of passion between women, in particular the connection between the girl's unconscious desire for her mother and an adult lesbian affair'. Thynne's analysis draws on Luce Irigaray's model of the mother-daughter dyad and the possibility of refiguring the language of the maternal body in order to produce a different romantic narrative. Both Thynne and Lawler's critiques point to a wider problem in looking to Freud and Lacan for explanations of romantic love: that is, the extent to which relationships between women (mothers and daughters, or lesbian relationships) cannot be accounted for adequately within such models.

Some feminist work on romance has turned instead to object relations theory for a model of the formations of gender and sexual identities in relation to the mother. Theorists such as Nancy Chodorow (1978 and 1989), Dorothy Dinnerstein (1976) and Jessica Benjamin (1990) have reworked Kleinian theory and other object relationists to produce an account of the constitution of femininity and masculinity in relation to the mother. Janice Radway's work, in particular, draws on Chodorow's model of feminine identities as more fluid and more susceptible to merging with the romantic other (Radway, 1984). Radway employs Chodorow's explanation for this fluidity of feminine identity boundaries: 'early and exclusive mothering of a female child ... tends to cement a daughter's identification with her mother, a state that later produces difficulties in the daughter's individuation' (Radway, 1984: 135). Radway suggests that there is 'a remarkable similarity' between Chodorow's account of 'the female personality development and the history of the ideal romantic heroine' (Radway, 1984: 135). Thus object relations theory might illuminate some of the ways in which female desires and pleasures in romantic narratives (for example, finding one's identity in another) operate in a culture primarily based upon patriarchal kinship structures.

The Dialogues of Romance

Another set of theories that we see contributing to future theorisations of romance and romantic love derives from the work of the Russian philosopher and literary critic, Mikhail Bakhtin. While 'Dialogic Theory' today encompasses a broad range of linguistic, literary, psychological, and philosophical formulations, these nevertheless share a common root in Bakhtin's belief that 'dialogue' is the 'basic building block' of human existence (see Clark and Holquist, 1984: 9). According to Bakhtin, words, like individuals, can only 'mean' through the reciprocating presence of another. As is stated in *Marxism and the Philosophy of Language* (1929):

> A word is a bridge thrown between myself and another. If one end of the bridge belongs to me, then the other depends on my addressee. A word is a territory shared by both addresser and addressee, by the speaker and his interlocutor. (Voloshinov, 1986: 86)

What is immediately striking about this quotation is its expressly 'romantic' vocabulary. Although conceived as a model of linguistic communication, the 'relationality' upon which all utterance is predicated necessarily invokes a new model of subjectivity and human relationships. The 'dialogic subject' has, indeed, been perceived as a useful alternative to certain psychoanalytic models, in as much as problematic universality is replaced by an emphasis on cultural/historical specificity. In contrast to most psychoanalytic accounts of subject and gender acquisition, dialogic theory does not associate subject development with distinct (and universally applicable) phases (such as, oedipal/pre-oedipal; imaginary/symbolic). Rather than being 'programmed' through the psychosexual traumas of early childhood, the dialogic subject is formed and re-formed through a never-ending process of socio-linguistic encounters with others (see **Stevi Jackson**). This emphasis on the socio-linguistic construction of the subject obviously relates superficially to Lacan, but commentators like Robert Stam have located a major difference between the two on the questions of 'agency' (Stam, 1989: 5). While the Lacanian subject, according to Stam, is doomed to an unsuccessful battle with the impersonal forces of the Symbolic Order, the dialogic subject is constantly modifying his/her subjectivity through interpersonal exchange.

If we consider what this socio-linguistic model of subjectivity might offer theorisations of romance, we find ourselves looking at a new, dynamic mapping of 'self-other relations' in which the individual's search for a reciprocating other is not necessarily predicated upon (pre)oedipal desire. Elsewhere, a dialogic reading has been offered of Adrienne Rich's 'Twenty-One Love Poems' (from *The Dream of a Common Language*) which explores the way in which the speaker's emotional development is inscribed through a complex range of relationships with other women (mothers/lovers/friends or other role models) (Pearce, 1994). A particular love-affair, then (such as the one described in this sonnet sequence), will be seen to exist in 'hidden polemic' with a broad collection of former relationships.[2] The notion of 'polemic' further alerts us to the fact that the encounter might not necessarily be friendly (!): all dialogues are power-inscribed, and it would be a mistake to read Bakhtinian 'reciprocity' as the code for a totally benign and democratic exchange of words/emotions (see Pearce 1994: 207). The dialogic model of relationships is also strongly resistant to idealisations of pseudo-maternal intimacy and merger (see account of object relations theory above): dialogue actively *depends* upon difference, and is the means by which difference is (positively) negotiated.

Another Bakhtinian concept which looks as though it might prove useful in future feminist theorisations of romance is the *chronotope*. Meaning literally 'time-space', chronotope is defined by Bakhtin as 'the intrinsic connectedness of temporal and spatial relations that are artistically expressed in literature' (Bakhtin, 1984: 84). As has been argued in an essay on 'The Chronotope of Romantic Love in

Contemporary Feminist Fiction' (Pearce, forthcoming), literary lovers are typically depicted as occupying an 'empty time' cut off from the diachronic processes of the material world, and that this time 'becomes artistically visible ... *through a distinctive spatial displacement*' (Bakhtin 1984: 84). In both popular romantic fiction and its feminist counterpart, it is clear that this 'other space/place' of romance (see **Diana Collecott** and **Jenny Wolmark**) is highly politicized, representing both an exotic 'otherness' (which is an expression of the lover's own desire for transformation: see discussion above) and a territory in which alternative sexualities/gender relations can be explored. By recognizing that romantic love constitutes a distinctive chronotope in this way, the feminist theorist can better understand the radical questionings of subjectivity and gender-identity that are interrogated through what, on the surface, might appear to be a simplistic expression of fantasy and wish-fulfilment. As the work of Modleski and Radway has shown, the desire(s) liberated through the process of falling in love are nearly always in excess of the love-object. Or, as Lucy Goodison put it, 'Really being in love means wanting to live in a different world' (Goodison, 1983).

Post/Modern Romance?

The variations on the oedipal scenarios of psychoanalysis discussed above, as well as the rescripting of the narrative of romance described in the previous section, point to the general question of how much feminism (along with other social forces) has transformed the meanings and the possibilities of romance in contemporary Western cultures. Is romance, in fact, one of the meta-narratives of modernity which, along with others, such as science (see Lyotard, 1984 and also **Sarah Franklin**), will increasingly fail to function as a stable category? Indeed, how might romantic discourse operate in our so-called postmodern culture in which meanings are apparently so quickly transformed and power so widely dispersed? Have people in general 'lost faith' in the power of love in a culture where one in three marriages ends in divorce and where princesses leave future kings to 'go it alone'? Or does the surprisingly high rate of remarriage indicate that the narrative compels many to try, try and try again? What do the marriage vows *mean* third time around? How sincere and trusting can we expect people to be in a culture which seems increasingly to offer individuals endless choices and variations through commodity consumption?

Perhaps Giddens (1992) is right (if rather romantic!) in his clai… intimacy has been transformed in late modernity. But how far would feminists agree with his generalisations about the emancipatory potential of the new democratization of the personal sphere? Characterising 'romantic love' as distinct from '*amour passion*', Giddens suggests that the former is characteristic of the move towards the self-reflexivity of modernity: 'romantic love presumes some degree of self-interrogation. How do I feel about the other? How does the other feel about me?' (Giddens, 1992: 44). As a result of dramatic social changes (such as the impact of feminism on gender divisions and expectations) Giddens argues that sexuality and reproduction are significantly no longer inextricable. Instead of tying romantic love into motherhood and life-long monogamy, then, contemporary culture enables people to seek love relationships for their own sake, in a dialogue with each other and with themselves. Indeed, Giddens suggests, this facilitates shifts away from a romantic love in which we idealise each other and project infantile fantasies onto our ideals, towards a new contingent or '*confluent*' love which jars with the 'forever', 'one-and-only' qualities of the romantic love complex (Giddens, 1992: 61). The 'pure relationship', for Giddens, is one which is for its own sake (and is not necessarily about kinship, reproduction or marriage) and offers the possibility for us to treat each other with mutual respect and to find a love that can be really personally satisfying.

The 'transformation of intimacy' and the fracturing of the 'grand narrative' of romance has opened up numerous new possibilities for women. According to Shere Hite's 1987 study *Women and Love: A Cultural Revolution in Progress*, in which she presents the results of interviews with 4,500 women, feminism has indeed impacted enormously upon women's experiences of romantic relationships. Many of the heterosexual women interviewed, for example, had much higher expectations of relationships with men in terms of reciprocity and 'equality' and found them frustratingly unsupportive, yet demanding: 96 per cent of women in the study felt they were giving more emotional support than they were getting from men (Hite, 1987: 806). As a result, the numbers of women dissatisfied in these relationships and willing to leave them was very striking: 98 per cent of women want fundamental changes in their marriage and 91 per cent of those divorced claimed it was their decision to leave the marriage, not their husbands' (Hite, 1987: 806, 872). Women's overwhelming dissatisfaction with men's emotional capabilities might be accounted for by the ways in which feminism has encouraged a sense of 'entitlement' amongst women in the last twenty years. Perhaps women are less likely to settle for so little from men and are increasingly demanding that they change their emotional behaviour accordingly. Hite suggests that whilst dissatisfaction might not be new, the subsequent behaviour of challenging men, making demands on them, and ultimately leaving them, is part of a 'cultural revolution in progress'. Given women's changing forms of participation in the so-called 'public sphere', their demand for men to take on new challenges in personal relationships seemed to many women in the study a late-twentieth-century inevitability. As gender differences are shown increasingly to be a cultural construction, rather than a biological imperative, so inequalities in heterosexual relationships would seem to have less and less foundation.

Hite's study also confirms the wide significance of lesbian relationships in the transformation of the meanings of love and romance. A high percentage of women (54 per cent) in lesbian relationships reported feeling positive about their sexuality (Hite, 1987: 894) and 46 per cent felt it to have been a choice for them (Hite, 1987: 896). Significantly, 96 per cent of those interviewed expressed satisfaction with how they were loved in their relationship and felt a sense of equality with their lovers. This is not to idealise lesbian relationships, whose problems are also well-documented by Hite, but rather to see these findings as indicative of some very radical social changes, particularly in terms of women's expectations of relationships today.

Romantic discourses in contemporary culture, then, clearly include a recognisable set of concepts which suggest that many women no longer accept their place within classic narrative trajectories (seeking to challenge men, transgressing the taboos of interracial relationships or exploring the possibilities of 'deviant' desires). Whilst many of the traditional gendered components may well continue to have significance (monogamy, betrayal, conflict and abandonment), the extent to which women and men take up their respective places in relation to them has been fundamentally called into question with the impact of feminism. The paradoxes of continuing the pursuit of happiness through romantic love, whilst simultaneously assuming it may not last for long, never mind forever, capture something of the contemporary dilemma for the feminist critic. If classic romance can be characterised as the quest for love delayed by a series of obstacles which desire must overcome, then postmodern romance might be conceptualised as the condition in which romance itself has become *the obstacle* which the desirable love relationship must overcome: surely everyone knows too much these days really to expect romance to last and has no-one to blame but themselves if they thought otherwise. Thus, the knowledge (and yet the disavowal) of the impossibility of 'true romance' can both be called upon with equal conviction in a culture in which the rhetoric of individual rights vies with that of self-sacrifice. For if our 'commonsense' increasingly tells us to be wary of life-long promises, while our social institutions continue to manufacture false hopes, it may be that the pleasures of romance will combine with a critical irony which enables us to keep a certain distance as we remember that we have 'been here before' (probably several times!).

In this introduction we have argued that if romance *does* have a common meaning across the multiple discourses and practices of contemporary culture, then it is its continued inscription as a narrative (romance is 'always already' a story). Our survey of the diverse 'narratives of romance' represented by this book also revealed, however, that there is no longer a *single* (foundational) story to which they all refer. In different texts/contexts, the structural properties of classic romance – action, sequence, contexts, closures – have become radically dislocated. Things do not necessarily happen in the expected order any more, and the roles/actions of the protagonists are being challenged by specificities of gender, class, race, and sexuality.

We believe that this re-writing of the narrative of romance in the culture(s) of post-modernity is also having profound consequences for its theorisation. Where, even in the 1980s, there was still a desire to 'explain' romantic love and its cultural representations in terms of a fixed structure or psychoanalytic projection, we feel that these models would be inadequate to account for the complexity of the emotional encounters described and analysed in many of the chapters which follow. Clearly, this is the reason why sociologists and anthropologists are calling for a new methodology for the examination of intimate relationships which will take account of cultural difference and change, and why feminist theorists, such as Stevi Jackson, are rejecting structuralist and psychoanalytic accounts of emotional/sexual desire which fail to take account of the specificity, complexity, and dynamism of its impact on our *adult* lives. In this respect, it would seem that discourse theory and dialogics offer two of the more useful ways forward, since both are theoretical models which emphasise the material (historical/cultural) situatedness of romance as well as acknowledging its provisionality. The lover's discourse may still be 'always already' textual, but both the texts which inform the discourse and the discourse itself are in a constant process of transformation.

We have structured this book very much with this tension in mind. Using the pattern of a romance narrative as our basic structure, we have grouped chapters around four metaphorical interpretations of the staging of this narrative – 'Encounters', 'Transformations', 'Negotiations' and 'Refusals'. We begin with 'Encounters' – the classic coming together of two subjects: in this case, feminism and romance. The chapters in this section offer different interventions into the theoretical debates surrounding this encounter. Stevi Jackson outlines the 'state of play' in these debates and suggests some new ways forward. Focusing particularly on heterosexual love, her chapter charts the feminist encounters with the subject of romance and calls for a new kind of cultural theory of the emotions to respond to changing configurations of romantic love. Sarah Franklin maps fresh terrain for future 'close encounters' by highlighting the romantic charge of scientific knowledge; deconstructing the usual ascription of romance as a feminine genre, this chapter examines the scientific quest to map the human genome as a postmodern romantic narrative. These new genetic sciences, she argues, are differently gendered from their bioscientific predecessors; in the shift in scientific paradigm from 'nature' to 'life itself', this transition promises to decouple a 'reproductive *telos* from heterosexuality'. Continuing the theme of decouplings and recouplings within this encounter, Rosalynn Voaden provocatively pairs Mills and Boon with medieval accounts of religious dedication, situating her analysis within a synthesis of the key components of romantic narratives. For Voaden, each genre (the modern romance and the medieval unitive vision) places woman on 'the threshhold between the potential and the actual', offering liminal possibilities within the parameters of conventional patriarchal constraints. Finally, Bridget Fowler suggests a fruitful encounter between feminism and the cultural theory of Pierre Bourdieu. Fowler outlines the place of 'middlebrow' romance within cultural analysis of class, taste and gender, suggesting that this forgotten middle ground in the high/popular culture divide offers women readers utopian fantasies of harmony, community and integration within the problematic universals of patriarchal ideology.

Following the classic romantic trajectory, our second section is entitled 'Transformations'. In the typical narrative each partner is transformed by the force of their passion for the other – they become a new person. However, once the initial fascination begins to wear off, each party enters the 'critical disillusionment' phase: the mismatch between the romantic ideal (held on to for as long as possible) and the actual person in the everyday begins to grate and irritate; gradually, each tries to change the other. Romance is thus transformative in two ways: another self might be revealed (or, some would say, produced), and/or the other might be moulded in accordance with our own desires. Taking 'Transformations' as a central metaphor of romance, the chapters in this second section deal with the transformative possibilities of romance and with the ways in which romance itself has been or might be transformed. Significantly, a substantial section of the book, the work represented here provides a radical challenge to what romance has offered women and explores new possibilities of recasting the traditional story.

Each chapter relates to this theme in different ways. Lizzie Thynne explores the possibility of representing lesbian desire through a new 'female symbolic' which moves beyond the oedipal constraints of the heterosexual romantic trajectory in her discussion of the film *Anne Trister*. The romantic script is rewritten here in both structure and originating myth, opening up inter-feminine possibilities for the connections between early childhood and adult love. Continuing this psychoanalytic theme, Sue Vice asks whether the phenomenon of the 'addicted lover' is 'an anomaly or simply an extreme example of how love works under patriarchy'. In a discussion of both cinematic and literary texts which represent 'obsessive' attractions, Sue Vice looks at how each transforms or reinforces conventional understandings of love, desire and romance. Questions of similarity and difference are central to all attempts to rewrite the romantic script, as Diana Collecot foregrounds in her study of Bryher's *Two Selves*. Here she explores the question of how some lesbian texts might fundamentally challenge both compulsory heterosexuality and the prescriptions of narrative closure. Gabriele Griffin raises important questions about the transformation of the classic 'quest' trajectory in relation to lesbian sexual practice in the age of HIV and AIDS: how is the apparent contradiction between 'safer sex' and the pleasures and dangers of erotic desire resolved in contemporary lesbian writing and publishing? A final exploration of transformation is Jenny Wolmark's investigation of how contemporary feminist science fiction undermines the rewriting of romance and its accompanying prescription of gender and sexual identities. Highlighting the postmodern instabilities of such fiction, Jenny Wolmark suggests that their new cyborg hybridities offer the possibility of moving beyond the rigidities of patriarchal binarisms.

A third and crucial stage in the romance trajectory is 'the negotiation'. Aware of potential problems and difficulties, even frustrations and inequalities, the two parties come together in an attempt at productive exchange. There is a self-reflexivity to this phase and each side is acutely aware of the power relations at stake. They are also aware that things may go either way: negotiations may lead to renewed and extended pleasures, or to the recognition that this is 'the beginning of the end'. The moment of negotiation is thus a pivotal one in the progress of romance. It serves here as a metaphor for the tricky manouverings which permeate romantic dialogues. In particular, it is used as a trope for one aspect of romantic exchange rarely satisfactorily debated: interracial romance. In this third section of the book, then, each chapter discusses the subject of 'Love Across the Tracks'. Initially in dialogue with each other as a panel presentation at the *Romance Revisited* conference, these contributions suggest how we might break the taboos around this subject and begin to address questions of power, fantasy and desire across constructions of 'racial' and 'ethnic' difference. Kathryn Perry suggests how the white sexual imagination has constituted racial others in accordance with its own psychic and social needs, and explores how this racist 'heritage' is negotiated in interracial relationships. Inge Blackman tells stories of inter-racial lesbian encounters, drawing on interview material, and maps out some of the limits and possibilities of such negotiations. Helen (charles) discusses this loaded negotiation in relation to the question of 'compromise'. Analysing a number of cultural texts which deal with interracial relationships, she interrogates the problems of representing the subject (on television, in fiction – or within Women's Studies) in a culture so heavily permeated by this taboo and its transgression. Felly Nkweto Simmonds suggests some of the ways in which interracial romance challenges the heart of romantic discourse and the public/private divide upon which it is premised. Reworking the feminist claim that the 'personal is political', this chapter highlights the paradox of the invisibility of interracial love in official public discourse and yet its visibility in a racist society where such encounters come under such vicious public scrutiny.

The final section of the book offers one kind of closure to this compelling trajectory: 'Refusals'. There are a number of possible reasons why a romance may come to an end: perhaps the excitement has worn off, the physical attraction subsided, the habits of a partner have appalled or horrified; perhaps another has intervened, new lusts surfaced, political challenges shifted identifications; or perhaps the relationship has just simply come to the end of its shelf-life. Whatever the reasons, loss, pain and separation loom on the horizon alongside the question of whether there will be a 'next time'. An alternative to the classic 'happy ending', refusing romance might be the *preferable* option for many feminists. This figurative category is used here to signal both accounts of how romance is resisted by particular people for a whole host of reasons, and how romance itself is used to facilitate refusals of other kinds of relationships. Thus we end this collection with several chapters which offer an account and evaluation of 'refusals' of, or through, romance and what they mean for a feminist analysis.

Celia Lury's chapter examines one of the most famous recent refusals: the romance of 'Charles and Di'. Herself refusing to enter the debate about what went wrong, Lury sets a rather different agenda which foregrounds the role of 'the public' in the construction of this royal romance. The active participation of the public in the writing and rewriting of the royal romance suggests new understandngs of national political life, and new pressures for the feminine object of scrutiny who seeks to participate in public life. The public debate about this fairy-tale romance turned modern tragedy raised questions about changing gender roles in a world in which feminist demands have made their mark on even the most privileged and protected of female figures. But have men kept abreast of such changes and can they respond to these challenging demands? Addressing this crucial question for the 1990s, Jean Duncombe and Dennis Marsden ask: 'Can Men Love?' Drawing on interviews with heterosexual couples, this chapter looks at the relationship between media narratives and people's individual trajectories and stagings of romance. In particular, it offers an investigation of the ways in which men refuse romantic conventions and at how women respond to such strategies. Wendy Langford's chapter similarly suggests that gender and power are central to heterosexual romance. Looking at the 'petnames' couples playfully call each other at a certain stage in their relationship, Langford argues that this apparently trivial and rather embarrassing game is not simply a harmless secret code for Valentine's ads, but is a widely-used strategy to escape from the problems of power imbalances between men and women in heterosexual couples. 'Snuglet-puglet and snuglet-piglet' then symbolize a kind of refusal of adult sexual identity and a retreat into genderless and childlike alter-personalities as an avoidance of conflict which might facilitate positive change.

Steph Lawler's chapter looks at a rather different kind of refusal: the rejection of one's mother in favour of another (more middle-class) substitute. Basing her argument on interviews about the mother/daughter relationship, Lawler reworks Freud's theory of the family romance to look at the historical conjuncture of class, gender and romantic fantasy in the widely articulated desire to replace one's mother with another. Extending this exploration of the intersections of class and gender in relation to romance, Judy Giles also uses ethnographic material to analyse how working-class women in interwar Britain remember refusing the discourse of romance in favour of a more pragmatic set of choices in relationships and marriage. Challenging the universality of romance narrative (and of some feminist theories of it), Giles offers a detailed case-study of the reflexivity and self-awareness with which her interviewees regarded the 'luxury' of believing in romance. Finally, Joan Forbes takes us further back in history to women's fiction writing at the end of the eighteenth century, which she analyses in terms of its anti-romantic discourse. Whilst not able to articulate an explicit challenge to romantic love, courtship or indeed marriage, the female characters in these texts nevertheless refuse to be seduced by the usual promises offered to women within classic romantic scenarios.

Should you be embarking upon this book with similar scepticism we would urge you to keep an open mind. Just remember: the fact that romantic love clearly is not what it used to be might give you the opportunity of writing or imagining another story.

Notes

[1] The formalist critic, Roman Jakobson, argued that all literary texts may be

distinguished by their 'dominant' stylistic devices, and that literary history may thus be characterised as a reactionary process in which texts continually replace the 'dominant' of their predecessors. For an account of Jakobson's theory, see Hawkes (1977), pp76–87.

[2] Bakhtin invents the term 'hidden polemic' to describe the way in which words and utterances are sometimes directed (often antagonistically or fearfully) towards the 'future answer' of a person/discourse not mentioned directly in the text (for a full explanation of this concept see Pearce, 1994: 51–4).

Bibliography

Althusser, L. (1971) 'Ideology and ideological state apparatuses', in *Lenin and Philosophy and Other Essays*, tr. B. Brewster, London: New Left Books.

Austen, J. (1818; this ed. 1965) *Persuasion*, Harmondsworth: Penguin.

Bakhtin, M. (1981) *The Dialogic Imagination*, ed. M. Holquist, tr. C. Emerson and M. Holquist, Austin, Texas: University of Texas Press.

Baldick, C. (1990) *The Concise Oxford Dictionary of Literary Terms*, Oxford: Oxford University Press.

Barthes, R. (1977) *A Lover's Discourse: Fragments*, Harmondsworth: Penguin.

Benjamin, J. (1990) *The Bonds of Love: Psychoanalysis, Feminism, and the Problem of Domination*, London: Virago.

Bronte, C. (1847; this ed. 1982) *Jane Eyre*, Harmondsworth: Penguin.

Bronte, E. (1847; this ed. 1965) *Wuthering Heights*, Harmondsworth: Penguin.

Chodorow, N. (1978) *The Reproduction of Mothering: Psychoanalysis and the Sociology of Gender*, Berkeley: University of California Press.

Chodorow, N. (1989) *Feminism and Psychoanalytic Theory*, New Haven: Yale University Press.

Clark, K. and M. Holquist (1984) *Mikhail Bakhtin*, Cambridge, Mass. and London: Harvard University Press.

de Beauvoir, S. (1949; this ed. 1987) *The Second Sex*, first published in translation 1953, Harmondsworth: Penguin Books.

Dinnerstein, D. (1976) *The Mermaid and the Minotaur: Sexual Arrangements and the Human Malaise*, New York: Harper and Row.

Eagleton, T. (1991) *Ideology: An Introduction*, London and New York: Verso.

Eliot, G. (1872; this ed. 1986) *Middlemarch*, Oxford: Oxford University Press.

Firestone, S. (1971; this ed. 1979) *The Dialectic of Sex: The Case for Feminist Revolution*, London: Women's Press.

Foucault, M. (1981) *The History of Sexuality: Volume 1: An Introduction*, tr. R. Hurley, Harmondsworth: Pelican.
Freud, S. (1909; this ed. 1977) 'Family Romance', in The Penguin Freud Library, Volume 7, *On Sexuality*, London: Penguin: 217–226.
Freud, S. (1912; this ed. 1977) 'On the Universal Tendency To Debasement in the Sphere of Love (Contribution to the Psychology of Love II), in The Penguin Freud Library, Volume 7, *On Sexuality*, 1977, London: Penguin: 243–260.
Giddens, A. (1992) *The Transformation of Intimacy: Sexuality, Love and Eroticism in Modern Societies*, Cambridge: Polity/Blackwell.
Goodison, L. (1983) 'Really being in love means wanting to live in a different world', in S. Cartledge and J. Ryan (eds) *Sex and Love: New Thoughts on Old Contradictions*, London: The Women's Press.
Greer, G. (1971) *The Female Eunuch*, St. Albans, Herts: Paladin.
Hawkes, T. (1977) *Structuralism and Semiotics*, London: Methuen.
Hite, S. (1987) *The New Hite Report: Women and Love: A Cultural Revolution in Progress*, London: Viking/Penguin.
Lacan, J. (1977) 'The mirror stage as formative of the function of the I', in *Ecrits: A Selection*, tr. Alan Sheridan, London: Tavistock.
Langford, W. (forthcoming) 'The Power of Love: Domination and Resistance in Heterosexual Love Relationships', Lancaster University: unpublished Ph.D. thesis.
Light, A. (1984) ' "Returning to Manderley": Romance Fiction, Female Sexuality and Class', *Feminist Review*, 16, 7-25.
Lyotard, J.F. (1984) *The Postmodern Condition: A Report on Knowledge* tr. Geoff Bennington and Brian Massumi, Manchester: Manchester University Press.
Millett, K. (1969) *Sexual Politics*, New York: Ballantine Books.
Mitchell, J. (1974) *Psychoanalysis and Feminism*, Harmondsworth: Penguin.
Mitchell, J. (1984) *Women: The Longest Revolution*, London: Virago.
Modleski, T. (1982) *Loving with a Vengeance: Mass-Produced Fantasies for Women*, London: Methuen.
Moi, T. (1985) *Sexual/Textual Politics*, London: Methuen.
Nead, L. (1988) *Myths of Sexuality*, Oxford: Basil Blackwell.
Pearce, L. (1994) *Reading Dialogics*, London and New York: Edward Arnold.
Pearce, L. (forthcoming) ' "Written in Tablets of Stone?": Roland Barthes, Jeanette Winterson, and the Discourse of Romantic Love', in S. Raitt (ed), *Volcanoes and Pearl Divers: Essays in Lesbian Feminist Studies*, London: Onlywomen Press.
Pearce, L. (forthcoming) 'Another Time/Another Place: The Chronotope

of Romantic Love in Contemporary Feminist Fiction', in Gina Wisker (ed) *Guns, Roses and Fatal Attractions: Reading Romantic Fiction*, London: Pluto Press.

Radford, J. (ed.) (1986) *The Progress of Romance*, Routledge and Kegan Paul: London.

Radway, J. (1984) *Reading the Romance: Women, Patriarchy, and Popular Literature*, Chapel Hill and London: The University of North Carolina Press.

Rich, A. (1978) *The Dream of a Common Language*, New York and London: Norton.

Richardson, S. (1740; this ed. 1980) *Pamela*, Harmondsworth: Penguin.

Rose, J. (1986) *Sexuality in the Field of Vision*, London: Verso.

Shakespeare, W. (1594; this ed. 1978) *Romeo and Juliet*, ed. P. Alexander, London and Glasgow: Collins.

Shakespeare, W. (1584; this ed. 1978) *Much Ado About Nothing*, ed. P. Alexander, London and Glasgow: Collins.

Stacey, J. (1990) 'Romance', in Annette Kuhn, with Susannah Radstone (eds) *The Women's Companion to International Film*, London: Virago, 345–6.

Stacey, J. (1995, forthcoming) ' "If You Don't Play, You Can't Win': *Desert Hearts* and the Popular Lesbian Romance Film', in Tamsin Wilton (ed.) *Immortal, Invisible: Lesbians and the Cinema*, (London: Routledge.

Stam, R. (1989) *Subversive Pleasures: Bakhtin, Cultural Criticism and Film*, Baltimore and London: Johns Hopkins University Press.

Taylor, H. (1989a) *Scarlett's Women: 'Gone With The Wind' and Its Female Fans*, London: Virago.

Taylor, H. (1989b) 'Romantic Readers', in Helen Carr (ed) *From My Guy to Sci-Fi: Genre and Women's Writing in the Postmodern World*, London: Pandora.

Tolstoy, L. N. (1878; this ed. 1954) *Anna Karenina*, Harmondsworth: Penguin.

Thompson, S. (1989) 'Search for tomorrow: or feminism and the reconstruction of teen romance', in Carole S. Vance (ed), *Pleasure and Danger: Exploring Female Sexuality*, London: Pandora, 1989.

Voloshinov, V. N. (1929; this ed. 1986) *Marxism and the Philosophy of Language*, tr. L. Matejka and I. R. Titunik, Cambridge, Mass: Harvard University Press.

Weedon, C. (1987) *Feminist Practice and Poststructuralist Theory*, Oxford: Basil Blackwell.

Encounters: Feminism Meets Romance

Women and Heterosexual Love: Complicity, Resistance and Change

Stevi Jackson

Romantic love has been somewhat neglected by feminists, despite the considerable attention that has recently been paid to its fictional representation. Research on women as readers and viewers of romance, however, does reveal that it has considerable emotional resonance for them. In order fully to appreciate both the appeal of such fiction and the place of romantic love in women's daily lives we need an analysis of love itself, the ways in which it is made sense of as an emotion and how it figures in women's understanding of their own and others' relationships. In particular, rather than treating romantic desires as given, we should consider the ways in which they are culturally constructed.

In this chapter I will suggest some lines of enquiry that might be pursued and indicate some of the theoretical and political questions which love and romance raise for feminists. In the space available I can do little more than provide a few signposts to directions that a critical analysis of love might take. My remarks are directed towards heterosexual love, since it is here that the political issues are brought into sharpest relief. It is in heterosexual relationships that romantic love has been institutionalized as the basis of marriage, and it is heterosexual love which dominates cultural representations of romance. Yet it is clear that contemporary ideals of romantic love, framed within the context of a heterosexual and patriarchal social and cultural order, also impinge on those who resist the constraints of compulsory heterosexuality.

There is nothing new in feminist critiques of love, which had their origin in the period of first wave feminism, for example in the work of Alexandra Kollontai (1919/1972). Later Simone de Beauvoir (1949) provided foundations for analyses of romantic love developed by early second wave feminists such as Comer (1974), Firestone (1972) and Greer (1970). These accounts were unambiguously critical of romantic love. It was the bait in the marriage trap; it served to justify our subordination to men and rendered us complicit in that subordination; it involved an unequal emotional exchange in which women gave more than they received; its exclusivity was taken as indicative of the emotional impoverishment of our lives; it diverted women's energies from more worthwhile pursuits. Where these writers considered romantic fiction, as in the case of Greer, it was represented simply as 'dope for dupes' – a means of brainwashing women into subservience. The emphasis, then, was unequivocally on the dangers of love and romance for women.

Since that time feminists have developed new perspectives, which take women's pleasure in romantic fiction more seriously and which offer more sophisticated accounts of women's reading practices. This shift in focus from the dangers of romance to its pleasures, however, risks clouding our critical vision. Part of the problem, as I see it, is that love itself has moved out of the picture. The emotion which romantic fiction represents and which is so central to its readers' responses to it remains relatively unexplored. Subjecting love itself to analysis may serve to sharpen our critical faculties.

I want to state very firmly that retaining a critical perspective on love and romance need not be simplistic. You do not have to see romance readers as cultural dupes in order to argue that romance is implicated in maintaining a cultural definition of love which is detrimental to women. Nor need we resort to a moralistic sackcloth-and-ashes feminism which enjoins strict avoidance of cultural products and practices which are less than ideologically sound. It is not necessary to deny the pleasures of romance or the euphoria of falling in love in order to be sceptical about romantic ideals and wary of their consequences. It is possible to recognise that love is a site of women's complicity in patriarchal relations while still noting that it can also be a site of resistance.

The Cultural Construction of Emotion

In saying that we should give greater consideration to romantic love as an emotion, I am not implying that there is something called 'love' that exists outside society and culture. Indeed I think it vitally important that as feminists we should contest ideological constructions of love which represent it as 'natural'. On Valentine's day 1993 BBC2 screened an evening of programmes on love, including one on the writing and marketing of Mills and Boon romances. We were told that their books sell millions all over the world and are translated into dozens of languages – proof that they speak to a universal feminine concern, that romantic love is a transhistorical, transcultural phenomenon. Feminists have learnt to be sceptical of such universalizing, naturalising claims. These romances derive from a specifically Western culture tradition – if they are being consumed world-wide we need to know why they are being read. It cannot simply be assumed that all women everywhere make sense of them in exactly the same way (Taylor, 1989b). We therefore need to develop analyses of love as a culturally constructed emotion and to explore its linkages to specific social orderings of intimate relationships.

Emotions should not be regarded as pre-social essences, but as socially ordered and linguistically mediated (Jagger, 1989; Hochschild, 1983). This means that they are also culturally variable. Recent anthropological work suggests that particular constructions of emotion, and indeed the category 'emotion' itself, are culturally specific (Rosaldo, 1984; Lutz and Abu-Lughod, 1990). As yet there has been little exploration of love from this perspective, but some of the insights of anthropologists are suggestive of possible interconnections between modern Western ideas of the self and of emotionality which might have implications for an analysis of love. Individualism is a key issue here: in particular the way in which Western introspection about our 'feelings' is linked to a definition of individuals in terms of unique subjectivities (Errington & Gewertz, 1987; Lutz, 1986; Abu-Lughod, 1990). This is particularly pertinent to the emotion we call romantic love since it assumes a coming together of two such unique subjects, each of whom should be the 'only one' for the other. While ideal love is often thought of as a merging of selves, it presupposes the prior existence of two distinct selves. Moreover to be 'in love' is not only to be intensely preoccupied with one's own inner feelings, but with those of the beloved (does s/he really love me, does s/he feel as I do?). Such concerns, taken for granted within Western discourses of the emotions, may be quite alien elsewhere (Errington & Gewertz, 1987; Abu-Lughod, 1990).

The construction of the self in terms of inner psychic processes may well be historically as well as culturally specific (Foucault, 1988; Rose, 1989). Moreover, the discourses around individual subjectivity which have emerged over the last few centuries have also been discourses around gender. Emotionality in general has been associated with the feminine, counterposed to masculine rationality (Lutz, 1990), while love in particular has been defined as part of the feminine sphere (Cancian, 1990). The link between romantic love and individualism has in the past been discussed primarily in terms of free choice of marriage partners (Goode, 1959; Macfarlane, 1987). More recently, however, more attention has been paid to shifting definitions of love itself, to its interconnections with ideals of self-realisation and to the gendered character of both love and the self (Cancian, 1990; Seidman, 1991; Giddens, 1992). This recent work draws extensively on feminist scholarship even where it is not directed by explicitly feminist agendas. What does emerge from the very different perspectives offered by Cancian, Seidman and Giddens, however, is that 'love' is not a fixed, unchanging emotion and that its shifting meanings are the outcome of gendered struggles. In particular love has been, for the last two centuries, a locus both of feminine complicity in and resistance to male domination.

Love, like all emotions, is not directly observable. We can, in the end, analyse only the ways in which it is talked and written about – the discourses around romantic love which circulate within our culture – but these I would argue construct our experience and understanding of love. This is not to deny that emotions are deeply, subjectively felt as embodied experience (see Lutz & Abu-Lughod, 1990: 12), nor that such discourses are embedded in observable social practices and material social realities. Whereas a strictly Foucauldian use of the term 'discourse' counterposes it to ideology (Foucault, 1980), I would argue that feminists need to retain a conceptualisation of discourses as ideological in their effects in that they can serve to conceal, legitimate or render palatable relations of subordination and domination. Such discourses can also be internally contradictory while at another level serving to hide such contradictions. This process is evident in modern romantic ideals.

Love's Contradictions

Romantic love hinges on the idea of 'falling in love', and on this 'fall' as a means for establishing an intimate and deep relationship. Yet being 'in love' is also seen as radically different from other forms of love – mysterious, inexplicable, irrational, uncontrollable, compelling and ecstatic. Even feminists often resort to mystical language to describe it. Haug, for example sees love as a means of retrieving 'the buried and forgotten stirrings of the soul' (Haug, 1987: 278). It appears to be experienced as a dramatic, deeply felt inner transformation, as something that lifts us above the mundane everyday world – which is of course part of its appeal and has led some feminists to defend it against its critics (see, for example Person, 1988; Baruch, 1991). It is different in kind from lasting, longer term affection and widely recognised as more transient.

There are fundamental contradictions between passionate, romantic attraction and longer term affectionate love, yet the first is supposed to provide the basis for the second: a disruptive, tumultuous emotion is ideally supposed to be the foundation of a secure and durable relationship. Feminists from Kollontai (1919/1972) to Firestone (1972) – as well as mainstream social theorists – have suggested that romantic love is not really about caring for another, but is self-centred and individualistic. To be in love is to make another the centre of your universe, but it also demands the same in return.

There is a strong suggestion in literary, psychoanalytic and social scientific writings that the excitement of love thrives only when obstacles are put in its way. Romantic love is fuelled by 'compulsion and denial' and 'gratification destroys the compulsion little by little' (Wilson, 1983: 42). Insecurity appears fundamental to being in love – it wears off once lovers feel secure. Again this makes it an unlikely basis for a committed relationship. So too does the oft noted tendency to romantic idealisation – the other we pursue so compulsively is frequently our own creation, the 'real' person we think we love may be no more than a pretext around which our fantasies are woven (Wilson, 1983; Baruch, 1991). Hence the transformative power of love: its ability to turn frogs into princes. The 'happy ever after' conclusion of fairy-tales and romances papers over the contradictions between these two forms of love. This narrative closure indicates that the excitement lies in the chase, not in the 'happily ever after'. One of the most obvious appeals of romance is that it enables readers to relive that excitement over and over again, without having to confront the fading and routinization of romantic passion. In real life we all too often discover that our prince was only a frog after all.

The passionate compulsiveness of love raises the issue of eroticized power and violence – a persistent theme both of pornography and romantic fiction. This is suggestive of an articulation between love and violence which is rarely explored – although the related linkages of sexuality with violence and love with sexuality have received considerable attention. Although the concept of love in some senses carries connotations antithetical to violence, in its passionate, romantic form it is not a gentle feeling. It is often characterised as violent, even ruthless (Bertilsson, 1986). 'More than wanting to cosset the beloved we may feel we want to eat them alive' (Goodison, 1983: 51–52). It can also be a pretext for violence which, if provoked by a jealous rage, can be read as proof of love – as can rape. Good reason, I think, to maintain our critical stance on the romantic construction of love, particularly since many of us are well aware of the painful experiences of women abused by those they had loved.

Although love relationships are often seen as egalitarian, the compulsiveness and insecurity of romantic passion implies a struggle for power. To be in love is to be powerless, at the mercy of the other, but it also holds out the promise of power, of enslaving the other in the bonds of love. This may be part of the specific appeal of love for women – that it is the only way they can hope to gain power over a man. Again this is a prevalent theme in romances – love tames and transforms the male beast, brings him to his knees (Modleski, 1984; Radway, 1987). Here the themes of complicity and resistance come into play – the desire for power over a man might be read as resistance. The power it delivers is, of course, illusory. It only lasts while the man is in the throes of romantic passion, after which the beast is likely to reassert himself (Langford, 1992). He may continue to be dependent on a woman's nurturance and she may continue to gain a sense of power in providing it – but the structural bases of power and inequality in heterosexual relationships remain untouched. What she is providing is emotional labour, which like domestic labour may offer her a sense of self-worth while simultaneously being exploitative (Bartky, 1990; Delphy and Leonard, 1992).

Love's Discontents

Once heterosexual love is routinized within a committed relationship, then, the asymmetry of gender may become all the more apparent. This again raises the question of women's resistance. Dissatisfaction with a lack of emotional reciprocity, with men's incapacity to give or display love, has emerged as a source of women's discontent in numerous studies of marriage and long term heterosexual relationships since the 1960s (see for example Komarovsky, 1962; Rubin, 1976; 1983; Mansfield & Collard, 1988; Duncombe & Marsden, 1993). It has also been used to explain the attraction of romantic fiction for women (Radway, 1987). This may be a way in which the ideal of companionate marriage based on romantic love sows the seeds of its own destruction – or at least the destruction of a specific relationship. Women appear to be more dissatisfied with the emotional than the material inequities of marriage and heterosexual relations (Mansfield and Collard, 1988; Duncombe & Marsden, 1993).

One potentially subversive aspect of romance fiction suggested by Radway (1987) is that it is a means by which women provide themselves with the nurturance lacking in their relationships with men. It is also clear from ethnographic studies like Radway's that when women talk about their reading and viewing preferences this can be an occasion for discussing gender differences, highlighting men's distance from the feminine emotional world and voicing their criticisms of the men in their lives (see also Gray, 1992). Rarely, however, does this lead to any explicit critique of heterosexual relationships. As Radway herself notes, the consumption of romantic fiction is an adaptation to discontent not a challenge to its source. It also sustains the ideal of romance which produced the discontent in the first place.

There is a further issue here. It is all too tempting to simply accept that men are emotional inadequates and thereby treat women's emotional desires and capacities as given, or even as a form of feminine superiority, particularly since women have for so long been undervalued because of our imputed emotionality. We should be very wary indeed of falling into such an essentialist stance for two reasons. First, what we are dealing with is not merely an imbalance of values, but a material, structural imbalance. Our nurturant capacities are closely interwoven with our location within patriarchal relations – we should be cautious of revalorizing what might be symptomatic of our subordination. More generally, we should not treat emotions as given.

Hence, whether we are talking about nurturant caring love or passionate romantic love, we need an explanation of the ways in which these emotions are constructed at the level of our subjectivities.

Earlier feminist accounts recognised that women's romantic desires were not merely an expression of some innate feminine proclivity, but often underestimated how deeply rooted in our psyches these desires were. Romance was a confidence trick which, once seen through, could be avoided, but which continued to dupe and ensnare less enlightened women. More recently the cultural dupe notion has been challenged, particularly in relation to romantic fiction.

Readers of romance are of course perfectly aware that it is not a realistic representation of the social world – indeed that is part of its attraction (Radway, 1987; Fowler, 1991). They know what they're reading and they know they can't hope to achieve this fantasy in reality. It is also the case, as numerous sociological studies tell us, that romantic aspirations in choice of life-partners are tempered with realism. The point, however, is that romanticism and realism can coexist at different levels of our subjectivities. It is perfectly possible to be critical of heterosexual monogamy, dismissive of romantic fantasy and still fall passionately in love: a fact to which many feminists can themselves testify (Jackson, 1993a; Gill & Walker, 1993). This should not surprise us since it is now widely recognised that our subjectivities are not coherent and consistent.[1] It is the awareness of such contradictions which has inspired much feminist writing on love and romance. Gradually feminists have broken the silence which surrounded our continued experience of 'unsound' desires, and have been willing to 'come out' as secret fans of romance (Kaplan, 1986; Modleski, 1991; Taylor, 1989b). Romantic ideals can be deeply embedded in our subjectivities even when we are critical of them.

Love, Romance and Subjectivity

Here I find myself confronting what seems to me a major gap in feminist theory – the lack of a convincing theory of subjectivity. It has become almost conventional to introduce psychoanalytic explanations at this point – perhaps because there is no well-developed alternative. Psychoanalysis has indeed been used to explain the attractions of romance reading for women. Radway's use of Chodorow's (1978) framework may provide a coherent explanation of why women wish to be nurtured and why men are incapable of providing that nurturance, but it doesn't explain why women are so attracted to tales of passionate, even violent, desire. Lacanian accounts certainly tackle desire in a way which is congruent with some of the features of romantic love which I have identified. Desire is constituted through lack, an inevitable product of our entry into language and culture and is intrinsically incapable of satisfaction (Mitchell & Rose, 1982). This, however, is conceptualised in terms of entry into language and culture *per se* – not of entering a specific culture. Desire, by implication, is an essential part of human social nature. Lacanian psychoanalysis does not admit of the possibility of emotions being structured differently in different cultural settings and thus imagines the whole world to be beset by the same desire – an assumption that anthropologists would make us wary of (Rosaldo, 1984; Errington & Gewertz, 1987; Lutz & Abu-Lughod, 1990).

I am not convinced, either, that the Lacanian account can deal with the specifics of the ways in which language structures emotional and sexual experience even within Western culture. Emotions are not simply 'felt' as internal states provoked by the unconscious sense of lost infantile satisfactions – they are actively structured and understood through culturally specific discourses. These discourses differentiate between love as nurture, being 'in love', lust and sexual arousal – all of which are conflated in the psychoanalytic concept of desire. Even if we were to accept that desires are shaped at an unconscious level, that this is what surfaces in our romantic fantasies, this cannot account for the specific content of our desires and fantasies. Fantasies do not emerge fully formed into our consciousness. They are actively constructed by us, in narrative form, drawing on the cultural resources to hand.

Lacanian psychoanalysis, while ostensibly an account of the cultural construction of emotion, locates 'desire' as an inner state and thus precludes the possibility of linking the experience of 'love' to specific cultural contexts and to the specific discourses and narratives which give shape to our emotions. Feminist accounts of the pleasures of romance reading within this type of psychoanalytic framework, for example Alison Light (1984) on *Rebecca* and Cora Kaplan (1986) on *The Thorn Birds*, seem to me to suggest that romantic fiction reflects, gives voice to or is constructed around a set of emotions which already exist. I would argue, on the contrary, that romantic narrative itself contributes to the cultural construction of love. I do not maintain, as some early critics of romance did, that it is simply a means of brainwashing women into subservience. Rather I am suggesting that this is but one of the resources from which we create a sense of what our emotions are. As Michelle Rosaldo argues, 'feelings are not substances to be discovered in our blood, but social practices organised by stories that we both enact and tell. They are structured by our forms of understanding' (Rosaldo, 1984: 243).

What I would suggest, and have discussed in more detail elsewhere (Jackson, 1993a; 1993b), is that we explore further the possibility that our subjectivities – including our emotions – are shaped by the social and cultural milieu we inhabit through processes which involve our active participation. We create for ourselves a sense of what our emotions are, of what being in love is, through positioning ourselves within discourses, constructing narratives of self, drawing on whatever cultural resources are available to us. This perspective allows us to recognise the constraints of the culture we inhabit while allowing for human agency and therefore avoiding the 'cultural dupe' syndrome, of admitting the possibility of both complicity in and resistance to patriarchal relations in the sphere of love.

Conclusion: Resistance, Complicity and Change

If, as I have suggested, emotions are culturally constructed, they are not fixed for all time. Recent accounts of love suggest that it has indeed changed its meaning over time and that this has come about in part because personal life has been the object of political, especially feminist struggle (Cancian, 1990; Baruch, 1991; Seidman, 1991; Giddens, 1992). Where these writings comment on current trends and begin to predict future changes, however, they frequently over-estimate the changes which are occurring.

A common strand running through these analyses is the claim that romantic love is being undermined as a result of changing sexual mores and women's demands for more equal relationships. For Baruch (1991) romantic love might meet its end once the denial it feeds upon gives way to too easy gratification of sexual desire, but may yet be revived by the anti-permissive climate consequent upon the spread of AIDS. While Seidman (1991; 1992) espouses a more libertarian and less romantic ethic than Baruch, he shares his view that libertarianism and romanticism are antithetical to each other, and that we are now witnessing a struggle between these opposing social currents. He argues the progressive sexualization of love during the twentieth century created the pre-conditions for its demise by valorizing sexual pleasure in its own right and therefore breaking the linkage between love and sexuality. Giddens (1992) sees these same trends as leading away from the romantic quest for the 'only one' with whom to share one's life towards the ideal of the 'pure relationship', more contingent than lifelong monogamy, lasting only as long as it is mutually satisfying. Women are leading this trend because they are refusing to continue to service men's emotional needs at the expense of their own. Similarly Cancian (1990) detects a move away from 'feminized' love, to a more androgynous form where men take more responsibility for the emotional well-being of their partners.

A less restrictive sexual morality does not, in itself, indicate that romantic love is losing its emotional salience, although it may well mean that love is less often regarded as a precondition for physical intimacy. Romanticism and libertarianism are not as mutually exclusive as Baruch and Seidman imply. It is not only moral strictures which place barriers in the way of the gratification of our desires, and romantic love is not in any case reducible to sexual desire. A libertarian ethic may be antithetical to a prescriptive form of romanticism which enjoins lifelong monogamy on lovers, but need not preclude falling in love. Young women's increased heterosexual activity is not necessarily evidence of an absence of romantic desires, although it may indicate a higher degree of realism about the durability of relationships founded upon them. Higher divorce rates, adultery and serial monogamy may indicate a continued search for romantic fulfilment rather than the abandonment of that quest. It may be that women are expecting more out of heterosexual relationships and are less likely to remain in them if these expectations are not realised. This does not mean, however, that in their search for the 'pure relationship' they regard their love for their partner as contingent and conditional at the outset, or that they have ceased to entertain romantic hopes. Given the lack of evidence that women's demands are currently being met, claims that a more egalitarian form of love is emerging seems absurdly over-optimistic and wilfully neglectful of the continued patriarchal structuring of heterosexuality.

It is erroneous to assume too close a correspondence between changes in patterns of sexual relationships and transformations of romantic desire. What may be happening is that the contradictions of romantic love are becoming more apparent with the partial erosion of its institutional supports. Now that premarital chastity and lifelong monogamy are no longer expected of women it becomes obvious that romantic love does not guarantee lasting conjugal happiness – but then it never has. This may lead us to modify our expectations of intimate relationships, may render them less durable, but it does not yet herald the demise of romantic desires.

Certainly the purveyors of romantic fiction are not suffering a contraction of their markets. Rather they are adapting their plots to suit shifts in sexual mores – but their more assertive, less virginal heroines are still seeking Mr. Right. There are, moreover, new markets being created, notably through book series for young readers. If, as I have suggested, the attraction of such romances both requires and helps constitute particular emotional responses, reports of the death of romantic love are certainly exaggerated.

Notes

[1] This insight is usually attributed to psychoanalytic and poststructuralist perspectives, but I would argue that most feminists have – at least implicitly – long recognised that this is the case (see Jackson 1992).

Bibliography

Abu-Lughod, L. (1990) 'Shifting politics in Bedouin love poetry', in C. Lutz & L. Abu-Lughod (eds) *Language and the Politics of Emotion*, Cambridge: Cambridge University Press.

Abu-Lughod, L. and Lutz, C. (1990) 'Introduction: emotion, discourse and the politics of everyday life', in C. Lutz & L. Abu-Lughod, *op cit*.

Bartky, S. (1990) *Femininity and Domination*, New York: Routledge.

Baruch, E.H. (1991) *Women, Love and Power*, New York: New York University Press.

Bertilsson, M. (1986) 'Love's Labour Lost? A sociological view', *Theory, Culture and Society*, 3,1: 19–35.

de Beauvoir, S. [1949] (1972) *The Second Sex*, Harmondsworth: Penguin.

Cancian, F. (1990) *Love in America*, Cambridge: Cambridge University Press.

Chodorow, N. (1978) *The Reproduction of Mothering*, Berkeley: University of California Press.

Comer, L. (1974) *Wedlocked Women*, Leeds: Feminist Books.

Delphy, C. and Leonard, D. (1992) *Familiar Exploitation*, Cambridge: Polity.

Duncombe, J. and Marsden, D., (1993) 'Love and intimacy: the gender division of emotion and "emotion work",' *Sociology* 27,2: 221–241.

Errington, F. and Gewertz, D. (1987) *Cultural Alternatives and a Feminist Anthropology*, Cambridge: Cambridge University Press.

Firestone, S. (1972) *The Dialectic of Sex*, London: Paladin.

Foucault, M. (1980) 'Truth and power' in C. Gordon (ed) *Michel Foucault: Power/Kowledge*, Brighton: Harvester.

Foucault, M. (1988) 'Technologies of the self', in L.H. Martin, H. Gutman & P.H. Hutton (eds) *Technologies of the Self*, London: Tavistock.

Fowler, B. (1991) *The Alienated Reader*, Hemel Hempstead: Harvester Wheatsheaf.

Giddens, A. (1992) *The Transformation of Intimacy*, Cambridge: Polity.

Gill, R. and Walker, R. (1993) 'Heterosexuality, feminism, contradiction: on being young, white heterosexual feminists in the 1990s', in S. Wilkinson & C. Kitzinger (eds) *Heterosexuality*, London: Sage.

Goode, W. (1959) 'The theoretical importance of love', *American Sociological Review*, 24,1.

Goodison, L. (1983) 'Really being in love means wanting to live in a different world', in S. Cartledge, and J. Ryan, (eds), *Sex and Love: New Thoughts on Old Contradictions*, London: Women's Press.

Gray, A. (1992) *Video Playtime: The Gendering of a Leisure Technology*, London: Routledge.

Haug, F. *et al* (1987) *Female Sexualization*, London: Verso.

Hochschild, A. (1983) *The Managed Heart*, Berkeley: University of California Press.

Jackson, S. (1992) 'The amazing deconstructing woman', *Trouble and Strife* 25: 25–31.

Jackson, S. (1993a) 'Even sociologists fall in love: an exploration in the sociology of emotions', *Sociology* 27,2: 201–220.

Jackson, S. (1993b) 'Love and romance as objects of feminist knowledge', in M. Kennedy, C. Lubelska & V. Walsh (eds) *Making Connections: Women's Studies, Women's Movements, Women's Lives*, London: Taylor & Francis.

Jagger, A. (1989) 'Love and knowledge: emotion in feminist epistemology', in A. Jagger and S. Bordo, (eds) *Gender/Body/Knowledge: Feminist Reconstructions of Being and Knowing*, New Brunswick: Rutgers University Press.

Kaplan, C. (1986) *Sea Changes*, London: Verso.

Kollontai, A. (1919; this ed. 1972) *Sexual Relations and the Class Struggle*, Bristol: Falling Wall Press.

Komaravsky, M. (1962) *Blue Collar Marriage*, New York: W.W. Norton.

Langford, W. (1992) 'Gender, power and self-esteem: women's poverty in the economy of love', unpublished paper presented to the Women's Studies Network (U.K.) Conference, University of Central Lancashire.

Light, A. (1984) ' "Returning to Manderley" – Romance fiction, female sexuality and class', *Feminist Review*, 16: 7–25.

Lutz, C. (1990) 'Engendered emotion: gender, power and the rhetoric of emotional control in American discourse', in C. Lutz & L. Abu-Lughod, *op. cit.*

Macfarlane, A. (1987) *The Culture of Capitalism*, Oxford: Basil Blackwell.

Mansfield, P. and Collard, J. (1988) *The Beginning of the Rest of Your Life*, London: Macmillan.

Mitchell, J. and Rose, J. (eds) (1982) *Feminine Sexuality: Jacques Lacan and the Ecole Freudienne*, London: Macmillan.

Modleski, T. (1984) *Loving With a Vengeance*, London: Methuen.

Modleski, T. (1991) *Feminism Without Women*, New York: Routledge.

Person, E.S. (1988) *Love and Fateful Encounters: The Power of Romantic Passion*, New York: W.W. Norton.

Radway, J. (1987) *Reading the Romance*, London: Verso.

Rosaldo, M. (1984) 'Towards an anthropology of self and feeling', in Shweder, R.A. and Levine R.A. (eds) *Culture Theory*, Cambridge: Cambridge University Press.

Rose, N. (1989) *Governing the Soul: The Shaping of the Private Self*, London: Routledge.

Rubin, L. (1976) *Worlds of Pain*, New York: Basic Books.

Rubin, L. (1983) *Intimate Strangers*, New York: Harper & Row.

Seidman, S. (1991) *Romantic Longings: Love in America 1830–1980*, New York: Routledge.

Seidman, S. (1992) *Embattled Eros: Sexual Politics and Ethics in Contemporary America*, New York: Routledge.

Taylor, H. (1989a) 'Romantic readers', in H. Carr (ed) *From My Guy to Sci-Fi*, London: Pandora.

Taylor, H. (1989b) *Scarlett's Women: Gone With The Wind and its Female Fans*, London: Virago.

Wilson, E. (1983) 'A new romanticism?' in Phillips, E. (ed) *The Left and the Erotic*, London: Lawrence & Wishart.

Romancing the Helix: Nature and Scientific Discovery

Sarah Franklin

Scientific pursuit is often described in terms of masculinity and adventure – as a domain of seminal breakthroughs, trail-blazing pioneers and uncharted territories. Such descriptions emphasise and valorize the enterprising activities of scientists as they busy about their colonising practices. They are, moreover, key moments in the gendering of scientific practice, its objects and its subjects.[1]

Though generically often counterposed to masculinity or adventure, the idea of romance is also very much a part of the scientific quest for understanding. Romance pervades the pleasures, fantasies and desires which inform the quest for scientific knowledge, complementing its adventurous techniques. Adventure and romance are not only generic conventions, but as such, they are devices of enchantment. Such devices are no less world-building for being either representational or phantasmatic. The theme of 'romance' is thus useful in providing a refashioned hermeneutical ground for engaging with the gender and science debate. Using the conventions of romance as an indexing or sighting device, I will address the question of whether the new genetic sciences can be seen as differently gendered from their antecedents. My aim here is to contrast the metanarratives indexed by the idea of 'nature' with those that reference emergent ideas of 'life', or what I have referred to as 'life itself'.

To do so, I will explore the scientific quest to 'unravel the secrets of life', to produce a map of the human genome, as a postmodern romantic narrative. Without overstating the unity of scientific enterprise (which is often more happily chaotic and benign than assumed by its interrogators) this tack allows me to explore (in a self-declaredly speculative mode) some components of the desires which have propelled forward the most monumental biophilia of the late twentieth century, that is, the Human Genome Initiative. My interest in these desires attends to their capacity to shapeshift not only organisms and descent lines, but cultural values and possible futures. Of particular interest, therefore, are the relations between scientific discovery and creation, or begetting. My reading of the Human Genome Project casts it as both progeny and parent in a genealogical rendering of science that posits its foundational moves always in dialogue with technologies of gender and generation (including discursive ones). In other words, I am here undertaking science studies as extended kinship theory.

Though pleasures are at issue, their pursuit is not always pleasing. But then, neither is the dictionary definition of romance as beatific as we might assume. Romance is defined as 'an atmosphere or tendency characterised by a sense of remoteness from … everyday life'. As a literary genre, it is classed as one which features 'highly imaginative unrealistic episodes forming the central theme'. It is further described as an 'exaggeration or picturesque falsehood' (OED).

The Human Genome Initiative

The Human Genome Initiative is the global scientific project to sequence the genes on the 23 pairs of human chromosomes which comprise the so-called blueprint of humanity, the handbook of man, the code of codes, the mystery or secret of life. It is the largest collective scientific undertaking ever pursued within the biosciences.[2] The aim, in pragmatic terms, is to unlock the secrets of the genes in order to alleviate the suffering caused by genetically-determined pathology, the scope of which continues rapidly to expand, as ever-greater potency is attributed to the gene as source, or origin, of human affliction. There is not a week that passes without reports of yet another discovery of a genetic root to conditions as obscure as shyness, now reportedly inherited.[3] The map of the genome, when it is complete, uncovered, unlocked, penetrated by the masterful authority of the scientific gaze, is imaged and imagined as a great cure-all. It is a quintessentially millennial venture, entirely suited to the late twentieth century.

It is, of course, also a modern, and even premodern romantic narrative, as of the chivalric genre. A romance, according to yet another dictionary definition, is a 'medieval tale, in verse, of some hero of chivalry'. This too characterises the Human Genome quest, often described as a search for the 'Holy Grail' of the biosciences, for that which is *most unattainable*.[4] This is nothing if not an overdetermined scientific venture: at once a product of postmodern premillenialism, the apotheosis of modern molecular biology and starkly medieval in its resonances.

As it is pre- and post- and modern, the Human Genome Initiative is also a site of tradition, novelty and, self-evidently, recombination. It is a classically romantic quest in its constitution of the gene as the object of passionate scientific attachment, beset by obstacles in the path of fulfilment, which must be overcome, and which provide the occasion to produce (romantic) heroism, by pitting the narrative agents 'against the odds'. Yet, this conventional quest narrative also suggests a departure from familiar themes insofar as it constitutes its object of desire in a manner somewhat at odds with bioscientific convention.[5]

Onlookers familiar with the feminist analysis of science will recognise in the Human Genome Initiative themes well charted by theorists, such as Carolyn Merchant, Evelyn Fox Keller or Ruth Hubbard, namely the conquest of nature by a definitively patriarchal apparatus which constitutes the unknown as distant, other, feminine and secretive, in need of a masculine ordering mechanism provided by detached, objective, rational scientific mastery. This is the critique of post-Enlightenment Baconian science provided by a host of feminist theorists against which is contrasted, for example, a 'feeling for the organism', as is said to characterise the work of more feminine biologists such as geneticist Barbara McClintock, who pursued an intimate, rather than distanced, attachment to their object (Keller, 1983).

But, as Donna Haraway points out, even the most patriarchal bioscience has always been romantic. She notes,

> Biology is inherently historical, and its form of discourse is inherently narrative. Biology as a way of knowing the world is kin to Romantic literature, with its discourse about organic form and function. Biology is the fiction appropriate to objects called

> organisms; biology fashions the facts 'discovered' from organic beings. Organisms perform for the biologist, who transforms that performance into a truth ... Romanticism passes into realism, and realism into naturalism, genius into progress, insight into fact. (Haraway, 1989: 4-5)

Like its epistemological antecedents in the life sciences, biogenetics is a transformative discourse, and, like nineteenth-century biology, it fashions facts out of the objects it selects and colonises according to an origin narrative of form and function, to further paraphrase Haraway. But what is different in the context of the Human Genome Initiative is the constitution and selection of the object. It is not the organism, but the gene, which is historicized as the point of origin, the narrative *telos*. It is not a *natural object* but an *informational flow* which is selected and produced as a certain type of object by this narrative trajectory.[6]

What is romantic, as is suggested by commentators such as Haraway, about the organism is its embeddedness in a liberal humanist ethos, to which the form and function (ie, the holism) of the organism is metonymically akin. It is, like the Hobbesian body politic, a whole made up of integrated parts and characterised by a bounded ontology. The gene is a very different entity. It is a fragment. The gene is like the postmodern subject, it is a partial segment, a location, a situated agency that relies on its context to express itself, but which can self-replicate, or mutate, into simulacra. It is from this perspective that I suggest a differently gendered moment of scientific hegemony becomes apparent.

The Human Genome Initiative is not so much concerned with Nature, or concepts of the natural, as its point of departure as it is concerned to unclothe, demystify and manage a new object of knowledge which is the concept of Life. It is from this refashioned point of departure that a different narrative, and, more to the point, a differently gendered narrative of scientific progress, emerges.[7]

The gender of post-Enlightenment Baconian science's 'nature' was definitively feminine. It had to be feminine, it had to be conquered, the conqueror had to be masculine, and the narrative trajectory, not to mention the necessary obstacle to romantic fulfilment, had to be instantiated by the reproduction of sexual difference this patriarchal fiction both authorised and relied upon. Nature, in this dialogic narrative construction, had to be oppositioned to Science, as did femininity to masculinity; the reproduction of these polarities inscribed as the relation of the active, knowing masculine subject to the passive feminine object of knowledge is what the feminist critique has named as both the gendering and the sexualization of the production of knowledge. Like genes, the polarised Baconian calculus instantiated an auto-replicating apparatus of co-constitutive subject and object positions, to the beat of the forward march of scientific progress (truth, reason, salvation) – and liberty and justice for all.

In the context of the Human Genome Initiative, the situation is both the same and different. Feminism describes well what is the same. What is the same is the controlling, managerial and hierarchical construction of scientific truth in the context of genetic science. A postmodern perspective becomes more useful in accounting for what is different. For it is in this context that gender becomes more of a receding horizon,[8] and as it recedes all sorts of other boundaries dissolve, in turn releasing different techniques for instrumentalizing knowledge.

Genes, Gender and Nature

The gene, or the concept of the gene, is not gendered in the same way that Nature was. The predominant trope or idiom for the gene is not natural but rather informational. Insofar as it belonged to the realm of the natural, the organism was feminized, as it was romanticised, for the two had been collapsed. The idea of the gene belongs more to an ontological universe defined by the idea of the life force – to a different construction of vitalism, in a sense. Vitalism, in the history of biology, describes the goal-directedness of design (or, put differently, that part of a system's self-referentiality that is in some sense inexplicable). Earlier vitalisms emphasised the determining influence of the whole upon the parts. This is the language of nature the organism speaks – it is a romantic notion, of the parts losing themselves in a greater whole. The fluidity of the organism is that of a system, whose parts interrelate into a complex function greater than the sum of its parts. This is its vitality.[9]

It is this view that the idea of the gene reverses. From the perspective of a geneticized ontology, the whole is not the sum of its parts, the parts summarize the whole. The gene is the essence – the segment reigns supreme. The fluidity of the gene is expressed not in the form of a complex organism, but as an information flow. It is described as a code, a cipher. Information is gendered differently from nature. It is more gender neutral. It is more sexless (see Oyama, 1985).

It is for this reason that the Human Genome Initiative raises some interesting questions for the feminist analysis of science, in terms of gendered definitions of the natural, in terms of romance, and in terms of the subject and object positions constructed by the interrelation of the scientific knower and the scientific known. Baconian science relied upon the reproductive metaphor of paternity – of seminal thoughts and fathers of invention, of penetrating gazes and fruitful outcomes. The reproductive imagery it deployed was premised upon the heterosexual model, in its emphasis on male sexual conquest in pursuit of the paternal reproductive function. Neither heterosexual masculinity nor rapacious 'Baconian' pursuit attach to the representation of the fecundity of the gene. It is precisely its self-replicating capacity which is definitive of the gene, as distinct from the organism. As Richard Dawkins states, 'the potential near-immortality of a gene, in the form of copies, is its defining property' (1976: 37).

By bypassing heterosexual reproduction, and drawing its analogies instead from the less gender-differentiated idiom of information, genetic science inevitably invites a different set of mergings. Whereas earlier versions of biology drew heavily on the imagery of a masculine science unveiling a feminine nature, and emphasised the fecundity of this coupling, the mergings which inspire the awe of biogeneticists are much more expansive and promiscuous. Informing this shift, there is again the indebtedness to a model of replication, rather than reproduction; to an idiom of information flow connecting generations, rather than of a blood tie; and to an interest in the secrets of life, rather than the facts of Nature. In the realm of genetic science, even species boundaries disintegrate, as in the modernist evolutionary accounts of human origins, which emphasise our proximity to apes.

As the infamous sociobiologist E.O. Wilson enthuses, 'We are literally kin to other organisms ... About 99 per cent of our genes are identical to the corresponding set in chimpanzees'. 'This does not diminish our humanity', he adds, 'it raises the status of non-human creatures' (1984: 130). He emphasises this fact in *Biophilia: the Human Bond with Other Species*, in which he argues that biology itself urges us to recognise the importance of biodiversity and consequently eco-awareness (see also Wilson, 1992).

As E.O. Wilson speculates on the mergings of the past, the scientist Lynn Margulis and science writer Dorian Sagan also see such mergings in the future. They argue that, 'We are beginning to see the biosphere not only as a continual struggle favoring the most vicious organisms but also as an endless dance of diversifying life forms, where partners triumph' (1991: 66).

Panhumanity and Autopaternity

With the formal approval in Britain in 1993 of human genetic engineering trials, the recombinant future promised by novel pedigrees and partnerships is undeniably in the offing. With its emphasis on the life flow as analogous to information circuitry, through which the map of the genome is being produced, the possibilities for merging are virtually infinite as well as simultaneously multiple. Yet, while such protean hybridity – the potential physically to become one with animals, plants and even machines – may appear promiscuous, it is arguably also unsexed by the nature of the bonding process, which is informational and disembodied.

It is partly in the context of the loss of the species boundary, through the merging of humanity with other life forms, that an exchange suggests itself. Trading organismic distinction for pan-species genetic information flow pulls the rug out from under the sex/gender system as we know it. It is the possession of a reproductive body, not the possession of a sexed subject position, which has already made of the male genitalia, once a sacrosanct haven from clinical scrutiny, a hot new topic on the agenda of reproductive biology – the human bench of real-time genetic science. Conception is redefined as the union of the genes,[10] whether or not they were preceded by a union of the organisms (as is increasingly an available option, not to say a service industry, in the business of assisted conception). With these and other instances of the displacement of Nature by Life, new possibilities for parity and substitutability of the sexes before the Techniques of the Clinic appear. But what is the trade?

At the same time that new genetic technologies are productive of new interspecies hybridities, thus blurring the boundaries of the human as a distinct genealogy or kind, there is also a consolidation of humanity as one through a renewed assertion of consanguinity within 'the family of man'. What can be described as an emergent *panhumanity* based on a new genetic essentialism is implicit in the denomination of the genome as the 'book of man'.[11] Likewise, racial differences are 'flattened' in the context of genomic pan-humanisation; as in the 'United Colours of Benetton' advertisement campaign, new definitions of purity (of colour and type) are simultaneously deployed to evoke mixture and inclusion.[12]

As race in the context of genetic sciences is both purified and reconstituted as a mixture of continuum, so sex and gender are both disarticulated from antecedent cultural matrices and refashioned along a different cultural logic. As race is both reasserted and *deracinated*, so too is gender both dissolved and *re-genealogised*. This occurs through a decoupling of paternity from heterosexuality in order to achieve what I describe as *autopaternity*. As the gene is primarily defined as an autoreplicant, the corresponding genealogy or pedigree is unilineal. Insofar as paternity has long been associated with the capacity to give form and shape to matter, analogous to the planting of the seed in the soil, the recovery of paternity in the context of genetic science is entirely familiar.[13] What is different is the capacity to redefine maternity along this model (as in cases of 'total surrogacy' whereby the embryo is provided by the commissioning couple, so that both partners contribute their 'seed' to the gestational surrogate). Sex/gender is also refigured in the context of information, where the gene, as 'author' of the message, becomes the agent of its own instrumentality, in a loop of self-determinism as telos that does away with the need for 'soil' (or matrix) altogether.

One could speculate, therefore, the following set of correlations:

nature	life
organism	gene
sexual coupling	self-replication
seed and soil	seed and seed
family of man	panhumanity
hetero-paternity	autopaternity
genealogy	information flow
bilateral or cagnatic	unilineal or recombinant

So far, I have suggested that the new genetic sciences might be understood as *differently gendered* from the biosciences premised on older constructs of 'the natural'. The shift I have attempted to outline is away from 'nature' as a foundational object for the biosciences towards an emergent model of life, or 'life itself'. The transitions indicated as pairs above mark out possible trajectories of emergent shifts in terms of science and paternity. The main difference indicated between the two columns is the decoupling of reproductive *telos* from heterosexuality.[14] The concept of autopaternity belongs to a different sex/gender system than does the 'hetero-paternity' it displaces. In this sense, the ways in which genetic sciences may be seen to have a 'degendering' effect in relation to previous accounts of the natural are offset by the regendering inscriptions of, for example, maternity as the mimesis of the male seed.

Here again, the question of romance works as a useful sighting device, enabling a reconsideration of the nature of desire at work in the pursuit of 'man's second genesis', or his birthing of himself, out of the womb of genomic creation. This desire is not so much to conquer nature as it is to create life itself. Is one of the exchanges at issue that for science to assume the maternal function of creating life it must reinscribe maternity as a paternal act? What are the consequences of such shifts for a technologized reproductive imaginary in a world of science we can still safely describe as a patriarchal establishment? Is another of the 'trades' working itself out in this context that, as many more women scientists occupy positions of leadership in the biosciences, particularly in reproductive medicine, but also in reproductive science as well as genetics, their role has to become more isomorphic with that of male scientists? Is science in this sense becoming a gendered performance, rather than an expression of preformed gender attributes? Finally, is the romance of discovery now made manifest as an act of begetting, in a move reminiscent of the many similarities between modern romantic love and older conventions of divine rapture?

Conclusion

To conclude, the project to map the human genome is, like scientific quests which have gone before it, a potent source of cultural imagination, especially in relation to the future, and inevitably inscribed by gender differences. Importantly, I have argued, the fetishisation of Life that is evident in the context of the Human Genome Initiative is not the Baconian romance with Nature revisited. It posits a very different narrative trajectory, in which a universe of unbounded couplings with plants, animals and machines is celebrated as ecological, emancipatory and pleasurable. We might call it in this sense a postmodern romance: a promiscuous pastiche of 'family resemblances' recombined, like elements from different architectural traditions, into a celebratory excess of novel reiteration. In this sense, reproduction in the context of the new genetic sciences is not so much 'enterprised-up' as it is 'camped-up', in a mocking re-presentation of 'the real thing' it simulates.

There is another sense in which the refiguring of discovery and paternity in the context of the Human Genome Project invokes an older, quintessentially patriarchal, tradition of insemination as the definitive act of begetting.[15] From this perspective, the romance between the scientific knower and the object that is known is not of the masculine aggressor conquering the feminine adversary, but instead a project of self-realisation. The obstacle in the path of fulfilment here is not elusiveness on the part of the quarry so much as the quasi-divinity of the matter at hand. Thus, a much older tradition of romance, or arguably its antecedent in the form of spiritual transcendence, is suggested.

In either instance, the conventions of romance work as a set of indices, charting the relations between science, discovery and creation. As the pursuit of genetic salvation accelerates in the remaining years of the Human Genome Initiative and beyond, the hermeneutical trope of reading its performance as a postmodern romance thus yields the possibility of pursuing its multilayered dimensions. As its inscriptions of life history, of human history and of inheritance flatten into binary bit space, the recombinant pedigree of genomic science becomes a palimpsest of mixed ancestry. This excess offers the possibility of some novel hybridities which may work to destabilize longstanding patterns of parenthood, procreation and kinship. Yet too celebratory a recognition of such possibilities obscures the extent to which familiar patterns, especially paternal ones, may be not only reinscribed, but re-embodied. Here, as ever, new sighting devices will be as essential as new technologies of encoding, in the formation of the reproductive imaginaries of future generations.

Notes

1 The gendered dimensions of science have been the subject of a rapidly expanding scholarly literature for at least two decades. Indeed the intersection between gender and science studies increasingly reveals how much these two fields are constitutive of one another. Carolyn Merchant's *The Death of Nature* (1980) related the feminization of nature to the rise of modern science which she characterised as quintessentially patriarchal. The work of scientist Evelyn Fox Keller critiqued scientific epistemology as masculinist within a more contemporary frame (1985). David Noble's recent and unambiguously

entitled *A World Without Women* (1992) charts the exclusion of women from the power-knowledge which is congealed as 'science', an argument paralleled by the work of Londa Schiebinger in both *The Mind Has No Sex?* (1989) and *Nature's Body* (1993). This is only an indicative list of titles, in no way representative of the breadth and depth of recent scholarship on gender and science. For an overview of the more philosophical dimensions of this debate from the mid 1980s, see Harding (1986). For counterpoints, see Franklin and McNeil (1988) and Haraway (1991). For more recent assessments see Harding (1991) and Haraway (1989, 1991).

2 For an introduction to the social, ethical and legal issues raised by the human genome initiative, see Kevles and Hood (eds) (1992) *The Code of Codes*. For a feminist critique see Hubbard and Wald (1993) *Exploding the Gene Myth*. For other introductory accounts, see Hall (1992), Levy (1992) and Wingerson (1990). The British Medical Association's *Our Genetic Future* (1992) provides one of the most accessible overviews of new genetic technologies.

3 For an account of the range of cultural contexts in which it is possible to trace the emergence of new forms of genetic essentialism, see Nelkin and Lindee (forthcoming), *Powers of the Gene: Heredity in American culture*. See also Franklin (1993a and b).

4 The Holy Grail both refers to the chalice used by Christ at the Last Supper, and is an allegorical term for the object of a prolonged and arduous quest. In particular, the search for the Holy Grail is also associated with the conventions of knighthood, such as bravery, honesty and courtesy, otherwise known as chivalry. That the object of the genome quest should be understood in terms of masculine codes of conduct related to battle and protection of the feminine sex (the chivalric code) is suggestive both of Noble's (1992) analysis of science in terms of christian clerical culture and Shapin and Schaffer's (1985) emphasis on masculine modesty as a component of scientific virtuosity in the rise of 'the experimental life' connected to modern science. See also Haraway (1993).

5 Accounts of the discovery of the double helix are many and celebrated, in particular of late on the occasion of the twentieth anniversary of this event. For an analysis of this account of discovery as a 'conventional quest narrative', see Franklin (1988).

6 The redefinition of the natural in the context of the new genetics has been the subject of commentary by anthropologists Paul Rabinow (1992) and Marilyn Strathern (1992). Both argue that 'nature' has lost its grounding function to the extent it has become something that can be added on to, or, as Strathern puts it, 'enterprised up'. Rabinow indexes this to a shift 'from sociobiology to biosociality' and describes the process as excessive or 'meta' modern. For Strathern the excess is that of consumer choice as an end or identity in itself,

coupled to technological innovation, producing a postmodern condition of loss. For a collection which explores these and other related anthropological debates concerning the status of nature and the natural, see *Naturalizing Power*, Delaney and Yanagisako (eds) (forthcoming).

[7] For analysis of the emergence of 'life' as a concept within science, see Georges Canguilhem, *A Vital Rationalist* (1994); Michel Foucault, *The Order of Things* (1970); Francois Jacob, *The Logic of Life* (1973); Steven Levy, *Artificial Life* (1992); Ernst Mayr, *The Growth of Biological Thought* (1992) and Carl Sagan, 'Life' in the *Encyclopaedia Britannica* (1992). For a discussion and critique of the way in which 'life itself' is being sacralised, see Barbara Duden, *Disembodying Women* (1993). For a juridically-based philosophical argument in favour of understanding life as essentially sacred and inexplicable, see Dworkin (1993). For a review of these and other accounts, see Franklin (forthcoming).

[8] I am grateful to Penny Harvey for this formulation. See also Duden, 1993.

[9] Vitalism is often contrasted to mechanism, the view of animation associated with the rise of modern science and positivist empiricism, or the experimental method. Whereas mechanism accounts for animation in terms of the function of parts, as in the ticking of a watch, vitalism carries with it more of a suggestion of mystery and inexplicability in relation to 'the life force'. Both vitalism and mechanism can be seen as important epistemic techniques in the context of genome science. Clearly, the impulse to provide a 'map' of the genes in order to influence phenotype articulates a parts-control-the-whole mechanism. Yet, the imagery of mystery, secrecy and divinity which also attaches to the genome, and descriptions of the project to map it as a 'second genesis', index older vitalistic models of life itself.

[10] Conception is now defined as the union of the genetic substance whereas fertilization is the union of the two gametes. In other words, for example, human fertilization would be the fusion of egg and sperm whereas conception would be the merging of their genetic substance. This distinction is now widely recognised, including within the Human Fertilisation and Embryology Act of 1990 (in Britain).

[11] The term 'panhumanity' as used here emerges out of discussions with Celia Lury and Jackie Stacey in the context of recent collaborative work on new forms of universalism associated with global culture.

[12] For analysis of Benetton advertising as productive of a global and transracial 'panhumanity' expressed through an appeal to consumer desires, see Lury (forthcoming). For an extension of this analysis of the 'Benetton effect' of racial flattening to international adoption, see Castaneda, 1994.

[13] For recent feminist discussions of paternity, see Delaney (1986) and Jay (1993).
[14] I am distinguishing the decoupling of a reproductive *telos* from heterosexuality in contrast to the separation of reproduction and (hetero)sexuality *per se*. Hence, I am describing how the very *purpose* of reproduction (if defined as autoreplication) can be separated from sexuality in the context of a geneticized model of regeneration.
[15] For a detailed discussion of begetting within the patriarchal tradition (and one from which this article takes direct inspiration) see Delaney, 1986 and 1993.

Bibliography

British Medical Association (1992) *Our Genetic Future: The Science and Ethics of Genetic Technology*, Oxford and New York: Oxford University Press.

Canguilhem, Georges (1994) *A Vital Rationalist*, New York: Zone Books.

Castaneda, Claudia (1994) 'Resignifying International Adoption', paper presented at the American Ethnological Society meetings, Los Angeles, 16 April.

Dawkins, Richard (1976) *The Selfish Gene*, Oxford: Oxford University Press.

Delaney, Carol (1986) 'The Meaning of Paternity in the Virgin Birth Debates', *Man* 21, 3: 494-513.

Delaney, Carol (1991) *The Seed and the Soil*, Berkeley: University of California Press.

Delaney, Carol (1993) 'Abraham and the Seeds of Patriarchy', public lecture, Harvard Divinity School, 22 April.

Delaney, Carol and Sylvia Yanagisako (eds) (forthcoming) *Naturalizing Power: Essays in honor of David Schneider*, Berkeley: University of California Press.

Duden, Barbara (1993) *Disembodying Women: Perspectives on Pregnancy and the Unborn*, trans. Lee Hoinacki, Cambridge and London: Harvard University Press.

Dworkin, Ronald (1993) *Life's Dominion*, New York: Harper Collins.

Foucault, M. (1970) *The Order of Things*, New York: Vintage.

Franklin, Sarah (forthcoming) 'Life', *Encyclopedia of Bioethics*, New York, NY: Macmillan.

Franklin, Sarah (1993a) 'Essentialism, Which Essentialism?: Some Implications of Reproductive and Genetic Techno-Science', *Journal of Homosexuality*, 24:3–4:27–40.

Franklin, Sarah (1993b) 'Life Itself', paper presented at Detradiationalisation conference, Centre for Cultural Values, Lancaster University, Lancaster, 9 July.

Franklin, Sarah (1988) 'Lifestory: the new gene as fetish object', in *Science as Culture*, 3:92–101.

Franklin, Sarah and McNeil Maureen, (1988) 'Reproductive Futures', *Feminist Studies* 14:3:545–61.

Hall, Stephen (1992) *Mapping the Next Millennium*, New York: Vintage.

Haraway, Donna (1993) 'Modest Witness as Second Millennium', paper presented at Association of Social Anthropologists (of Great Britain) Decennial meeting, Oxford, 30 July.

Haraway, Donna (1989) *Primate Visions*, New York: Routledge.

Haraway, Donna (1991) *Simians, Cyborgs and Women*, New York: Routledge.

Harding, Sandra (1986) *The Science Question in Feminism*, Ithaca: Cornell University Press.

Harding, Sandra (1991) *Whose Science, Whose Knowledge*, Ithaca, Cornell University Press.

Hubbard, Ruth and Wald Elijah (1993) *Exploding the Gene Myth*, Cambridge, MA: Harvard University Press.

Jacob, Francois (1973) *The Logic of Life*, trans. Betty Spillman, Princeton: Princeton University. Press.

Jay, Nancy (1992) *Throughout Your Generations Forever: Sacrifice, Religion and Paternity*, Chicago: University of Chicago Press.

Keller, Evelyn Fox (1985) *Reflections on Gender and Science*, New Haven: Yale University Press.

Keller, Evelyn Fox (1983) *A Feeling for the Organism*, New York: W H Freeman.

Kevles, D. and L. Hood (eds) (1992) *The Code of Codes*, Cambridge, Harvard University Press.

Latour, Bruno (1993) *We Have Never Been Modern*, trans. Catherine Porter, Cambridge: Harvard University Press.

Levy, Steven (1992) *Artificial Life*, New York: Vintage.

Lury, Celia (forthcoming) 'The United Colours of Diversity', in Franklin, Lury and Stacey, *Second Nature*.

Margulis, Lynn and Sagan, Dorion (1991) 'Microcosmos', in C. Barlow (ed) *From Gaia to Selfish Genes*, Cambridge: MIT Press, 57–66.

Mayr, Ernst (1992) *The Growth of Biological Thought*, Cambridge: Harvard University Press.

Merchant, Carolyn (1980) *The Death of Nature: Women, Ecology and Scientific Revolution*, New York: Harper Row.

Nelkin, Dorothy and Susan Lindee (forthcoming) *Powers of the Gene: Heredity in American Culture*.

Noble, David (1992) *A World Without Women*, Oxford: Oxford University Press.

Oyama, Susan (1985) *The Ontogony of Information*, Cambridge: Cambridge University Press.

Rabinow, P. (1992) 'Artificiality and Enlightenment From Sociobiology to Biosociology' in J. Crary and S. Kwinter (eds) *Incorporations*, New York: Zone Books: 234-52.

Sagan, Carl (1992) 'Life', *Encyclopaedia Britannica*, 15th ed., vol. 22, 979–996.

Schiebinger, Londa (1989) *The Mind Has No Sex?*, Cambridge: Harvard University Press.

Schiebinger, Londa (1993) *Nature's Body*, Cambridge: Harvard University Press.

Shapin, Steven and Simon Schaffer (1985) *Leviathan and the Air-pump*, Princeton: Princeton University Press.

Strathern, Marilyn (1992) *Reproducing the Future*, Manchester: Manchester University Press.

Wilson, E.O. (1992) *The Diversity of Life*, New York: Norton.

Wilson, E.O. (1984) *Biophilia*, Cambridge: Harvard University Press.

Wingerson, Lois (1990) *Mapping Our Genes*, New York: Plume.

The Language of Love: Medieval Erotic Vision and Modern Romance Fiction

Rosalynn Voaden

Oscar Wilde said that it is every woman's tragedy that her past is always her lover and her future always her husband (Wilde, 1925: 184). This chapter will explore two literary genres in which women succeed in avoiding that tragedy, genres where the woman is forever poised on the threshold between the potential and the actual, where she is always the lover and never the wife. Between these sheets (of paper), Mills and Boon will join with the Medieval Mystic, or at least the erotic visions of the medieval mystic. The two genres may seem strange bedfellows – like politics, academia does make strange ones – but these two representations of women's experience do have certain resonances, adhere to similar conventions, and present women in similar ways. This is not to suggest that medieval erotic visions were precursors of modern popular romances; rather it is to argue that certain parallels in the construction of women in these widely differing representations are due to their conception within the larger patriarchal environments of church and romance.

This chapter will concentrate on three of the many parallels between modern romance fiction and medieval unitive vision.[1] The first, 'Women in Limbo', deals with the position of the heroine in both these dramas; the second, 'The Ideal Couple', looks at the presentation of both hero and heroine and the relationship between them; the third, 'The Progress of the Plot', traces the similarities in plot structure between the two genres.

Women in Limbo

It is in their exclusive focus on a woman's brief moment on the threshold that significant points of comparison can be found between modern popular romance fiction and medieval visions. During the period of courtship, before her singularity is subsumed into the duplicity of marriage, the spotlight is on a woman; what she does, the experiences she has and the decisions she makes at this time elicit interest, attention, speculation from family and friends – not to mention unwanted advice. It is a sad fact of our society that, as Northrop Frye put it, 'The heroine who becomes a bride, and eventually, one assumes, a mother, on the last page of a romance ... by her marriage ... completes the cycle and passes out of the story' (Heilbrun, 1988: 86). In other words, the romance ends with marriage. So it is little wonder that millions of women choose to relive vicariously their own brief flowering in the improbable romances of the Violettas, Alexis and Cosimas of Mills and Boon novels.

In the late Middle Ages, women's piety was affective and highly Christocentric, focusing on the humanity of Christ to a far greater degree than did that of men.[2] This Christocentric piety is reflected in the visionary experiences of late medieval women. Devotion to the Passion of Christ often inspired unitive visions, where the visionary yearned to be united with the bleeding body of the crucified Christ. In many cases, the language used to express these unitive visions is sexual, and highly erotic. It is language drawn from the Song of Songs, from courtly love literature and troubadour lyrics. This borrowed discourse was used to give voice to the intensity of yearning for fulfilment in Christ which was a major part of women's spiritual experience in the late Middle Ages.

Caroline Bynum, in her essay 'Women's Stories, Women's Symbols', argues that Victor Turner's application of the concept of liminality – a moment of suspension of normal rules and roles, a crossing of boundaries and violating of norms – to non-primitive societies is only valid for men's experience; she contends that women are fully liminal only to men (Bynum, 1991: 49). I would argue, however, that there are certain moments in women's lives, threshold moments, which are ritualistic and dramatic, in which there is a degree of reversal of power and attention, moments which occupy a position on the edge of women's normal life experience, and that these moments can be classified as liminal. One of these moments is courtship; another is the visionary experience. The visionary, by definition, occupies a liminal position – she is intermediary between earth and heaven, between God and humanity, between the celestial and the material. Normal rules and roles are suspended; this is not to say that she is totally free to do as she likes, and neither is the courted woman, as we shall see later. However, meditation on Christ's humanity, and identification of herself as bride of Christ, reinforce the liminality of her visionary experiences, allowing her to be eternally positioned in that moment of consummation. Jacques de Vitry, a prominent churchman who chronicled the lives of several beguines at the beginning of the thirteenth-century, describes seeing '… some of these [holy] women dissolved with such a particular and marvellous love toward God that they languished with desire and for years had rarely been able to rise from their beds' (Petroff, 1986: 174).[3] A reflection part way through the romance novel *A Mistake In Identity* describes the allure of balancing on the threshold of fulfilment: 'She wanted the moment to last forever, so that he would always be coming toward her and she waiting for him' (Jones, 1986: 199). One critic remarks that this 'permanent state of foreplay' may well correspond to most women's experience of sex as better in anticipation than in action (Jones, 1986: 200). Whereas modern romance, and the book, end with marriage, for the medieval holy woman the last chapter could be replayed over and over again. Modern romance ends with happily ever after – medieval visions end with happily ever here and after.

Apart from the re-run value of the medieval vision, the scenarios for both romance fiction and unitive vision are essentially the same. The focus is on the woman. Although the hero is the centre of the story, he merely facilitates the action. Usually he is rather wooden, flat, a mirror, in medieval terms a *speculum*, which reflects the heroine's own emotional turmoil. It is her experiences which form the story. For once in her life, she is the heroine; she has achieved a position of power in a culture which habitually denies power to women. It is a brief moment of glory, evanescent and enchanted – made so by the very limits set upon it. Even if it is only temporarily, she is watched, she is listened to, her exploits have significance. Hermine (sic) Black, a romance novelist, says, 'A love-story is the most important thing in the world … I think a woman in love is a terribly important thing' (Anderson, 1974: 265). Medieval visionaries were similarly important – their experiences were written down, circulated and read widely by both men and women. They had the attention of their spiritual confessor, their fellow nuns or holy women, of lay audiences. Undeniably, not all the attention the visionary received was positive – heretics were often visionaries whose stories had the wrong readers – and the wrong ending. But a successful visionary could return to that liminal space and time where she had the freedom to explore her own spirituality in ways that might not conform fully to the conventions of the patriarchal society, just as the modern romance heroine can, briefly, explore her own sexuality outside of the narrow constraints of marriage and motherhood.

But the period of courtship comes with a price. Just because a woman is in limbo doesn't mean she is free. As Carolyn Heilbrun says, in *Writing a Woman's Life*, 'Women are allowed this brief period in the limelight – and it [courtship] is the part of their lives most constantly and vividly enacted in a myriad of representations – to encourage the acceptance of a lifetime of marginality' (Heilbrun, 1988: 21). And that is why the romance ends with marriage. Irene Roberts, romantic novelist, states this emphatically.

> It is not, and never has been, the function of a romantic novelist to continue further than the first dawning and final declaration of true love ... It would take the gilt off the gingerbread to follow the romantic dream with realism. How sad to watch the heroine, now married and pregnant, trying to do up her shoes ... Her frantic search now is not for the blossoming of love, but for a packet of indigestion tablets. No! Penelope is best left where she is – wide-eyed and happy and quite, quite beautiful in her wedding gown (Anderson, 1974: 244).

This representation of the *molestiae nuptiarum*, the pains of marriage, echoes vividly the advice handed out some eight hundred years earlier by the author of *Hali Meidhad*, a treatise encouraging women to dedicate their virginity to God. After a passage outlining in gory detail the risks of marriage – he might be a brute, and even if he isn't you have to be sure to feed him on time, and sleep with him – the author concludes: 'By God, woman, even if not for the love of God, the hope of heaven or the fear of hell, you should shun this act [of sexual intercourse] above all things, for the integrity of your flesh, out of consideration for your body and the health of your body' (Millett 1982: 17).[4] For both the romance heroine and the medieval mystic the life after closure, after consummation, is never realised, never written about.

The Ideal Couple

In both popular romance fiction and medieval unitive vision, appearance is terribly important – the body features prominently. In both the perfect body meets the perfect body, though the bruised and bleeding body of Christ, and the emaciated, flagellated body of the visionary, are equally remote from the impossibly beautiful bodies of the romantic hero and heroine which form our modern notion of perfection. The bodily representations in both genres exemplify physical ideals for the culture. In the epilogue to *Holy Anorexia*, a study of women and fasting in the Middle Ages by Rudolph Bell, psychiatrist William Davis comments that holiness represented an ideal state of being in medieval culture (Bell, 1985: 181). Similarly, in our culture, physical beauty and fitness and the lifestyle that produces those states are seen as ideal. The romance heroine is like the Virgin Mary in that she represents an ideal of womanhood, endorsed by the dominant culture, which it is impossible for real women to attain. The Virgin Mary is immaculately conceived, eternally virgin, meek, mild, and in most representations, beautiful: one has only to consider Michelangelo's *Pietà*. Similarly, the romance heroine is, of course, beautiful – she never has a hair out of place, she always knows her place, she is submissive and charming. She has the needs, dependencies and temperament of a child with the sexual allure and capacity of an adult woman. In the words of a popular song from the 1970s: 'She looks just like a woman, but she feels just like a little girl.'

The situations of the medieval visionary and the romance heroine are similar. The heroine is often an orphan, or far away from her family. Friends are few, and never turn up at inopportune moments. If she has a job, it is quite vague and makes few demands on her time, leaving her free for the full-time pursuit of being pursued. Her social isolation increases her dependence on the hero, and emphasises her powerlessness and the imbalance between them. Often the hero is described as acting like a father or a brother to the heroine. In medieval visions, Christ adopts a variety of familial roles; as well as being lover or bridegroom, he is frequently mother, sometimes father, sometimes even brother. The medieval holy woman was cut off from the world; family ties and responsibilities were nonexistent or severely attenuated; her whole focus was on Christ, and on being receptive to Christ. Both the visionary and the romance heroine are voids in a vacuum, dedicated to reading the hero and being receptive to him.

Both are presented as virtuous; holy women were, of course, models of virtue, tending lepers, feeding the poor, ironing their hair shirts. Similarly, romance heroines are thoroughly nice women; dangerous drivers and secret tipplers don't get a look-in. For example, in the Mills and Boon novel *No Gentle Seduction*, the heroine, Lexi, is the epitome of niceness – she even gives a pregnant woman her place in the queue for the bathroom (Bianchin, 1991: 121).

The hero also turns out to be 'nice', in the end, but initially his sardonic demeanour confuses the heroine, who is not overly burdened with intellect. He is always handsome, and outstanding in every way; he is a noted surgeon, a dynamic and successful executive, a Scottish laird, a famous artist. He 'has an innate ability to project an aura of power' (Bianchin, 1991: 115), is always powerful, much more powerful than the heroine, who is often overawed by his attention, and by the circles that he moves in. The parallels here with the experience of medieval holy women are suggestive. Mechthild of Magdeburg has a vision of the soul as a poor maid at the court of heaven.

> God lays the soul in his glowing heart so that He, the great God, and she, the humble maid, embrace and are one as water with wine. Then she is overcome and beside herself for weakness and can no more (Petroff, 1986: 215).

Like God, the romantic hero is always in control, especially of the heroine and her emotions.

> I don't know what would have happened if we hadn't been interrupted at that point, because he was about to step forward again [to kiss her], and I am quite sure I couldn't have done much about it. He might have been able to control the situation, but I should have been helpless (Anderson 1974: 231).

Will she be ravished, or will the innate decency of the hero save her from herself? This seems an appropriate point to move into the third area of comparison.

The Progress of the Plot

So far this chapter has considered the liminal position of the heroine, and the presentation of hero and heroine. It will now plunge into the heart of the matter – the inevitable, orchestrated movement from

'Hello' to 'How was it for you?' The development of the plot of both romance fiction and medieval erotic vision can be broken into five stages: 'Preparing for Love'; 'How to Tell a Hero'; 'He Loves me, He Loves Me Not'; 'The Declaration of Love', and then the climactic moment, which shall presently be left nameless, and cloaked in euphemism when the time comes.

So, the first stage: the preparation of love. Caroline Bynum states: 'We should not be misled by modern notions of ... brides as images of passivity. When the [medieval holy] woman saw herself as bride or lover, the image was deeply active and fully sensual' (Bynum, 1991: 48). As mentioned above, holy women dedicated their lives to being receptive to Christ, to becoming voids to be filled by the divine essence. Paradoxically, this was an active pursuit of passivity, a humbling of the self in order to be chosen and elevated, a denial of the self in order to be endowed with an identity; it was the purpose of their whole life and being, whether or not they ultimately achieved mystical union. Similarly, romance heroines have spent their whole lives preparing for this liminal moment; they have no need to prepare for life after marriage, because at that point their choices end; the shape and progress of life is then determined by the man. As one critic points out:

> ... the heroine of the novels can achieve happiness only by undergoing a complex process of self-subversion, during which she sacrifices her aggressive instincts, her 'pride', and – nearly – her life (Modleski, 1982: 37).

In some sense she does sacrifice her life. Like the medieval visionary, she becomes a blank sheet, a wax tablet which receives the imprint of the male. She can then read herself there, through the male gaze, and know who she is. The romance heroine, like many women, has spent her adolescent years searching for a husband rather than an identity. The medieval holy woman and the romance heroine both have their identities supplied by the man in their life.

Once the woman has prepared, she waits. Waiting becomes eroticized, it is a state of readiness, an anticipation of fulfilment. It is a necessary stage on the way to the happy ending; it is also a stage which reinforces the essential passivity of women. The man – or Christ – has no need to prepare or wait. He is just there, in control, perfect as he is, with no doubts that he will get what he wants. He does not have to wait to be chosen; he can pick and choose.

The difficulties of waiting to be chosen lead us to the next stage of the plot: 'How to Tell a Hero'. Medieval visionaries were tormented by the fear that what they took for Christ was really a 'devil in disguise'. This fear was reinforced by the ecclesiastical perception that women lacked discernment, a perception derived from Eve's inability to tell Satan from a snake in the grass. There were treatises enumerating the criteria of a true vision to help the poor benighted visionary read the signs and correctly identify her Lord and Saviour. Similarly, the romance heroine is frantically engaged in reading the signs; in both cases this reading consists of decoding the hero's behaviour and utterances, and interpreting and categorizing her own feelings and behaviour. Both visionary and heroine are engaged in watching the hero and themselves, and both are afraid to trust their own perception.

The inability of the heroine and the visionary to trust their own perceptions leads us to the next stage of the plot where the problems involved in 'How to Tell a Hero' are compounded. This is the stage of 'He Loves Me, He Loves Me Not'. Built into the plot of romance fictions is some artificial rupture which impedes the smooth course of true love. Usually based on some misunderstanding, the hero and heroine, who have overcome their initial difficulties and are getting on swimmingly, separate in hurt, anger and non-communication. The heroine, who by this time has given her heart, is desolated; the hero is temporarily out of the picture, and, although we learn later that his manly features masked similar anguish, the focus of the novel is on the heroine's despair. Once again she is playing a waiting game, and although she can, and does, eventually put herself in the hero's way again, the reconciliation is ultimately in his control. Lexi, in *No Gentle Seduction*, suffers thus: 'The days were bad enough, but the nights were worse, for then she lay awake, aware with each passing hour of a deep aching sense of loss' (Bianchin, 1991: 175).

This stage in romance fiction is analogous to the mystics' 'Dark Night of the Soul', a period of spiritual dryness when the soul feels abandoned by God for reasons beyond comprehension. All the visionary can do is mourn and wait in a state of painful receptivity. Mechtild of Hackeborn underwent a period of seven days 'with no savour or sweet thought of God. And because of that, she fell into so much grief that she sometimes cried so pitifully and loudly for God, her lover, that the sound of her sorrowing and crying could be heard throughout the entire house' (Halligan, 1979: 380).

Fortunately, this stage presages 'The Declaration of Love', when hero and heroine rediscover each other and know without any shadow of a doubt that they are made for each other. For Lexi, '[a]ll the self-doubts, the pain, were gone, and in its place was love – everlasting' (Bianchin, 1991: 189). For Mechtild of Hackeborn, 'our Lord, of his pity and goodness ... came and filled her full of such plentiful comfort and sweetness that often she lay as if dead, with her eyes closed ... ravished by the bodily feelings, with all her affections occupied by God, and all that time fed by the joy of his presence' (Halligan, 1979: 380).

'The Declaration of Love' stage is quite short, since now there is nothing standing in the way of 'the final embrace [which] left her secure in the knowledge that he was her reason for living – that together they belonged, almost as if fate itself had decreed it' (Jones, 1986: 205). In some romance fiction, the reader is left, like the heroine, poised on the edge of consummation. Others, especially more recent works, 'go all the way', with coy descriptions – 'his maleness', 'the heart of her femininity'. Consummation is, of course, rapturous, simultaneous and complete, no disappointments, no argument over who sleeps on which side of the bed, just silken nightgowns and total fulfilment. However, for orgasmic intensity, medieval visions can outdo any Mills and Boon yet written. Hadewijch of Brabant describes her experience of union with Christ as follows.

> With that he came in the form and clothing of a Man ... wonderful and beautiful and with glorious face, he ... took me entirely in his arms, and pressed me to him; and all my members felt his in full felicity, in accordance with the desire of my heart and my humanity ... I could no longer recognize or perceive him outside me, and I could no longer distinguish him within me. Then it was to me as if we were one without difference (Petroff, 1986: 196).

We have now reached the climax, the moment of consummation. There is nothing more to say; the story ends here.

However, every climax has its anti-climax, and my story is not quite finished. While I hope that this voyage from the sublime to the ridiculous and back has been entertaining, I also hope that by exploring the readily accessible construction of women in modern romance fiction and discerning its parallel in medieval women's unitive visions, it has become evident, as Mary Jacobus claims, that 'Women's access to discourse involves submission to phallocentricity' (Jacobus,

1986: 29). Both modern romance fiction and medieval unitive visions present what the culture that produced them has deemed to be the ideal relationship: between God and soul in the Middle Ages, and between a man and a woman now. Both are expressed in terms which present the establishment of this relationship as the pinnacle and pivotal experience of a woman's life, in terms which imply that in achieving this culmination she had discovered her own identity and her own reality. Paradoxically, the only discourses available to women to express this most profound of life experiences are the patriarchal discourses of church and romance, discourses which define women as passive, powerless, and corporeal. The result of this discursive restriction is that a woman's search for identity is represented as being achieved through identification with a powerful, compensatory other – either a divine husband, or one of the more mundane variety. While modern romance fiction and medieval unitive visions may both put women briefly in the spotlight, it is still the male who occupies centre stage.

Notes

[1] This term is used to designate mystical union with Christ or with God.

[2] Affective piety consisted of an emotional and sensual identification with the events of Christ's life, particularly the Nativity and the Passion.

[3] Beguines were women who made individual vows to live a religious life, while remaining in the community. They lived together in self-supporting groups, principally in Northern Europe. The movement began in the twelfth century.

[4] My translation.

Bibliography

Anderson, R. (1974) *The Purple Heart Throbs: The Sub-Literature of Love*, London: Hodder & Stoughton.

Bell, R. (1985) *Holy Anorexia*, Chicago: University of Chicago Press.

Bianchin, H. (1991) *No Gentle Seduction*, Richmond: Mills and Boon.

Bynum, C. (1991) *Fragmentation and Redemption: Essays on Gender and the Human Body in Medieval Religion*, New York: Zone Books.

Frye, N. (1976) *The Secular Scripture: A Study of the Structure of Romance*, Cambridge: Harvard University Press.

Halligan, T. (ed) (1979) *The Booke of Gostlye Grace of Mechtild of Hackeborn*, Toronto: Pontifical Institute of Mediaeval Studies.

Heilbrun, C. (1988) *Writing a Woman's Life*, New York: Ballantine.
Jacobus, M. (ed) (1986) *Reading Woman: Essays in Feminist Criticism*, London: Methuen.
Jones, A.R. (1986) 'Mills and Boon Meets Feminism', in Jean Radford (ed) *The Progress of Romance: The Politics of Popular Fiction*, London: Routledge and Kegan Paul.
Millett, B. (ed) (1982) *Hali Meidhad*, Oxford: Early English Text Society.
Modleski, T. (1982) *Loving With A Vengeance: Mass Produced Fantasies for Women*, Hamden: Archon Books.
Petroff, E. (1986) *Medieval Women's Visionary Literature*, New York: Oxford University Press.
Wilde, O. (1925) *An Ideal Husband*, London: Methuen.

Literature Beyond Modernism: Middlebrow and Popular Romance

Bridget Fowler

What is popular women's fiction? It is a mistake to think you know in advance, that you can tell from the blurb or the covers what the content will be. I want to focus here on the ideological and artistic diversity of romance subgenres. It is usual to delineate the romance as the formulaic 'theory' of the practice of female dependence, whether from a feminist or a literary perspective (Greer, 1970: 171–90; Cawelti, 1976:16). In this chapter I want to claim that the popular literature of romance can, under certain conditions, be creative and innovative, although at other times it can be ossified and indeed, formulaic. Further, the ideological structure of contemporary middlebrow and popular romance is more complex and heterogeneous than is usually supposed. This is particularly apparent in relation to the new social groups chosen as protagonists, in which heroes may be dustbinmen or miners, and heroines shopkeepers or the children of poor immigrants. It is also apparent in the representations of gender relations. Often a problematising sub-text works within the main narrative and its normative closures. Thus in the case of the two examples selected below, the narrative pivot of Steele's *Daddy* (1989) is the desire of married women for further learning, while Andrews' *Heaven* (1985) encodes resistance to new forms of degraded domestic labour.

It is helpful to situate popular and middlebrow romance in terms of the divisions of the cultural field proposed by Pierre Bourdieu (1984,

1993a). Especially crucial here is his distinction between the post-1850 sphere of restricted production – in which market principles are denied and in which both popular realism and bourgeois art are rejected – and the sphere of expanded or early twentieth-century mass cultural production, devoid of consecrated culture (1993a: 38–9). However, I want to suggest that this approach lacks an adequate gender perspective and that adding this in vitally affects our understanding of the cultural boundaries between high and low. The argument developed below is that women have been marginal within modernist literature and that this gives us additional grounds for assuming that the genre of popular romance, located, as it is, outside the canons of modernity, has more internal diversity than is commonly supposed.

Bourdieu's richest and most suggestive exploration of popular aesthetics is to be found in his study of the visual field of photography (1990a). It is through this opening, I suggest, that a parallel analysis could be developed to discover the principles which lead some popular novels, including romantic fiction, to be appropriated enthusiastically by the working class and some to be seen with indifference. Most tellingly, Bourdieu remarks that peasants and workers do not share the same source of interest in photography as the bourgeoisie; theirs is not the romantic gaze, with its desire for solitude, its pastoral vision of the village, and search for fresh ways of representing nature. The different material experience of workers and peasants is registered in their distance from these forms of romanticism. Photography is used to aid the visual memory of the whole social group, from the depictions of extended kin to those of the honeymooning couple. The social group is reaffirmed by capturing the subjects in predictable poses at the most obligatory sites, such as the Eiffel Tower. The use of conventional perspective and the encoding within it of the traditional world of kinship permits the photograph to operate as an art which acts as an 'accumulator' of collective consciousness, transcending the physical separation of the widespread family. My understanding is that some of the romances and sagas which are greeted with most popular affection are motivated by a similar collective aesthetic: Catherine Cookson is the paradigmatic case here.

This in turn raises the issue of gender. A proto-feminist study of gender certainly exists in Bourdieu. For example, he has suggested recently that the multivocal writing of Woolf's *To the Lighthouse* possesses the discursive linguistic structures of the dominated gender (1993b:173). But he fails to elaborate on how gender operates as a massive fault-line through modern societies, structuring even the avant-garde, with its repudiation of mass taste. For the boundary between modernism and low culture has been routinely fortified by the stigmatization of the kitsch which *women* read, both in key sectors of modernist writing and through critics' theories of the 'Great Divide'. Thus Bourdieu's archetypal modernist is Flaubert (1993a: chs. 4–7), and his Madame Bovary has, of course, fed her fatally-heightened aspirations towards both the aristocracy and the erotic on her youthful fairy tales and her serialised women's magazine stories (p12). Now Bourdieu is well aware that high art has raided popular forms in its quest for revitalization (1984: ch.1). However, he has not detailed the practices through which modern art and literature have remained the province of the male gender. It was, after all, as late as 1903 that Otto Weininger wrote 'femaleness can never include genius' (Battersby, 1989:113).

Traces of the Gender Divide in Literary Production

There is much evidence to suggest that, from the modernist period onwards, women writers have been excluded from the literary avant-garde (Huyssen, 1986: 49–51; Wilson, 1992; Wolff, 1985). Fresh data appertaining to contemporary women writers would also seem to bear this out.

Contrary to expectation, a relatively high proportion of twentieth-century women authors of popular texts were educated at universities and therefore have some 'cultural capital'. For example, the biographies of romance and Gothic writers support the view that these forms are overwhelmingly the province of women (Vinson, 1983). But they also show that a much higher proportion than expected of both British writers (33 per cent), and American writers (72 per cent) had university degrees and therefore possessed a key pre-requisite of entry into the legitimate literary world.[1] We can speculate that the twentieth-century popular genres have included relatively more 'refugee' women writers who have been rejected from the serious literary world, and that as men they would have attained entry more easily.

There is also the question of access to market alternatives, specifically, the Arts Councils' literature awards in the last ten years. We already know that the Arts Councils support financially only what their panels construct as 'serious writing' (McGuigan, 1981:96–7)). But what is less commonly known is that subsidies in both Scotland and England have continued to be given more frequently to men than to women, despite the relatively favourable recent climate for women (Arts Council, 1981–91). Thus, during the period 1981–1991, 67 per cent of the Bursaries and Writing Fellowships went to men. And 73 per cent of the grants to publishers were given for texts written by men.[2] That this is not an aberrant period is shown by McGuigan's analysis of public support for literature in the 1970s, which indicates that 56 novels by men received subsidies but only 24 by women (1981: 23–9).

A 1992 interview study of 24 writers in the West of Scotland gives further evidence of the extremely precarious material existence at present for women writers of all kinds. This reports a typical return for writing of £2000 p.a., with only three authors earning as much as £10,000 to £13,000. The group studied included established Scottish writers such as Agnes Owens and Janet Galloway. Predictably, the romantic fiction writers are the category with the highest incomes (Audain, 1992).

In contrast, the Public Lending Right lists show that the texts by women predominate amongst those that are most lent in public libraries. The list for 1991–2 reveals that 61 per cent of the most frequently lent authors were women. The most frequently loaned authors are often, but not invariably, writing in popular genres, and among them women figure strongly.

In light of this, I suggest that we look again at Bourdieu's category of 'popular culture' and middlebrow writing. The relatively unfavourable conditions for women's success in 'serious literature' may well have had the consequence of grouping within popular genres quite heterogeneous writers. It could also explain the re-emergence within these genres of motifs which testify to an underlying complexity of class and gender perspectives, or which incorporate a fraught or contradictory relationship to ideological thought. My argument is that this was particularly true in the past but is still detectable now.

New Forms of the Romance

Little has been done to map the vast terrain of contemporary popular women's writing, let alone develop adequate accounts of the reception of such texts. This variety has been recognised in Jean Franco's recent research. She shows that in contemporary Mexico there are two genres addressing 'lower' class women: first, Spanish translations of the Mills and Boon/Harlequin romances – and, second, photonovels (Franco 1986). The latter show the romantic promise to be an illusion, and, employing a realism reminiscent of the cynical voice of older women, warn against hard-drinking, violent Mexican men. Heroines in this genre are depicted as solitary workers. Yet, as Franco acknowledges, these newer popular narratives also veil the fact that their heroines' emancipation from machismo and the family may serve to expose them more starkly to another form of exploitation – free labour itself. As Marx observed: 'the period of time for which [s]he is free to sell [her] labour is also the period of time for which [s]he is forced to sell it' (Marx 1867:415).

I will limit myself here to an examination of two recent novels (*Daddy*, by Danielle Steele, and *Heaven*, by Virginia Andrews) to show some new forms of the romance in the 1990s. Both are organised around the structure of the traditional romantic story. However, they differ widely in many respects. In Bourdieu's terms *Daddy* is best-selling 'bourgeois art'. It is organised around the cult of economic success and belongs to the 'school of good sense', which Bourdieu describes as subjecting the most frenzied Romanticism to the tastes and norms of the bourgeoisie, celebrating marriage, good management of property, the honourable placement of children in life' (1993a:166). *Heaven* has some elements of Bourdieu's 'popular art' embedded within it, including melodrama and a simple morally-grounded solidarity.

Danielle Steele's *Daddy*

The narrative is taken up first by Sarah Watson, married for eighteen years to Oliver Watson, an advertising executive. Once a 1960s student radical, she has uneasily accommodated to the corporation lifestyle she earlier questioned, softened by great sex and the possession of all the classic signs of the American good life: monogrammed furs, jewels, a swimming pool. In her dealings with a colicky first baby and an unwanted third pregnancy she mounts a transient moment of rebellion against her suburban destiny, but this fades with the arrival of a housekeeper and time for her own writing. Yet when her youngest is nine she drops the bombshell that she is returning to Harvard for a post-graduate degree. Despite the anguish of husband and children – they cry for ten pages – she leaves.

Oliver then assumes the narrative. The reader is distanced from

Sarah as from a false heroine, her project increasingly being diminished as an egotistic whim which lacks any serious rationale.

Her departure becomes in his eyes an abandonment, a desertion comparable to that of a soldier from his country in the First World War. The image of the family dream now switches to one of a domestic nightmare. Oliver, commuting late, is powerless to prevent the disintegration into chaos: the youngest boy becomes a bedwetter, the oldest sacrifices a Harvard place to work at two jobs to keep his now pregnant working-class girlfriend, his mother succumbs to the ravages of Alzheimer's disease.

Later, resigned to the total absence of Sarah, Oliver seeks solace in an anarchic affair with the talented but rootless Megan – with whom he can make love for virtuoso 10 hour sessions but who knows only how to heat up moussaka from the delicatessen – a fateful sign – and who is devoid of interest in his children.

Sarah's Bohemian existence with her young French lover is ended when he is killed in a car-crash. An older (magazine) genre of family story would have engineered reunion at this point. But the last moment of reconciliation with Oliver never comes. Instead his company moves him to head their new L.A. branch: his success is now unsurpassed but his inner loneliness unhealed. It is here, in the unlikely anomic setting of Hollywood, that he meets Charlotte. She is not merely the foremost actress of a noteworthy TV drama series, but she is a self-effacing country woman: unaffectedly drawn to his children, religious, her own house all oak beams and farmhouse kitchen. This ideally-adaptable woman combines the moment of modernity with her continued acting but also represents the old-fashioned Nebraska values of kin, cooking, the house. Her marriage to Oliver is a personal utopia in which the dichotomy between working wife and family are magically resolved. Together they recreate the lost paradise of the family.

What are we to make of this *male-centred* woman's narrative? At first sight it appears that the traditional heroine has been transformed into the person of Oliver. But Oliver is hardly a new man and the role reversal that makes him solely responsible for his children is presented purely negatively as a crisis, recalling a motif which in earlier women's fiction is the domestic suffering which *a wife* experiences at the hands of an unredeemable alcoholic or gambler. Moreover, although the narrative is first presented with liberal tolerance as Sarah's story – her awakening to her own needs – her actions are quickly converted into all the signs of excess, of classic family neglect, unthinkable amid the material plenitude of her existence. Finally, tied to Sarah's monstrous self-absorption are her other signifiers: jeans, cosmopolitanism and Vietnam protests, which, at the end, are seen as insidious rather than chic. For while these are signs of youthful rebellion, they are also signs of a long history of American dissent, and it is the work of the narrative to mobilise the central protagonists' commitments to family, work ethic and religion so as to satirize such an oppositional code.

Virginia Andrews' *Heaven*

This novel is the work of an author 'who died in 1986 and who wrote seven novels before she died and five afterwards' (*The Independent*, 16.2.91). *Heaven* is the heroine's name but the narrative figures also semi-religious landscapes of heaven and hell. Like Dante's vision these are representations of the different circles of hell, and the recurrent infractions of paedophilia, incest and lust, like the medieval images, gain much of their horror from their Old Testament resonance.

The novel is one of a series which has elements of a modern Cinderella: an epic of rags to riches and romantic love. But what distinguishes it as combining new elements of popular culture is that its images of oppression and poverty are emblematic of parts of modern America. For it is set amongst 'hillbilly scum' in the west Virginian mountains, with the heroine's father a half-Indian illicit whisky-dealer. Its narrative is driven by a sense of deficiency which is part of a wider dystopia of de-industrialization. The novel's motifs of unprofitable rural crafts and illicit commodities derive from its location in the semi-periphery, while the lost industrial past is recalled by the heroine in her continuous memories of the pickaxe sounds made by dying miners, trapped underground beneath her shack.

This is a world shaped *by* but not *in* modernity: says Heaven, 'To think of central heating, double sinks and flushing toilets made me realise just how poor we really were' (p22).

Throughout the novel, there are images of fundamentalism, the complement of the harsh material world. Yet religion is linked to a recurrent breakdown of the sexual order: girls use their sexuality for power, the local minister sleeps with the heroine's nymphet sister and his wife buys their baby. Heaven's father becomes ill from venereal disease.

At their lowest point, the children are abandoned by their parents, starve on dry biscuits and are forced to steal for survival. The family is then severed as the dissolute father returns, selling off each child to childless couples. The heroine is sold to one such couple to be an indoor slave.

Thus the scene shifts from poverty to middle class cosiness and to representations of discontent and oppression within abundance. Heaven is incarcerated in a household where all values have become objectified in the form of a wild dance of consumer goods (dishwasher, ten televisions, etc.), and where her endless labour is to dust every one of a thousand ornaments, every item in a bursting fridge, until she is exhausted. Neglect of duty is punished in a bath of carbolic that raises her skin. This is the mad nightmare of commodity fetishism.

Virginia Andrews retains the husk of the romance form. Her episodes of harmony have all the familiar components of a dreamed landscape (the grand house, the statues in the garden, the maze). But her narratives also represent new experiences of dispossession and oppression. In this way the pastoral form associated with the romance is inverted: the West Virginian countryside in *Heaven* is a wilderness (with wild animals threatening children and rural unemployment), so that the privileged city woman fails to thrive amid the excess, and even the personality of the strong male disintegrates in its barren wastes. This women's fiction, then, deals with the underside of family life usually present in romance in idealised form. Its images of lack are those of extreme situations but its crude, melodramatic force may well derive from the harshness of inequalities seen in the Appalachian Mountains. For these are the regressive fantasies of the semi-proletarianised world of the 'other America'.

Conclusion

There is a predominance of women writers within both the middlebrow and popular forms, and this was especially so in the first half of this century. Retrospectively, we can often see that the mandarin view of what is culturally significant within a given period underestimates these sub-literary fields – both in terms of the degree of diversity of the genre and the diversity of ideological meaning within them in their continued potential for writing of artistic quality.[3] In this context, writers' disavowal of 'art' and the implicit choice of a contract to 'entertain' should not always delude us into taking these at face value. Unfortunately, this kind of writing – both its production and reception – is largely uncharted.

As is evidenced by the Steele text, the complex types co-existing within the middlebrow category itself are difficult to theorise. For example, is this category distinguished by its 'petty-bourgeois' ascetic morality, or by its display of an élite life-style for a wider audience, as in Ian Fleming's thrillers? It is also problematic, of course, to differentiate between the popular and the middlebrow. For example, these texts contain moments of 'carnival reversal' (Bourdieu, 1984:491), but such moments are usually transient, and do not form part of the final settlement of the narrative. Equally, popular representations of an unsubordinated female sexuality, which rupture the patriarchal order, are often expressed in coded terms and placed within wider controlling narratives that normalise their deviance. The revelation of the frustrations and rage engendered by patriarchy is a strong subterranean current of women's writing from *Villette* (Bronte, 1853) to a middlebrow novel like *Rebecca*: (Du Maurier, 1938). At its most powerful, it embeds the personal within a wider social perspective.

It is often within popular forms – such as romantic fiction – that there appear for the first time symbolic representations of certain social groups. Subordinate strata, such as migrant workers or working women, celebrate within these narratives their own existence and value. I would suggest, for example, that much of the attraction of Cookson is her positive evaluation of the direct and pithy nature of 'lower-class' speech, championing these qualities against the gentility and power of dominant languages (see, *inter alia*, Cookson, 1991). Equally, Virginia Andrews' images of scarcity and deliverance, however crudely drawn, have a resonance for those who have had an existence close to material necessity. Finally, these texts are further evidence that the capacity of the romantic narrative to provide the figures of utopia, particularly those of an imagined community, is crucial to its ability to operate effectively as ideology (Ricoeur, 1978; Jameson, 1981:286). For the romance offers – like the good family photograph – an image of integration of the social group, with the harmonious couple at its centre. In doing so, of course, its ideological elements continue to legitimate the existing order.

Notes

[1] The figures are calculated from the biographies of 160 British and 98

American authors collected in Vinson (1983).

[2] The totals are calculated from the reported awards to individuals. Until analysis of rejected applications has been undertaken, it cannot be assumed that active discrimination has taken place.

[3] Du Maurier can be viewed in this light; see, for example, *Rebecca*.

Bibliography

Andrews, V. (1985) *Heaven*, London: Collins.

Arts Council of Great Britain (1981–91) *Annual Reports*, London.

Audain, L. (1992) *Time to Write: Women's Writing and Women's Work*, M.A. diss., University of Glasgow.

Battersby, C. (1989) *Gender and Genius: Towards a Feminist Aesthetics*, London: The Women's Press.

Bourdieu, P. (1984) *Distinction: A Social Critique of the Judgement of Taste*, London: Routledge.

Bourdieu, P., Boltanski, I., Castel, R. and Chamboredon, J–C. (1990a) *Photography, A Middlebrow Art*, Cambridge: Cambridge University Press.

Bourdieu, P. (1990b) *The Logic of Practice*, Cambridge: Polity.

Bourdieu, P. (1993a) *The Field of Cultural Production*, Cambridge: Polity.

Bourdieu, P. and Wacquant, L. (1993b) *An Invitation to Reflexive Sociology*, Cambridge: Polity.

Cawelti, J. (1976) *Adventure, Mystery, Romance*, Chicago: University of Chicago Press.

Cookson, C. (1991) *Bill Bailey*, London: Corgi.

Du Maurier, D. (1938; this ed. 1992) *Rebecca*, London: Gollancz.

Franco, J. (1986) 'The Incorporation of Women: A Comparison of North American and Mexican Popular Narratives', in Modleski (ed.) *Studies in Entertainment*, Bloomington: Indiana University Press.

Greer, G. (1971; this ed. 1976) *The Female Eunuch*, London: Paladin.

Huyssen, A. (1986) *The Great Divide*, London: Macmillan.

Jameson, F. (1981) *The Political Unconscious*, London: Methuen.

Marx, K., (1867; this ed. 1976) *Capital*, Vol.I, Harmondsworth: Penguin.

McGuigan, J. (1981) *Writers and the Arts Council*, London: Arts Council of Great Britain.

Ricoeur, P. (1978) 'Imagination in Discourse and Action', in G. Robinson and J. Rundell (eds) *Rethinking Imagination*, London: Routledge.

Steele, J. (1989) *Daddy*, London: Corgi.

Vinson, J. (1983; 2nd ed.) *Biographies of Twentieth-Century Romance and*

Gothic Writing, London: St. James Press.
Wilson, E. (1992) 'The Invisible Flaneur', *New Left Review*, 191.
Wolff, J. (1985) 'The Invisible Flaneuse: Women and the Literature of Modernity', *Theory, Culture and Society*, 2, 3.

Transformations: Rewriting Romance

The Space Between: Daughters and Lovers in *Anne Trister*

Lizzie Thynne

Hitchcock's film of *Rebecca* (USA, 1940) is one of Hollywood's greatest romances – but who is the girl really in love with: is it Max or is it Rebecca? It is Rebecca's elusive but all powerful presence, which dominates the film through the mise-en-scene, music and dialogue, though we never see an image of her. Her influence creates a crisis of identification for the nameless heroine through an overwhelming desire to be like her seductive forbear – independent, daring, sophisticated and beautiful.[1] At the resolution, the girl must repudiate her initial identification and align herself with Max's view of his first wife as evil and hateful. The film attempts to demonize the erotic components of same-sex desire by projecting them onto the sinister figure of Danny, Mrs Danvers, who, like her mistress, haunts Manderley, fetishizing Rebecca's furnishings, possessions and in particular her underwear.

Romance narratives typically revolve around a potential heterosexual love relationship which must overcome a series of obstacles before being fulfilled or tragically unfulfilled, as for example, in *Letter from an Unknown Woman* (Max Ophuls, USA, 1948).[2] For the girl in *Rebecca* the main obstacle to her happy union with Max is another woman, or at least the potent memory of another woman. This obstacle is apparently overcome when Rebecca's immorality and heartlessness are revealed to the girl and she realizes that he had come to despise his first wife. Yet the disavowal of Rebecca makes for too neat an ending – Rebecca's appeal has been too manifest to be so easily disposed of. The repression of her memory is not entirely successful because what many spectators remember is the girl's and (through her, their own) fascination – with her ghostly predecessor. The course of the narrative is self-consciously Freudian, the opening sequence intimating a return through a dream to the scene of the heroine's early life. Freud argued that in her journey to maturity, the girl must transfer her affections from her first love, her mother, to her father, even though as Freud acknowledged, and the film suggests, this process is fraught with difficulties and contradictions. The ending of *Rebecca* seeks to re-establish normality with the girl safely in Max's arms, what Freud describes as 'the final normal female attitude' (Freud, 1977: 376).

Lea Pool's romance *Anne Trister* (Canada, 1986), rejects the teleology which informs much classic and modern romance where maturity is equated with heterosexual union. The other most widely seen romances featuring lesbians, *Desert Hearts* (Donna Deitch, USA 1985) and *Lianna* (John Sayles, USA 1982) also reverse the woman's rite of passage in this way, having their heroines move from heterosexuality to homosexuality. In the case of these two films, though, as in *Personal Best* (Robert Towne, USA 1982), the transition is marked by the sexual initiation of the protagonist by a more experienced female lover. Mandy Merck argues in her discussion of *Lianna*:

> the cinematic convention, the 'love scene' [is assigned] a particular symbolic function: the ability to represent 'lesbian experience'. (If this seems completely natural, consider whether the cinema's heterosexual embraces function in the same way ...) (Merck, 1986: 169)

By contrast, *Anne Trister* looks at some of the other emotional dimensions of passion between women, in particular the connection between the girl's early unconscious desire for her mother and an adult lesbian affair. Pool explores this connection through a particular use of space, mise-en-scene and metaphor. My discussion of this film is informed by Luce Irigaray's engagement with neo-Freudian psychoanalysis. She highlights the need for a 'female homosexual economy' (Whitford, 1991: 44) based on the articulation rather than repudiation of the initial link with the mother, and her construction of a female symbolic helps illuminate the process of symbolization in *Anne Trister*.[3]

Many lesbians have resisted the notion that desire between women has anything to do with mother-love, apparently because the association has commonly been used to dismiss lesbianism as an immature and/or pathological sexuality.[4] I am not proposing that there is any direct equivalence between the two, but that reconceptualizing this primary relationship of our early life is an important part of validating the choice of a female love-object in later life. I believe that psychoanalysis is a valuable tool in exploring the unconscious roots of our desires but, as Irigaray and others have argued, its terms need to change to allow for less constricting notions of difference and sexuality.

In the Freudian and Lacanian accounts of subjectivity, separation from the mother is tied to her relegation to the status of object/lack because lacking the penis/phallus. The infant's acquisition of a distinct identity is made conditional on its recognition of the phallus as primary signifier, that which marks out the difference between the sexes. As Frank Krutnik summarizes:

> The male subject's acceptance of his destiny as a man requires a patent denigration and denial of the possibilities of satisfaction and identity which lie beyond the phallus. The mother literally embodies the pre-Oedipal regime and through the Oedipus complex, the female organs, womb, breast and vagina become recast as signifiers of phallic lack rather than productive feminine presence ... The denigration of the mother functions as strategy whereby the importance of her earlier nurturing role, and the child's very reliance on her as a fundamental mirror for his own identity can be disavowed. (Krutnik, 1991: 83)

What, then, happens to the little girl in this phallic regime? Since the entry into language and culture is predicated on the recognition of the phallus as primary signifier of sexual difference and the presence of the father as the representative of a wider social network, she too submits to this law (see Lacan, 1977). In doing so, Irigaray argues, she relinquishes the possibility of her own emergence as a specifically female subject; her connection with a subject like herself – her mother – finds no representation in a language based on the male metaphor of the phallus. For women, giving up their first love of the mother is to 'sever them from the roots of their identity and subjectivity' (Irigaray, 1991: 105).[5] She does not deny the need for the mother-child dyad to be broken in order for the girl to participate in a cultural and linguistic order beyond her – what she does question is why the phallus/penis should have this special place in securing/marking the subject's place in the social. In the Freudian and Lacanian systems woman represents lack, she represents the danger of castration for the male, his 'having' has meaning only in relation to her 'not having'. Irigaray's project is to create a different set of meanings, where differences necessarily still exist but without this hierarchy of male and female, where woman can exist for herself and not only in relation to a masculine norm. What is needed is a feminine symbolic where the language that stands in for the original loss of her mother as primary object is not masculine symbols and imagery but a language which allows for female identification. She tries to break the neo-Freudian link between language and the phallus, creating instead a language which embodies the connection with the mother's body recalled in the title of her work 'Corps à corps avec la mère' ('Body against body in relation to the mother'). She asserts: 'We need to discover a language that's not a substitute for the corps à corps as the paternal language seeks to be, but which accompanies that bodily experience, clothing it in words that do not erase but speak the body' (Irigaray, 1992: 18). In the male psychic economy, woman is categorized only as mother; in order to exist the woman must oust/substitute her own mother. This situation has negative consequences for our relationships with other women; since there is room for only one 'mother', together we may therefore become our own worst enemies, embroiled in self-destruction and envy. Irigaray proposes an alternative: distinguished from each other and yet similar (as in her image of femininity as two lips) we can be contiguous with our mothers, *with* them instead of being in rivalry for their place. This association, rather than substitution, can provide the basis for solidarity with and love for other women. Because Irigaray's writing refuses the sexual status quo it provides an invaluable tool for the analysis of women's cinema which is also trying to imagine a new sexual order.

Both *Anne Trister* and Pool's recent short *Rispondetemi* (1992) juxtapose childhood and adult experiences of sexuality. In the former, Anne, a young Jewish art student, goes on a journey to Montreal from Switzerland to recover from the death of her father, who is buried in the Israeli desert. She leaves behind her long-term lover, Pierre, and her mother. In Montreal, she meets Alix, an older woman who is professor of child psychology, and Simon, an old friend of her father who finds her a disused warehouse to use as a studio. The loss of her father repeats for Anne her earlier loss of her mother who was always too busy to look after her. Alix seems to provide the nurturance and support that Anne needs and she soon falls in love with her. Visual echoes of gestures and actions across the film highlight the connection between this relationship and that of mother and daughter. In the opening shot, Anne lies, back to camera, sobbing over her father's death while her mother sits looking on in the background, physically and emotionally distant, unable to comfort her. In the penultimate sequence, this shot is mirrored in a scene between Anne and Alix. Anne is again weeping over another loss – this time the demolition of her studio and with it the vast *trompe l'oeil* mural she had painted. Alix at first sits beyond her and then climbs onto the bed to comfort her. The scene culminates in a kiss as they start to make love. The connection between the two moments is clear but the progress of Anne and Alix's relationship in the interim has made it clear that this is no simple regression – unlike the 'pre-verbal, pre-oedipal narcissism' (Williams, 1986: 150) of the lesbian affair in *Personal Best*, which is succeeded by the protagonist's concluding heterosexual relationship. By contrast, Anne does not follow this path by transposing her love to a man, maturity is not equated with becoming straight. Instead the echoes of a mother-daughter relationship in the affair are mediated through the exchange of symbols (the painting, the desert, sand) between them which represent that link while also allowing them to establish boundaries and not merely mirror or merge with each other. This establishment of a threshold[6] is also achieved through different ways of making space – a process in which both women are engaged, either literally or figuratively – Anne through her work as a painter and Alix in her work as a therapist, where she tries to restore the child, Sarah's, trust and ability to communicate. Sarah's and Anne's initial desire to possess Alix are compared. Anne forces a kiss on Alix when she visits her (just as Anne's mother clung to her daughter on her departure from Switzerland). Accompanied by the sound of children's voices and then a heart-beat (recalling the mother's heart-beat in the womb) Sarah tries to reach inside Alix's shirt to touch her breast. Alix refuses these gestures. Sarah withdraws into a corner but Alix re-establishes the connection in a symbolic way by taking her hand. Irigaray's thoughts on the different ways in which the little girl deals

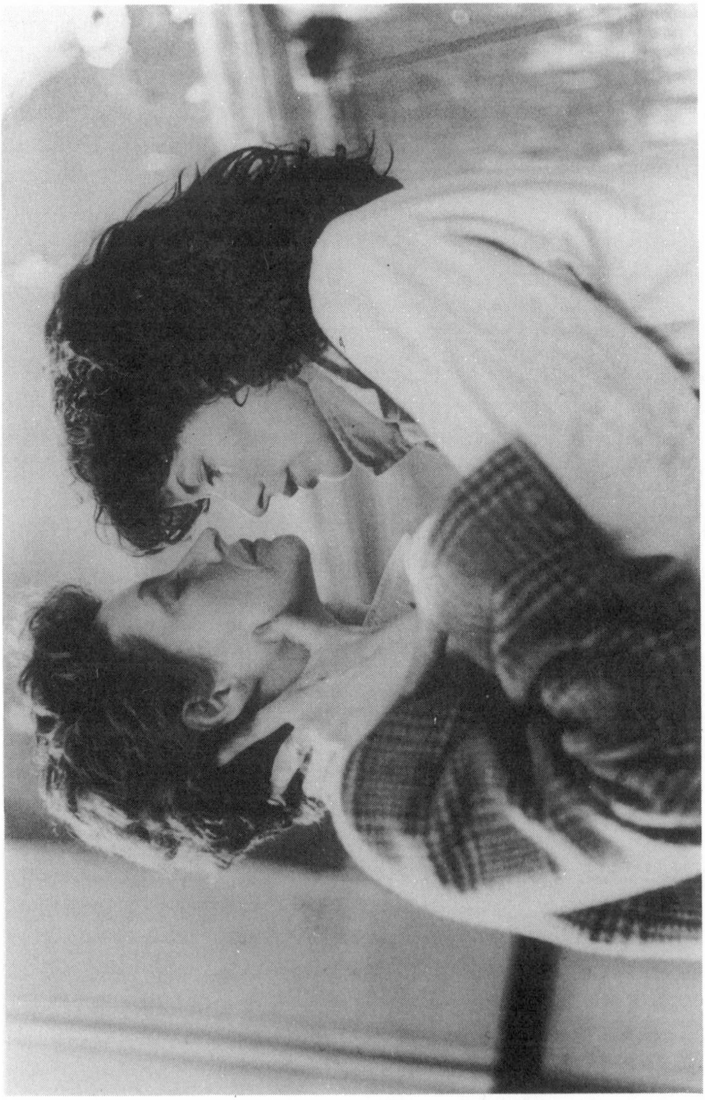

Figure 1: Anne (Albane Guilhe) forces a kiss on Alix (Louise Marleau) when she visits her studio.
Photo courtesy Contemporary Films.

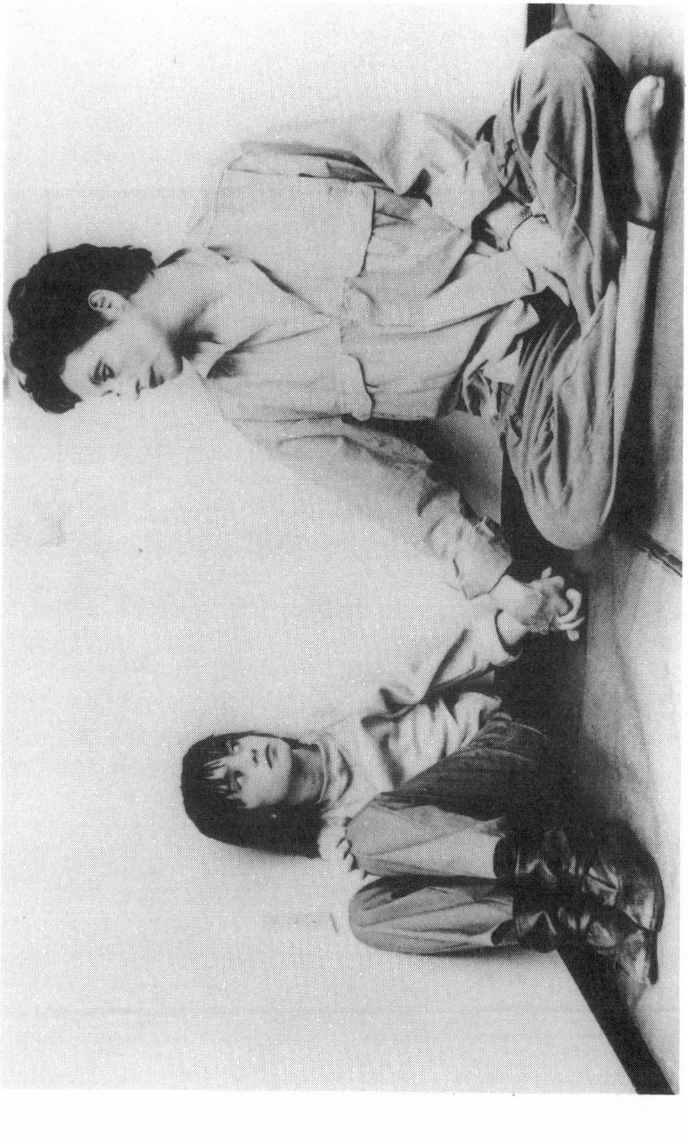

Figure 2: Alix re-establishes a connection symbolically by taking Sarah's hand.
Photo courtesy Contemporary Films.

with the absence of her mother are a useful reference point here. According to Freud, the boy masters the absence of his mother through substituting an object for her in the 'fort-da' game, a notion which Freud theorised on observing a baby boy throwing a cotton reel from his cot and then retrieving it (Freud, 1955). The reel stands in for the mother's body and as such becomes one of the boy's first experiences of language, accompanied by the verbal description 'fort' (gone) and 'da' (there). The girl's gestures, Irigaray argues, aren't the same because her mother's sex is the same as hers and she can't have the objective status of a cotton reel. To see her mother as an object is to become an object herself. She says there are three possible reactions on the part of the young girl to the absence of her mother:

> 1. She is overcome by distress if deprived of the mother, she's lost, she can't survive, she neither speaks nor eats and is anorexic in every way.
> 2. She plays with a doll, transferring the maternal affects to a quasi-subject which allows her to create a symbolic space.
> 3. She dances, thereby creating for herself a vital subjective space.
>
> (Irigaray, 1989: 32)

In her therapy sessions Sarah uses her toy bears ('quasi-subjects') to represent herself and her relationship to her mother. Initially she bandages one and unbandages it. Then she paints its outline. In the same scene, cross-cut with Anne's attempt to spoil her mural with white paint after Alix won't kiss her, she daubs the bear red. Later she wreaks her anger and hatred, her sense of abandonment, on the body of Alix (taping her mouth, tying her to a chair and calling her a 'bad mommy'). When she becomes violent, Alix tells her to pretend, not to play for real. The game and the bear become a way of articulating limits between the woman and the girl so that there is a 'space for sublimation'. 'In analysis between two female subjects, this space is necessary', Irigaray argues, 'to combat the limit of the transference [which] would appear to be this distanceless proximity between mother and daughter, distanceless because no symbolic process can account for it' (Irigary, 1991: 107).

Faced by the loss of identity threatened by bereavement, Anne too creates a 'vital subjective space' for herself. No longer content with the 'standard format' of canvas she paints red outlines on the window panes of her art school, just as Sarah later draws round her bear in red;

in Montreal she paints windows onto the walls of her studio giving them the impression of three dimensionality. The studio thus embodies both attachment to the past, the walls defining a closed space, combined with the desire to go beyond it – through the optical illusion of a space outside. The hall she is given to paint is initially a shell, deserted like the derelict building which she wanders through near the beginning of the film. The grafitti in the first building shows two adults and a child, reinforcing the idea of the place as representing her past infantile life and sense of abandonment. When Alix, initially unable to respond to Anne's advances, moves in with her lover Thomas, Anne is again left in an empty space, repeating the trauma of separation. This time it is Alix's apartment, denuded of furniture. After Pierre's arrival from Switzerland, she leaves him in the flat to go to her studio where her painting is finished. This space seems to her more like home; Alix has helped her to produce it through their work together on the model design – a process which Anne describes as 'two little girls making a doll's house'. It is a space claimed in the teeth of resistance from Thomas, Alix's boyfriend, who, when Anne is given the warehouse, cajoles her to trade it for his own much smaller workshop.

Both the male lovers in the film want the women to represent home for them, to be their space, although neither is shown as particularly 'sexist' in an obvious sense. Thomas pressurizes Alix into living with him, away from her own place. When Anne claims Alix's attention, he threatens Anne causing her to have an accident. Pierre sends Anne the story of a small boy, clearly representing himself, who leaves his mother, gets lost in the vast expanses of the world, wreaks havoc and then returns to her womb – it is a fantasy of an impossible return to her body as a secure place for his identity. Since, for men, women unconsciously constitute the phantasized body of the mother, Irigaray argues, they do not exist as subjects for themselves (Irigaray, 1985). Pool gives her women characters symbolic shared spaces where mutual recognition is possible. When Alix comes to see Anne's mural at her studio their conversation is given in voice-over as they look admiringly at each other. This mutual gaze recalls that of mother and child in the pleasurable bonding of infancy before speech begins but this moment of mutuality is not presented as a simple romantic resolution, each fully comprehending the other.[7] Instead, it is succeeded by Alix's confusion and surprise at Anne's attempt to kiss her. Similarly, the studio is not a permanent refuge for Anne – she cannot return to the home it represents – but its symbolic value is perpetuated in the other shared image, the desert, which is also spatial and signifies her connection with the other woman. There is no fixed 'home' for Anne's identity – her studio is demolished while she is in hospital recovering from the accident. Pool's rather clichéd use of a fluttering dove bruising its wings as it tries to escape the studio via the false windows indicates that while it creates an illusion of freedom her obsession with the space has also made it a prison. The project has become exhausting and out of proportion. The *trompe l'oeil* structure she has painted is only a place of transition between the blank desert where her father's funeral is held in the opening sequence and the flowering one which she returns to at the end.

If her environmental painting reconnects her with her girlhood home, the desert suggests the freedom to become autonomous. It is another imaginary space which she shares with Alix. Other recent features looking at the relationship of two women have put them into open spaces – suggesting a new place for female desire beyond the confines of domestic interiors. The landscape previously colonized by men trying to conquer nature and native peoples, often designated as feminine, becomes the arena of women: Thelma and Louise (Ridley Scott, 1991) speed across the desert on the run from patriarchal law; in *Salmonberries* (Percy Adlon, USA/Germany, 1991) Kotz (kd lang) lures Roswitha out of her warm but constricting haven to glide through the spectacular snowscapes of Alaska. Similarly for Anne, Canada is a thrilling expanse after the confines of Switzerland.

The blizzard which falls the first night she spends with Alix is the frozen counterpart of the desert sandstorms. Alix tells Anne her 'desert stories' – of the time when she went to the Arabian desert to forget the past, spent days hearing only Arabic and stuffed her suitcase full of the beautiful rocks she found. As Anne's father is buried in the desert, for her it evokes death but Alix's experience suggests its beauty. Its openness and formlessness are also full of possibilities. When Anne returns there at the end of the film she sends Alix a handful of sand and a super 8 film of herself. Sand as a symbol suggests change and fluidity – as such, it is an appropriate image for female sexuality characterised as open-ended and flowing as opposed to the goal-orientated solidity of male sexuality. Alix lets the sand slip through her fingers – it is not an object that can be fixed and held.[8] She projects the super 8 movie; it shows the desert in bloom and then Anne places herself smiling in front of the camera, moving backwards and forwards to make sure she is in frame, with her father's tomb behind her. She is both a subject – in shooting the film – and the object of Alix's loving look as she watches it. The super 8 picture is only part of an otherwise dark screen, suggesting that Anne has found her own limits in relation to the void, through her relationship with the older woman. (Earlier in the film Sarah refuses Alix's look by splattering the screen through which she is observed at the clinic – she refuses the position of object and only progresses when Alix interacts with her directly). The final image of self-representation for the look of another woman completes the film's project of charting a course for the female subject, in the words of the closing song 'celle qui n'a jamais parlée' ('she who has never spoken').

Five languages are either spoken or referred to in the film – French, English, Yiddish, Italian and Arabic – but the key moments between the women characters are wordless, suggesting the Irigarayan notion that women are in exile from language as it does not figure their bodies and their sexuality. The multiplicity of languages also reinforces the idea that Anne lacks a home. Her exile as a woman has affinities with the Jewish experience of not belonging, an experience suffered by director Pool's father, a Polish Jew, and Anne's father in the film, who spoke ten languages but, comments Anne, 'none of them well'. In her short film, *Rispondetemi* (1992), Pool uses the differences between languages to signify the difference of female desire. A lesbian couple are involved in a car crash in which one is killed and the other is rushed to hospital, barely alive. As the medics battle to save her, childhood experiences of abuse and memories/fantasies of her lover flash through her mind. Seduced by her father, she is distant from her mother when he beats his wife. Finally, still a child, she seems reconciled with her mother. Damaged by her father's sexual exploitation of her, her expression of affection for her mother has sexual overtones to which her mother responds only with a reassuring hug. The reconciliation with her mother is a prelude to her last memory – lying on her bed with her lover, who repeats the Italian words 'rispondetemi' ('answer me'). At this point she crosses the threshold from near-death to life and we know she will survive. As in *Anne Trister*, the links are suggestively drawn between a language which is other than the dominant one, love between women and between mother and daughter.

The endings of Pool's films avoid a conventional romantic conclusion – there is no final union either with each other or with a man, nor is there the self-destruction which concludes many films about lesbian affairs (such as *Another Way* Karoly Makk, Hungary, 1982 and

The Loudest Whisper, William Wyler, USA, 1961). Instead, two women are left separate but with the vital connection between them still represented through a medium – an Italian song, sand – which suggests the possibility of another language for desire, a language which will be able to figure the mother's body and not only that of the father. In the course of *Anne Trister*, the protagonist is reunited with the lost object of her childhood love, her mother, – both literally (she writes to her with a new affection) and figuratively through loving a body like her own in her affair with Alix. The depiction of the lovers' relationship avoids the pre-oedipal merging or mirroring to which much screen lesbianism has been condemned. Instead it is articulated through shared images and objects – a symbolic dimension of non-phallic signifiers. The final scene – Alix's projection of Anne's film of herself – reiterates the idea of a new feminine symbolic. Here the diegetic spectator is not caught up in seeing or disavowing the absence of the phallus as in the traditional voyeuristic and fetishistic regimes of the cinema, but is engaged in a more equal exchange between the looker and the looked at. Anne decides where to place herself in the frame and what to show, Alix controls the mechanism of projection. Not confined to securing masculine identity as does the passive image of the woman 'to-be-looked-at', they emerge through the cinematic metaphors of the active spectator and the film-maker, as autonomous female subjects speaking to each other in a medium they have made their own.

Special thanks to Linda Anderson for her inspiration in writing this article.

Notes

[1] Some critics, notably Teresa de Lauretis, query the notion that identification with or wish to be like an ideal female figure is continuous with the choice of a female love object (See de Lauretis 1991: 261–263). I agree however with Kaja Silverman's argument that there is an intersection of desire for, and identification (Silverman, 1988: 154).

[2] The conventions of Hollywood romance are usefully summarized in Stacey, 1990.

[3] I have drawn here on Margaret Whitford's overview of Irigaray's writing in Whitford, 1991, esp. pp169–191 and the following works by Irigaray: 'Body

against body in relation to the mother' (Irigaray, 1992); *Speculum* (Irigaray, 1985) and *This Sex Which Is Not One* (Irigaray, 1985b).

[4] This point is discussed further in Ryan, 1983: 196–209.

[5] Silverman argues that 'Irigaray sees the female subject's libidinal discontents as the inevitable result of distance from the mother and hence conceptualizes closeness as the remedy for these discontents.' (Silverman, 1988: 152) Although this may be true of *This Sex Which Is Not One*, elsewhere, as Silverman acknowledges, (for example in 'Body against body') Irigaray points to the existence of necessary boundaries between mother and daughter.

[6] The 'threshold' is an image for the relations between subjects which suggests there is no rigid boundary or hierarchy but rather a border which can be crossed and re-crossed. It refers to the morphology of women's bodies, which are not closed, as is the ideal masculine body, but allow penetration, the birth of children, etc. The openness of women's bodies, has, of course, been seen as a threat to patriarchal control, awakening fears of engulfment or trespass (see Whitford, 1991: 159–161).

[7] E. Ann Kaplan notes that 'this mutual gazing is not of the subject – object kind that reduces one of the parties to the place of submission' (Kaplan, 1983: 205).

[8] As a counter to Lacanian phallomorphism, Irigaray proposes a different set of metaphors for sexuality which more closely evoke the female body – at least two lips, mucous – images which suggest multiplicity, fluidity, lack of distinction between inside and outside. Other women's films have used the aqueous to represent women's bodily/erotic experience, eg, Ulrike Zimmermann's *Touristinnen* (Germany, 1986) which features a sexual game between a female harbour worker and a mermaid, shot partly underwater; Maya Deren's *At Land* (USA, 1944) where the protagonist finds herself beached from the sea onto the alien territory of land.

Bibliography

Freud, Sigmund (1955) 'Beyond the Pleasure Principle', in *The Standard Edition of the Complete Psychological Works of Sigmund Freud* vol. XVIII, ed. and trans. James Strachey, London: Hogarth Press and the Institute of Psychoanalysis.

Freud, Sigmund (1977) 'Female Sexuality' in *On Sexuality: Three Essays on the Theory of Sexuality* Angela Richards (ed) Harmondsworth: Penguin.

Irigaray, Luce (1985a) *Speculum of the Other Woman*, trans. Gillian Gill, Ithaca: Cornell University Press.

Irigaray, Luce (1985b) *This Sex Which Is Not One*, trans. Carolyn Porter with Carolyn Burke, Ithaca: Cornell University Press.

Irigaray, Luce (1989) 'The Gesture in Psychoanalysis', trans. Elizabeth Guild, in Teresa Brennan (ed) *Between Feminism and Psychoanalysis*, London and New York: Routledge.

Irigaray, Luce (1991) 'The Limits of the Transference', in Margaret Whitford (ed) *The Irigaray Reader*, Oxford: Blackwell.

Irigaray, Luce (1992) 'Body against body in relation to the mother', in her *Sexes and Genealogies*, trans. Gillian Gill, New York: Columbia University Press.

Kaplan, E. Ann (1983) *Women and Film: Both Sides of the Camera*, London and New York: Methuen.

Krutnik, Frank (1991) *In a Lonely Street: Film Noir, Genre and Masculinity*, London and New York: Routledge.

Lacan, J. (1977) *Ecrits*, London: Tavistock.

de Lauretis, Teresa (1991) 'Film and the Visible', in Bad Object Choices (ed), *How Do I Look: Queer Film and Video*, Seattle: Bay Press.

Raillard, Florence (1986) 'Une Femme Se Penche Sur Son Passe', *Le Matin*, 23 July, p16.

Ryan, Joanna (1983) 'Psychoanalysis and Women Loving Women', in Sue Cartledge and Joanna Ryan (eds) *Sex and Love: New Thoughts on Old Contradictions*, London: Women's Press.

Silverman, Kaja (1988) *The Acoustic Mirror: The Female Voice in Psychoanalysis and Cinema*, Bloomington and Indiana: Indiana University Press.

Stacey, Jackie (1990) 'Romance', in Annette Kuhn with Susannah Radstone (eds) *The Women's Companion to International Film*, London: Virago.

Whitford, Margaret (1991) *Luce Irigaray: Philosophy in the Feminine*, London and New York: Routledge.

Williams, Linda (1986) 'Personal Best: Women in Love', in Charlotte Brunsden (ed) *Films for Women*, London: British Film Institute.

Addicted to Love

Sue Vice

This chapter is an investigation into whether the phenomenon of the 'addicted lover', or erotomaniac, who is a staple literary figure and one also documented in sociological studies, is an anomaly or is simply an extreme example of how love works under patriarchy. An examination of some representative texts, in which the gender and sexuality of the protagonist and loved one vary, suggests that the addicted lover, who needs an endless series of 'fixes' to cope with their love-problem, is indeed a representative and not an extraordinary figure. Both Lacanian psychoanalysis and psychoanalytically inclined narrative theory (for instance, Brooks, 1985) support this conclusion, which becomes especially clear in literary texts about addicted lovers: it is the structure of such texts, rather than their infinitely interchangeable content, which is engaging to the reader, who becomes analogously addicted through the act of reading.

This investigation arises out of a course I teach on Literature and Addiction, in which questions about the links between addiction and signification are raised in relation to texts about (and by) alcoholics, junkies, hallucinators, food or starvation devotees, and love-addicts.[1] Whereas the serial nature of addiction is fairly clear in relation to alcohol in Jean Rhys' *Good Morning, Midnight* (1939), for instance, or to heroin in William Burroughs' *Junky* (1953), the notion of addiction in relation to romance is rather more complicated, especially when the romance is textualized. Is 'obsession' a more accurate label, if the lover is unable to relinquish an unsuitable or doomed relationship, suggesting that instead of a series of unsuitable objects (whether loved ones, bottles or tabs) there is only one, if an unpossessable one? And what of the 'serial lover', Mozart's Don Giovanni figure, who unrolls a huge list of sexual conquests from every European country: is this pattern more similar to the addicted one in suggesting an endless substitutability, an unwillingness to put an end to a stream of interchangeable objects?

The texts I have chosen to try and establish whether there is such a thing as an addictive structure to romance also raise the issue, implicit in the example of Don Giovanni, of how the gender and sexual orientation of lover and loved one affect the model. The term 'addiction' if applied to the Don, or to Milan Kundera's character Tomas in *The Unbearable Lightness of Being* (1982), who contrasts love for his wife Teresa to love-making, which he practices with an endless stream of other women, sounds simply like a patriarchal power-play taken to its logical conclusion. Applied to women, however, as Robin Norwood does in her book *Women Who Love Too Much* (1986), and Charlotte Davis Kasl in *Women, Sex and Addiction* (1990), the term is used to suggest self-victimization: a particular view of femininity also taken to its logical conclusion. It goes without saying that these women who love too much love men; as Susan Faludi points out in her book *Backlash: The Undeclared War Against Women* (1992), Norwood 'asks why so many [women] "choose" abusive men, but not why there are so many abusive men to choose from' (p380).

The texts I am going to discuss are Thomas Mann's *Death in Venice* (1912), Yukio Mishima's *Thirst for Love* (1950), Josephine Hart's *Damage* (1993), and Jane Rule's *Desert of the Heart* (1964). In each, except Rule's novel, love is pathological and can only result in death; the subject can only orientate her or himself, in addictive fashion, in relation to something outside the self, which appears to offer the opportunity for incorporation or possession, like a glass of whisky, but which also remains autonomous, like the bottle.

In *Death in Venice*, the nature of the romantic attachment is both classical and oddly modern, composed as it is of Platonic elements combined with an emphasis on the male gaze. Laura Mulvey, in her classic essay 'Visual Pleasure and Narrative Cinema', uses psychoanalytic theory to argue that in cinema the three gazes constructed on screen (of audience, camera and character) are all masculine, and the object of the gaze invariably female – which begs the question of how female identification with the screen operates (see Silverman 1988 for an alternative view). However, in this case the object of the three gazes is a male figure, albeit a feminine one. Gustav Aschenbach, the lover (if that is the correct term), is a writer, and links his preoccupation with the barely adolescent Tadzio to the aesthetic: 'with an outburst of rapture, he told himself that what he saw was beauty's very essence; form as divine thought, the single and pure perfection which resides in the mind, of which an image and likeness, rare and holy, was here raised up for adoration' (p46).

This etherealizing impulse exists in the distance there is between older man and young boy; they never speak, and Aschenbach's passion is, at least until the end, surprisingly un-goal-oriented. Roland Barthes comments on this construction of distance in his *A Lover's Discourse*, a particularly helpful work in approaching love-addicted texts because Barthes emphasizes the structural over the psychological. He says, 'Two myths have persuaded us that love could, *should* be sublimated in aesthetic creation: the Socratic myth (loving serves to "engender a host of beautiful discourses") and the romantic myth (I shall produce an immortal work by writing my passion)' (p97). Aschenbach invokes the Socratic myth several times in *Death in Venice* (pp47, 48), but the only text to emerge out of his interest is the one in which he himself is objectified and dies.

The glance – a stolen, secretive fragment of the gaze – in the text is primarily Aschenbach's, as the reader cannot tell that Tadzio sees or knows; in Luchino Visconti's film of the novel (1971) this is different, and the young boy, apparently conscious of himself as an aesthetic object, catches and returns the older man's look. This is an interesting effect in a film which relies upon, as well as represents, the spectator's gaze. This gaze is directed at the previously unknown actor Björn Andersen, who plays Tadzio, and whose pre-pubertal feminine looks made him a five-minute wonder when the film was released. It is unusual to find a film which constructs a voyeuristic character and audience, and then directs this scopic drive at a male, not a female, figure.

However, as Steve Neale has suggested in an article about David Puttnam's film *Chariots of Fire* (1982), an aversion of the gaze away from rather than towards male bodies in that film actually reasserts patriarchal priorities. Men who looked at other men while running competitively in *Chariots of Fire* often lose momentum and lose the race; as Neale puts it, 'winning, defined in accordance with the narrative and thematic structure of *Chariots of Fire* as achieving a stable identity within phallic authority, is dependent upon a suppression of the look at one's male sexual peers ... the achievement of an Oedipal resolution in accordance with the principles of a patriarchal society is dependent upon a repression not only of women and female desire, but also of male homosexual desire' (p36). Jacques Lacan suggests that the male gaze can only be directed at women, not other men, to the extent that even if what is before him is masculine the voyeur will feminize it, because he is trying, paradoxically, to assure himself of a lack: 'What the voyeur is looking for and finds is merely a shadow ... not ... the phallus, but precisely its absence' (1977b: 182).

In *Death in Venice* the voyeuristic impulse remains at the level of the look and never tries to realize its penetrative origins by killing what it sees, as often happens to female objects of the male gaze in films, including classics of the genre *Psycho* (Alfred Hitchcock 1960) and *Peeping Tom* (Michael Powell 1960). However, the opposite of the spiritual and Platonic love Aschenbach assures himself he feels for Tadzio is represented in the text by the corruption and decay of the plague in Venice. When this love does take a bodily form, it is in a sick body. The moment after Aschenbach thinks, ' "I love you!" ', the 'sickness' of Venice comes to his attention as a putrefying, sweet smell (p55), and as hidden rottenness, a secret which he identifies with his own secret love: 'the city's evil secret mingled with the one in the depths of his heart – and he ... owned to himself, not without horror, that he could not exist were the lad to pass from his sight' (p57). When Aschenbach dies at the end of the book, the plague and his love have become interchangeable, and his final sight of Tadzio is of a deathly figure: 'the pale and lovely Summoner out there smiled at him and beckoned' (p79). In our AIDS-conscious era, a text like this which uses illness as a metaphor for love, and vice versa, has an interestingly anachronistic resonance.

Mishima's novel *Thirst for Love*, its very title invoking a connection between (alcoholic) addiction and romance, has some structural affinities with *Death in Venice*. First, it also concerns an unconsummatable love, although this time impossible for class reasons; second, its historical moment is post-atom bomb, a calamity the text recalls in its landscape and in the uneasy class relations which (in)form the obsession, as the state of pre-First World War Europe constitutes it in *Death in Venice*; third, the emotional progress of the protagonist, a widow called Etsuko, also involves pleasure taken in illness and pain; and, lastly, the text can only resolve itself through a death, this time a sudden removal of the troublesome drug rather than of the addict: it is Saburo, the loved one, who dies, and at Etsuko's hands.

It is perhaps clearer in *Thirst for Love* that the nature of the love-relation in the text also constitutes its form. An instantly successful love would mean a short, or at least unproblematic, story. A love story which precludes success can only end arbitrarily, in death, as addictive texts often do, giving themselves the opportunity to unravel at great length: it is literally a case of kill or cure: Marilyn Farwell describes such a narrative trajectory as a re-enactment of the heterosexual act (p95). As Peter Brooks puts it in *Reading for the Plot*, 'Incest is only the exemplary version of a temptation from which the protagonist and the text must be led away, into detour, not the cure that prolongs narrative (p110). For incest, read the self-cancelling over-sameness of a perfect match, a meeting of souls; the text which ends in marriage. Etsuko prolongs her own story, but can only do so through choosing a love-object which she cannot possess; not only is Saburo engaged to someone else, so that jealousy for Etsuko becomes synonymous with love, but he is also a farm worker.

It is rare to encounter narratives of obssessive love which have a female protagonist: the film *Fatal Attraction* (Adrian Lyne, 1987) is a revealing counter-example, in which the woman in question is unmistakably pathologized for her passion. In *Thirst for Love*, Saburo's lower class status acts as a substitute for gender difference: Etsuko thinks, 'His lovely poverty! That above all attracted her. In Etsuko's eyes his poverty played the part usually played by shyness in a girl' (p71). Saburo may be male, but Etsuko is in a position of greater economic power, able to send his fiancée away and finally to take his life. This unlikely empowerment of a woman, and the representation of female desire, operate as the kind of potentially disruptive contradiction discussed by Marilyn Farwell in her essay, 'Heterosexual Plots and Lesbian Subtexts', but, as in some of the texts she discusses, the implications cannot be drawn out in *Thirst for Love* without the text destroying itself (Farwell, 1990: 97). Even in a warped heterosexual format like that in *Thirst for Love*, the very representation of female desire, Farwell suggests, can threaten the 'stranglehold' of heterosexuality on narrative (p93).

As in *Death in Venice*, there is a strict distance maintained between lover and (possibly unknowing) loved one in *Thirst for Love*. Etsuko emphasizes this by anonymously scratching Saburo's back with her fingernails at a festival; he does not guess it was her behind him in the crowd. This is not simply a tale of unrequited love, but of a love carefully contrived to allow no consummation; like Aschenbach,

Etsuko does not want a conventional ending. At the end, when Saburo makes advances towards Etsuko, this is not the prelude to a happy ending, but the last thing Etsuko wants from her distant lover. As René Girard puts it in *Deceit, Desire and the Novel*, the lover addicted to unsuccessful romance 'grows tired of a futile undertaking but the treasure is too precious for him to give up. So he begins to look for a stone which is too heavy to lift' (1965: 176). (Note that, according to Girard's argument, the masculine is used advisedly; see Moi, 1982, for a discussion of his male-centred view.) In this kind of addictive love-relation, fear of success more than failure ensures the choice of an impossible object. As Etsuko's brother-in-law says in *Thirst for Love*, ' "Sometimes jiltings run in series – like miscarriages. Her nervous system has got into the habit of it, I suppose, and when she falls in love it has to end in a miscarriage" ' (p96).

It could be said that this is the nature of desire in the symbolic order. According to Lacan, the child gains the ability to use language at the expense of losing its undifferentiated union with the mother, and its memory of, and urge to return to, this state constitute the unconscious. Language and desire operate according to the same motion of deferral: in both, a transcendent or ultimately satisfying signified is sought for at the end of an endless chain of signifiers. These signifiers can be either the words which stand in for the objects whose absence they signify, or lovers, who stand in for the true object of love, the mother. As Elizabeth Grosz says, 'In adult life, genital sexual relations are attempts to satisfy this impossible demand, the demand to be/to have the phallus for and through the other[2] (1990: 133), where 'the phallus' means what will complete me and what the other will be completed by.

Etsuko's and Aschenbach's stories of impossible desire are therefore not exceptional but exemplary. As Lacan says, 'desire is the desire of the Other': what lovers can give each other is their desire, that is, the unfulfillable in each other. Terry Eagleton summarizes this by rewriting the 'love cry' (Barthes, 1978: 147) of 'I love you' as, 'It's you who can't satisfy me! How privileged and unique I am to be the one to remind you that it isn't me you want ...' (1986). This makes textuality and sexuality intimately compatible, as both depend on the same metonymic structure, as Lacan puts it, 'a forward drive in the signifying chain, an insistence of meaning toward the occulted objects of desire' (quoted in Brooks, 1985: 51). Desire is always already textual; and expecting it to be satisfied is like expecting to reach the signified at the end of a chain of signifiers in a text. Thus unrequited –

or unrequitable – love is desire's most authentic expression.

Josephine Hart's infamous novel *Damage* (1993) expresses this last fact particularly paradigmatically. Both novel and film have been extremely popular; this is of course partly due to the sensational nature of the relationship portrayed: it is an *amour fou* between an older man and his son's lover, which (in the novel at least) features elements of eroticized power relations. Stephen Fleming ties up his lover Anna, and gags her, as an expression of their soul-matedness; this means that Anna cannot see what is happening when her fiancé, Stephen's son, accidentally comes upon them *in flagrante*.

However, this is not the whole story; even as soft porn the novel is curiously hollow, and this, it seems, is really why it is so compelling. It is a structure without a content; the whole point of Stephen and Anna's love is that it is both without apparent motivation yet – or therefore – all-consuming. The text makes a virtue of this; after a brief introduction at a party where they 'recognize' each other, Anna has only to ring Stephen up and say, 'It's Anna', for him to make an immediate appointment to meet and copulate – which they do without further exchange of words (p37). This may be a titillating (or 'lurid', as Jonathan Romney put it in his *Sight and Sound* review of the film) scenario; it also belongs to the same pattern we have already noted in the Mann and Mishima novels, that these stories of doomed desire have no content which is not also structure. Hart's novel conforms to this particularly clearly because it is both apparently very content-ful (it features incest, adultery, and a Tory junior health minister running naked down the stairs of a public building to take his dead son in his arms) and very empty. It concerns a love which cannot reach any satisfactory end except death; as such it is curiously similar to the medieval tradition of courtly love, which Lacan suggests, in 'God and the Jouissance of The Woman' (1982b), makes a virtue out of necessity. No love relation can ever reach fruition, so courtly love, in which elaborate rituals surround a male lover's celebration of his mistress's inaccessibility, is its fullest expression.

Finally, Jane Rule's *Desert of the Heart* takes place amid the paraphernalia and constructs of heterosexual love within the symbolic order, in particular the divorce town of Reno, but manages to some extent to leave them behind. In terms of the addictive pattern, Ann appears to have chosen an equivocal, rather than definitely inaccessible, love object; one who is in a transitional state herself. No death is necessary to terminate an interminable love and therefore text;

instead, the novel ends indeterminately, with the two women approaching the courtroom where Evelyn will pick up her divorce decree: 'And they turned and walked back up the steps toward their own image, reflected in the great, glass doors' (p244). This moment possibly represents Evelyn's entry into another kind of novel, as this one ends before the two women in effect walk through the mirror which, in Lacanian terms, is what allows for the subject's traumatic construction in the symbolic order (1977a). Logically, they will emerge in a world and a kind of writing more expressive of the imaginary, the realm inhabited by the infant before the intrusion of the father.

Evelyn has now escaped the 'long detour of marriage' (p173); instead of ending with heterosexual union, *Desert of the Heart* starts with its dissolution, and presents Evelyn's marriage as a narrative error. Ann sees marriage overtly in narrative terms: ' "I don't really understand how people take the marriage vows. How did you? It's one thing to forsake the past, but how can you forsake the future?" ' (p176). Marriage apparently makes for a poor story. Marilyn Farwell makes the same connection Ann makes, between social and narrative disruption occasioned by the fact and representation of women bonding. Definitions of 'lesbian' include disruption of the 'binary structures of male/female, subject/object, presence/absence of Western narratives', which provide Farwell with the basis for her theory of 'a lesbian narrative space as a disruptive space of sameness as opposed to difference' (p93).

As Bonnie Zimmerman points out, the novel's final image is one of relationship, not reflection (p108): the reflection of the two women in the plate-glass is described as 'their image', not 'their images', and they are side by side, not face to face, walking together towards the glass. The flattening out of the mirror so that it connects rather than divides implies an attitude to the symbolic order quite different from other texts devoted to love. Eschewing the paradigm of ending desire through death, the women in *Desert of the Heart* travel the other way, back through the mirror and away from what Lacan calls 'the comedy of copulation' which characterizes heterosexual relationships (1982a: 84).

Desert of the Heart raises and then questions what Gillian Spraggs identifies as the patriarchal discourses of Christianity and judgemental psychoanalysis in appearing to employ but then actually discarding imagery of Hell and Eden, and of mirroring and maternity, in lesbian relationships (1992: 117). Habits of defining lesbians as women with unresolved Oedipal crises or having regressed to infantile sexuality are thus challenged, as Zimmerman points out (1992: 94).

While not wanting to present this particular text as utopian, the ways in which *Desert of the Heart* deals with its subject of a different, rather than a doomed, love are revealing. It offers a textual version of a sameness in love which does not lead to the over-cancelling sameness, the dead-end, of marriage or incest (the 'successful' love relation); nor to the wearying endlessness of the addicted heterosexual lover, replaying over and over again the inaccessibility of the signified implied by a constant stream of signifiers.

Desert of the Heart is a narrative without a previously rehearsed script, which does not already know how it will end. Ann makes this clear when she tells her friend Silver, ' "Joe can make an honest woman of you. I'm not in the same position with Evelyn" ' (p213). This comment clarifies the difference between this novel and others about passion. Here, female bonding is not merely the 'subtext' of a heterosexual one (see Abel 1983 for a discussion of *Mrs Dalloway* in exactly such terms), nor is the label 'lesbian' only metaphorical. Marilyn Farwell, whose terms these are, calls the ability of female desire to disrupt conventional narrative a 'lesbian space' (102 n2), and this space takes on a geographically and psychologically material form in Rule's novel: the love which can undo heterosexual assumptions has its being in the desert and in the casinos of Reno. Evelyn knows that Frances, Ann's landlady, 'wanted love for Ann and did not much care how she got it' (p222); but, as we have seen, how Ann goes about getting it makes all the difference to herself and to the form of the narrative, which ends tentatively, almost before the romance begins. In this respect it is very different from, and less closed than, the other novels we have considered, where ending meant death. Here it means life, and uncertainty.

Thanks to Alex George and Lynne Pearce for help in completing this paper, to Sylvia Harvey and Jolyon Pike for suggesting particular texts, and also to the students who took the course.

Notes

[1] I have borrowed the name of Robert Palmer's hit single for my title here.

Bibliography

Abel, E. (1983) 'Narrative Structure(s) and Female Development: The Case of *Mrs Dalloway*', in E. Abel, M. Hirsch and E. Langland (eds) *The Voyage In: Fictions of Female Development*, Hanover: University Press of New England.
Barthes, R. (1978) *A Lover's Discourse: Fragments*, New York: Hill & Wang.
Brooks, P. (1985) *Reading for the Plot*, Oxford: Oxford University Press.
Burroughs, W. (1953; this ed. 1977) *Junky*, Harmondsworth: Penguin.
Eagleton, T. (1986), unpublished seminar presentation.
Faludi, S. (1992) *Backlash: The Undeclared War Against Women*, London: Chatto & Windus.
Farwell, M. R. (1990) 'Heterosexual Plots and Lesbian Subtexts: Toward a Theory of Lesbian Narrative Space', in Karla Jay and Joanne Glasgow (eds) *Lesbian Texts and Contexts: Radical Revisions*, London: Onlywomen.
Girard, R. (1965) *Deceit, Desire and the Novel*, Baltimore: Johns Hopkins University Press.
Grosz, E. (1990) *Jacques Lacan: A Feminist Introduction*, London: Routledge.
Hart, J. (1991; this ed. 1993) *Damage*, London: Arrow Books.
Kasl, C. D. (1990) *Women, Sex and Addiction*, London: Mandarin.
Kundera, M. (1982) *The Unbearable Lightness of Being*, London: Faber.
Lacan, J. (1977a) 'The mirror stage as formative of the function of the "I" ', *Ecrits: A Selection*, London: Tavistock.
Lacan, J. (1977b) *Four Fundamental Concepts of Psychoanalysis*, London: Hogarth Press.
Lacan, J. (1982a) 'The Meaning of the Phallus', in J. Mitchell and J. Rose (eds) *Feminine Sexuality: Jacques Lacan and the Ecole Freudienne*, London: Macmillan.
Lacan, J. (1982b) 'God and the Jouissance of The Woman', in J. Mitchell and J. Rose (eds) *Feminine Sexuality: Jacques Lacan and the Ecole Freudienne*, London: Macmillan.
Mann, T. (1912; this ed. 1955) *Death in Venice*, Harmondsworth: Penguin.
Mishima, Y. (1950; this ed. 1978) *Thirst for Love*, Harmondsworth: Penguin.
Moi, T. (1982) 'The Missing Mother: The Oedipal Rivalries of René Girard', *Diacritics* 12, summer.
Mulvey, L. (1975; this ed. 1989) 'Visual Pleasure and Narrative Cinema', *Visual and Other Pleasures*, Bloomington: Indiana University Press.
Neale, S. (1982) ' "Chariots of Fire", Images of Men', *Screen* 23, 3/4.
Norwood, R. (1986) *Women Who Love Too Much*, London: Arrow Books.

Rhys, J. (1939; this ed. 1969) *Good Morning, Midnight*, Harmondsworth: Penguin.

Romney, J. (1993) '*Damage*', *Sight and Sound*, February, 3, 2.

Rule, J. (1964; this ed. 1990) *Desert of the Heart*, London: Pandora.

Silverman, K. (1988) *The Acoustic Mirror: The Female Voice in Psychoanalysis and Cinema*, Bloomington: Indiana University Press.

Spraggs, G. (1992) 'Hell and the Mirror: a Reading of *Desert of the Heart*', in S. Munt (ed.) *New Lesbian Criticism*, Hemel Hempstead: Harvester.

Zimmerman, B. (1992) *The Safe Sea of Women: Lesbian Fiction*, London: Onlywomen.

Bryher's *Two Selves* as Lesbian Romance

Diana Collecott

> 'What happened to your novel?'
> 'Oh, that. I dropped it on some publishers.'
> 'Did they take it?'
> 'No. Wrote me after they'd had the thing two months to go and see them ... Asked me to give it a romantic ending and take it back to them.'
> 'Are you going to?'
> 'No. I don't feel romantic. And I have to feel things before I can write them.' (Bryher 1923: 119–20)

This exchange, between two young women named Doreen and Nancy, takes place within a few pages of the ending of Bryher's *Two Selves*. Published in 1923, *Two Selves* is the sequel to Bryher's autobiographical novel *Development*, which appeared in 1920. In both books, Nancy is the fictional *persona* (or mask) of the author, whose given name was Annie Winifred Ellerman, and Doreen represents her girlhood friend Doris Banfield. From about 1909, these two spent their summer holidays together on the Scilly Isles, where Winifred fell in love with the tiny island of Bryher and took its name for her writing signature. Her second and third novels appeared over the single name 'Bryher', by which she was then known to her friends in Britain, the United States and expatriate Paris. In that inner circle of writers and artists, she was also by then known as a lesbian: the devoted lover of the poet 'H.D.', whom she had met with her friend Doris in Cornwall in the summer of 1918.

'H.D.' was, like 'Bryher', a writing signature: the initials of Hilda Doolittle, who had left her parents' home in Pennsylvania to settle in London, and had been promoted there as 'H.D.: Imagiste' by Ezra Pound, to launch a new poetic movement (see Friedman, 1990: 38–9). Hilda had married, in 1913, her fellow Imagist Richard Aldington; however, within a few years they were separated by war and by extra-marital affairs. In the summer of 1918, Richard Aldington was with the British Expeditionary Force in France and Hilda Aldington was living in Cornwall with Cecil Gray. By mid-July, when Bryher traced her there, H.D. was three months pregnant with a child conceived with Gray. Neither Gray nor Aldington would be father to this daughter, who was brought up jointly by H.D. and Bryher, and legally adopted by her second mother in 1928 (Friedman, 1986: 132).

H.D.'s biographer, Barbara Guest, tells us that H.D. and Bryher celebrated, every remaining year of their lives, the anniversary of their meeting on 17 July 1918. In 1925, for instance, H.D. dedicated her poem 'Halcyon' to Bryher, with the words, 'For July 17, 1925/Because of July 17, 1918' (Guest, 1984: 177). Such inscriptions remind us that theirs was not only a relationship between writers, but a writing relationship. Between that first meeting and the baby's birth in March 1919, it took shape in letters where discussion of their own and others' writings and translations registers the complex position of H.D. as married woman, expectant mother and exemplary 'Imagiste', and encodes Bryher's desperation with her family as well as her passionate pursuit of H.D.[1] From this correspondence we learn that in March 1919 Bryher, at H.D.'s suggestion, consulted the psychologist Havelock Ellis about 'the question of whether I was a boy sort of escaped into the wrong body'; Ellis's response, apparently extrapolated from the experience of his wife Edith Lees, was to confirm Bryher's sense that 'I am just a girl by accident ...'. Bryher reports this first consultation to H.D. in a tone which suggests that, at the same time as constructing a writing personality for herself as 'Bryher', she was also actively reconstructing the feminine *persona*, which was required of her in the Edwardian Ellerman household, as a boyish alter-ego whom H.D. could tolerate and even encourage. It is telling that Winifred's parents called her 'Dolly', while H.D.'s nickname for her was 'Boy' (Guest 1984: 112).

Changes of name are usually perceived as marking sharp boundaries between the genders (feminine and masculine), and also between the literary genres of autobiography and fiction. But, just as H.D. persistently sites her writing on physical, sexual and psychic 'borderlines' (H.D. 1983: xi), so Bryher's life and work challenge the mutual exclusivity of categories such as 'self' and 'other', 'male' and 'female', 'heterosexual' and 'homosexual'. In her writings of this period, Bryher tests the limits of gender – while evading the issue of sexuality – as she would later do in a series of imaginative historical novels with young male heroes (Bryher, 1952, 1953, 1954, 1960). For instance, her essay 'The Girl-Page in Elizabethan Literature' (Bryher, 1920b) is a spirited exploration of cross-dressed roles in the plays and romances of Shakespeare's era. Acknowledging disguise as a common plot-device, it shows a shrewd awareness of genre. Combined with this is an awareness of gender that points to parallels between the late sixteenth-century and the early twentieth-century as times of expansion and experiment for men, but of containment and vulnerability for women. Thus Bryher identifies a literary tradition for Nancy's dream of 'Breeches and short hair and freedom....' – her 'romance' that 'If she had been a boy life would have lain at her feet' (Bryher, 1923: 48, 97, 98).

Selves and Others

The silencing of what Bryher felt to be her true self – the self who could write books (not merely read them) and act on her desires – is the starting-point for *Two Selves*. It begins:

> Two selves. Jammed against each other, disjointed and ill-fitting. An obedient Nancy with heavy plaits tied over two ears that answered 'yes, no, yes, no,' according as the wind blew. A boy, a brain, that planned adventures and sought wisdom ... (p5)

The heroine of H.D.'s autobiographical novel *Her* is driven to 'dementia' by the contradiction between her sense of herself as subject and her cultural object-status as a female; textually, this is enacted in abrupt juxtapositions of the two pronouns 'I' and 'her', in such paradoxical statements as 'I am Her' (H.D., 1984: 3). Similarly, in *Two Selves*, Bryher's protagonist is paralyzed by the contradictory demands of the sex-gender system as it was mediated by the paternal household: 'boy, girl'; 'yes, no'. What saves her from outright rebellion is that,

> She, herself, could escape into her other self. Swing her legs over a chair and shout 'to hell with marriage, patriotism, duty, they are lies, lies, lies.' (When no one was listening, of course). (p82).

Throughout *Two Selves*, Bryher presents Nancy's 'other self' as a writing self which runs together gender and desire: 'She had wanted to be a boy and write a book', is her blunt way of putting it (p82). The fact that both selfhood and authorship are normatively masculine in patriarchal culture undoubtedly influenced Bryher's reluctance to make a clear distinction between sex and gender. Yet Nancy's confusion is historically plausible; it embraces her need for verbal as well as sexual expression: 'She had no words to make them understand'; her being was 'hidden in silence' (p6). Only slowly does it dawn on Nancy that her desire to write encodes other desires: 'worlds or selves to be touched, smelt, tasted and accepted' (p33). Reflecting on Nancy's adolescence, Bryher writes: 'She still wanted the same things in more intense a way' (p82).

Finding a Friend

From the very first chapter of *Two Selves*, Nancy's keenest desire has been for 'a friend'; the gender of this friend is unknown, and will not be revealed until the end of the book. Thus the sequel to *Development* (whose working title was 'Adventure') takes the form of a romantic quest. Chapter One, quoted above, opens with the words 'Two selves' and continues:

> If she had friendship ever it would be immediate, inevitable. There would be no recognition of each other. Simply a placing together of two lives (p7).

The entire trajectory of the plot is traced in this transition between 'two selves' and 'two lives': it begins with a chapter called 'Two Selves', and ends with a chapter called 'Meeting'. Thus the novel's overall title has a double meaning: the hero will only heal the 'split' within herself by meeting with an other self (p17). Nancy imagines that the 'placing together of two lives' will be, romantically, 'inevitable': 'There would be no recognition of each other' (p7). This statement seems to affirm by denial the trope of recognition that is crucial to lesbian fiction and autobiography, 'After all,' to quote Audre Lorde, 'doesn't it take one to know one?' (Lorde, 1983: 180). Throughout H.D.'s *Her*, the eyes of female lovers meet and they gaze into each other's faces. In fact, the plot of *Two Selves* is directed precisely towards a moment of recognition. It ultimately occurs in the very last words of the last chapter, which are spoken by the new-found friend: 'I was waiting for you to come' (p126).

This simple statement is presented as the answer to Nancy's questions, the response to her yearnings. Earlier, we have read of how she found her own longing expressed in poetry:

> 'It was for you I watched dawn rise, for you. It was for you I learnt. I wait as the wind waits that shakes in the pines.'
>
> ... She listened. Her ears strained till to feel was simply to hear. A step on the stair. Yet the door never opened....
>
> Life made no answer. (p98).

Towards the end of Nancy's quest, she is near despair:

> A poet near. Would she answer? It was too late anyhow. Too late to have a friend ... Speak one's own thoughts. Be answered. Too late. (p120).

Jacques Derrida remarked: 'it is the ear of the other that signs. The ear of the other says me to me and constitutes the *autos* of my autobiography.' (Derrida, 1985: 51). The implication that the self is not only validated but completed by the other who, so to speak, signs one's own text, resonates strongly with the ending of *Two Selves*. The final page reads:

> This was the place. She knocked.
>
> She was too old to be disappointed if an elderly woman in glasses bustled out. Poets, of course, were not what they wrote about. It was the mind that mattered.
>
> A tall figure opened the door. Young. A spear flower if a spear could bloom. She looked up into eyes that had the sea in them, the fire and colour and the splendour of it. A voice all wind and gull notes said:
>
> 'I was waiting for you to come'. (p126).

Even at this climactic moment, Bryher handles her *persona* with a face-saving irony: 'Poets, of course, were not what they wrote about ...'. Yet it was the poetry of H.D., with its pervasive images of meeting-points and borderlines, that prepared Bryher for their actual meeting, on the very threshold of the Cornish cottage depicted in the novel. Until shortly before their meeting, she did not know the gender or the identity marked (or masked) by the initials 'H.D.' She only knew the 'voice all wind and gull notes' of poems like 'The Shrine', 'Loss' and 'Sea Gods' (H.D. 1983: 7, 21, 29). It is that voice which 'signs' the text of *Two Selves*. Moreover, the figure of the gull, or the gull-like voice, is used reciprocally by Bryher and H.D. in texts that celebrate this meeting, as if it were a mutual signature.

Gulls wheeling over the sea connote a specific kind of freedom to both women. In the unconscious code of *Two Selves*, Bryher elides this freedom with poetry: 'Poetry is ... Gulls. Sand. And sea ... Nice to be a gull and fly – free – free – untrammelled of persons' (pp 68–9). In a similar vein, she writes: 'Beauty was escape; beauty was another world. Greek chariots, the rainbow of the ships' (p124). H.D. connected such beauty and freedom not only with leaving home but with having a first lesbian relationship; in 1929, she looked forward to even 'more freedom ... more and more freedom', and recalled standing on the deck of a ship in New York harbour in 1911, about to set sail for Europe with Frances Gregg: 'I was part of all beauty being free ... going with a friend I loved.' (H.D. 1929: 39). For H.D. who, like Bryher, conceals the gender of her 'friend', expansive terms like 'beauty' and 'freedom' include and even encode the experience of same-sex love. Moreover, in poems like 'I Said (To W.B.)' and 'We Two', (H.D., 1983: 322; 164), which were about her relationship with Bryher (see Friedman, 1986: 131; Collecott, 1992: 104–10), H.D. insists on the combined strength needed by lesbian lovers to resist the pressures of what Adrienne Rich would later call 'compulsory heterosexuality' (Rich, 1987: 23–75). This resistance is surely implied by Bryher in her recurrent images of gulls against the wind. The gull is, as we shall see, a repeated motif in her 'Eros of the Sea', while in H.D.'s 'Halcyon', dedicated to Bryher, we read:

> Why am I vague, unsure
> until you are blown,
> unexpected, small, quaint, unnoticable,
> a grey gull,
> into a room.
>
> (H.D. 1983: 270–1)

The Quest for an Ending

Bryher's uncertainty, in her late twenties, about how to handle such momentous material, is evident in the final chapter of *Two Selves*. This begins with Nancy and Doreen preparing to sleep outdoors on the roof of their Cornish lodging. Although it is war-time, the scene is set for an episode more reminiscent of Angela Brazil than of 'Boy's' favourite author, G.A. Henty.

> 'Strange she should be so near,' said Nancy, thinking of the letter she had just posted.
>
> 'Oh, Cornwall's a great place for poets,' Doreen said, too calmly.
>
> 'If she doesn't answer, I'm going to fall into the cove and she can hardly refuse to let me sit by her fire and dry my clothes.'
>
> 'You could say you had seen a spy signalling from the cliffs and would she mind if you watched from her garden.' (p118).

The adolescent banter is an uncomfortable reminder of Bryher's search for a fictional form in which to write about love between women. As Alison Hennegan remarks, in her introduction to Rosemary Manning's *The Chinese Garden*, 'It comes as no surprise that homosexual and bisexual authors should so often have chosen to write school novels' (Manning, 1984: 8). Unfortunately, this most accessible model carries with it the risk of trivializing Nancy's longings into a school-girl 'crush' or 'passion'. Hence the rapid modulation of Bryher's story into a more desperate mode in which Nancy contemplates not a girlish jape but an act of suicide:

> Better not try to find a friend. Better drown under the cliffs … Better be done with it, under the cliff, forget the anemones, the sea call, the adventures. One choke of water and no fight more [sic]. (p125).

Choking on her own emotion, Nancy projects herself as a sacrificial victim. But, as the tragic quest regains ascendancy over the comic school-story, Bryher finds her stride in a poetic style that combines nostalgic romanticism with an imagistic modernism reminiscent of H.D.: 'under the cliff/forget the anemones/the sea call'

Bryher published two volumes of memoirs in addition to her early *romans à clef* (Bryher, 1962, 1972). Both excise any hint of homosexuality, although the first, subtitled 'A Writer's Memoirs', is shot through with the author's devotion to H.D. In this book, *The Heart to Artemis*, written and published some forty years after *Two Selves*, Bryher recalls her discovery of H.D.'s poetry, and her first meeting with the poet:

> There will always be one book among all others that makes us aware of ourselves; for me, it is *Sea Garden* by H.D. I learned it by heart from cover to cover ... It was not until some months later that I discovered from Amy Lowell's *Tendencies in Modern American Poetry* that H.D. was a woman and American.
>
> We did not spend that summer in Scilly ... but as a special favour Doris and I were allowed to go by ourselves to Zennor for a week or two, to run wild on the cliffs. Just as I had left London, Mr Shorter had got H.D.'s address from May Sinclair who was a mutual friend and I discovered to my amazement that she was staying in the neighbourhood. I asked permission to call ... I hung about waiting for the postman until, in due course, I was invited to tea.
>
> It was July 17, 1918. I had had to abstract myself from my surroundings in order to survive at all. To wish to create was a sin against the consciousness of the time. Yet I wanted things to be real, I did not want to dream. The gorse was out, I was walking across some of the most ancient ground in Cornwall, I could hear the roar of the sea. I reached a cottage with the familiar, yellow covers of a dozen French books piled up against the window sill. I knew then that it must be the right place and knocked.
>
> The door opened and I started in surprise. I had seen the face before, on a Greek statue or in some indefinable territory of the mind. We were meeting again after a long absence but not for the first time ... (Bryher, 1962: 187–8).

While the memory itself is moving, there is none of that Lawrentian 'ebb and flow of ... consciousness' which makes the earlier fictional version so much more vivid. There Nancy's inner feelings of despair and desire, and her alertness to colour and texture in the outer world, meet at the very moment when 'A tall figure opened the door'; indeed, they come together in this figure whose 'eyes ... had the sea in them', and whose 'voice [was] all wind and gull notes'. In the later memoir, by contrast, we hear only the public voice of an older Bryher: 'I wanted things to be real, I did not want to dream.'

The Kiss

After her death in 1983, over twenty years after the death of H.D., Bryher's dreams came (as the phrase is) into the public domain. The Bryher archive at Yale includes typescripts of poetry written over forty years, much of it unpublished and some of it addressed to H.D. They also include the prose-poem already cited, 'Eros of the Sea'; this was probably composed about 1920, since it is filed with Bryher's notes on H.D. of that date. The same file contains fragments of prose and poetry which constellate around their meeting in 1918 and resonate with the description of it in *Two Selves*. One reads: 'Her eyes had the sea in them, its movement, its tranquillity'; another ends: 'We cried out for the sea, the touch of it, the soft sand or even softer weed'. These almost Sapphic fragments evoke H.D.'s own poetry, especially in *Hymen*, which was completed in 1919 and inscribed 'For Bryher and Perdita' (H.D. 1983: 101, 616n).

In 'Eros of the Sea' – which is dedicated to H.D. 'For her gift of Greek' – Bryher has a female supplicant invoking the young male god whom H.D. addresses in *Hymen* (H.D. 1983: 133–4). Yet the setting is not Greek, but Cornish: a place of sea-pools and rock-ledges reminiscent of the liminal landscapes of H.D.'s *Sea Garden*. Moreover the figure of Eros has qualities that Bryher also assigned to H.D. in that Cornish setting: 'His eyes – filled with the sea – followed the circling gulls'. When, at the supplicant's plea, he rises like Aphrodite from the sea, 'She trembled back from the wonder of his body – afraid...afraid ...' (Bryher, 1990: 9). This erotic text, which covers less than five pages of typescript, climaxes with a kiss. In these final lines, Eros is the first to speak:

> '... Tell me your desire?'
>
> Words died. All her body spoke its longing but her lips could not utter her request. Yet dream had not betrayed her. This was the end of hope – to wait for the sea, to drown, not to re-enter the desolation she had left. How could she, having looked on Beauty, live? ...
>
> He moved to her – a wild gull – with eyes she dared not face. Wild eyes – wild wings – above her. Her head bent – back. Flutter of wings, flutter of more than wings, toward her face ...
>
> 'O ripple of bird-notes
> On my throat.'
>
> (Bryher, 1990: 10)

'Eros of the Sea' is romantic poetry of a decadent, or at least *symboliste* kind. Among the longer pieces of typescript filed with it are more naturalistic versions of the same scene, which appear to represent transitional stages between the prose-poem and the published text of *Two Selves*. In these versions, the beloved body is not that of a male god, but of a woman, 'Helga'. In Bryher's next novel, *West*, the H.D. figure unnamed in *Two Selves* is called 'Helga Doorn'. (This was H.D.'s cinematic name – inspired, no doubt, by her infatuation with the young Greta Garbo – and also the pen-name on the title-page of her bisexual novel *Her* (Friedman, 1990: 132)). It is hardly surprising that, in some of her typescripts, Bryher abbreviates this name to the initial 'H.':

> She turned to spend her last hour with beauty and her first.
>
> She was sure it was best. One dive – she need never fear bondage more ... To her amazement, H. was crying, short bird-sobs quivering the body. It had never occurred to her H. could possibly care.
>
> Without word, without protest, H. moved to her with eyes she dared not face. Wild eyes, wild wings; head bent back. Flutter of lips, flutter of more than lips, towards her mouth.
>
> O ripple of bird-notes
> on my throat.
>
> (Bryher 1990: 11–12)

An identical coda and near-identical motifs – of dread and desire, suicide by drowning, and the lover's bird-like flutter – connect this passage with that from 'Eros of the Sea'. In it, the young female supplicant or lover is named Nancy, which suggests that this fragment may have been intended for, or deleted from, an early draft of *Two Selves*.

Other fragments of prose, some of them literally cut from longer typescripts, offer heterosexual versions of the same scene. In one, Helga's lover is a young man, Ernest, a Henty-like hero whose name is as unequivocally masculine as 'Nancy' is contemptuously effeminate. (In a subsequent autobiographical novel, *Manchester*, Bryher would use the Ernest *persona* 'to narrate her passion for Elizabeth Bergner' (Friedman, 1990: 421)). It is evident then that, around 1920, Bryher was experimenting with gender as well as genre, in trying to find expression for an episode of fantasy or experience that she would write and re-write at different stages of her life. Moreover, she was also experimenting with ways of representing female sexuality in these carefully coded narratives. Catharine Stimpson has pointed out that 'the kiss' is a staple of lesbian fiction in English, adding that, because lesbian writing has 'shared with women's writing in general a reticence about explicitly representing sexual activity, the kiss has vast metonymic responsibility'. (Stimpson, 1989: 99). Citing Gertrude Stein's *Q.E.D.* and Virginia Woolf's *Mrs Dalloway*, Stimpson asks:

> Does the kiss encode transgression or permissibility? Singularity or repeatability? Impossibility or possibility? ... Does the kiss predict the beginning of the end, or the end of the beginning, of a lesbian erotic enterprise? Or is it the event that literally embraces contradictions? (Stimpson, 1988: 100).

Writing Beyond the Ending

'Once upon a time,' writes Rachel DuPlessis, 'the end, the rightful end, of women in novels was ... marriage ... or ... death. These were both resolutions of romance' (DuPlessis, 1985: 1). She goes on to argue, in *Writing Beyond the Ending*, that 'the marriage/death closure in the romance plot is a "place" where ideology meets narrative and produces a meaning-laden figure of some sort' (DuPlessis, 1985: 19). We have seen how Bryher, writing and re-writing her account of July 17, 1918, approaches such a point of closure: 'This was the place. She knocked ... A tall figure opened the door' (*Two Selves*); 'I knew then that it must be the right place and knocked. The door opened ...' (*The Heart to Artemis*). The entire novel, and the chapter of the memoir, stop at this threshold, without retreating from it into threatened death, or stepping over it into marriage. In both books, the 'meaning-laden figure of some sort', which Rachel DuPlessis envisages as the meeting-place of narrative and ideology in romance, materialises on that threshold as the body of a woman, a poet, who is eventually identified as H.D. The presence of same-sex desire at this crucial moment – this moment of 'Meeting', which is also potentially a moment of obliteration – interrupts the plot's movement towards any possible closure of a conventional kind. Marriage, as Bryher well knew, is the supreme convention: in literature as in society, it upholds what Judith Butler calls the 'institution of a compulsory and naturalized heterosexuality' (Butler, 1990: 22). Nevertheless, as Duplessis observes, 'the erotic and emotional intensity of women's friendships cuts the Gordian knots of both heterosexuality and narrative convention' (DuPlessis, 1985: 149). It is this subversive female sexuality that Marilyn Farwell sees as essential to 'lesbian narrative space as a disruptive space of sameness, as opposed to difference, which has structured most Western narratives' (Farwell, 1990: 93, 102n).

For a closet lesbian writing around 1920, such a space had no discursive existence, no acknowledged presence in the narratives of the dominant culture. Its reality was internalized (to quote Bryher) 'in some indefinable territory of the mind', or even annihilated: a black-hole into which one might disappear. For centuries, what Friedman and DuPlessis call 'the ferocity of the taboo against same-sex relationships' (Friedman and DuPlessis 1990: 208) had reduced Sappho's poetic works to fragments and sent Bryher to the Elizabethan dramatists in search of female friendships played by boy-actors in 'breeches parts'. The 'space of sameness' existed only in women's love-letters to each other (which were frequently obliterated) and in the fantasies Virginia Woolf invoked when she wrote to Vita Sackville-West, before embarking on *Orlando*: 'I lie in bed, making up stories about you' (Woolf, 1980b: 342). Even today, and in North America, Elizabeth Meese can say:

> When I write about lesbian: writing [sic], I take my life in my hands as my text. Or is it that I take my text as my life in my search for a language capable of expressing what those words – lesbian: writing – mean.... (Jay and Glasgow, 1990: 71–2).

This context, or rather this absence of context, the absence of texts, makes the anonymous presence of the female figure at the ending of *Two Selves* all the more laden with meaning. We have seen this meeting as a joint signature on the texts of their lives: it was also a sign that these lives would continue to be writing lives. Yet despite the fact that she wrote a sequel, *West*, and at least part of a further volume, *South*, Bryher would never in her published prose write inwardly of the long and complex relationship which followed that meeting. It is in the unpublished work that we can now glimpse the space that lies 'beyond the ending' of *Two Selves*: perhaps literally so, given the possibility that some passages were excised from the typescript of the novel. That space or place is marked by the erotic kiss which features in at least three extant versions of the story; we can read the kiss as a sign of a different kind of closure: one not only beyond the bounds of heterosexual convention, but radically disruptive of it.

At the beginning of this chapter, I quoted Nancy's account of her publishers' request that she re-write the conclusion of her first novel, giving it 'a romantic ending'. Her glib response, bypassing the implication of compulsory heterosexuality, is 'I don't feel romantic. And I have to feel things before I can write them.' Between Bryher's initial writing of the ending of her first novel, and beginning to write her second, the meeting had occurred which would give the plot of *Two Selves* its direction and be the 'place' in which Nancy's feelings have meaning and at which the text ends. That ending will only 'feel romantic' to the reader who is prepared to go with her into an as yet unwritten narrative space: the space of a lesbian relationship that is both feared and desired.

An early version of this paper was given at the day-school on autobiography, Women's Lives, Women's Times, at the Department of Women's Studies, University of York, in January 1991.

Notes

[1] Both sides of the substantial Bryher/H.D. correspondence are in the Beinecke Rare Book and Manuscript Library at Yale University. For permission to quote from Bryher's letter to H.D. of 20 March 1919, and from unpublished manuscripts in her 'H.D.' file, I am indebted to the Trustees of the Beinecke Library and to the Estates of Bryher and H.D.

Bibliography

Bryher (1914) [as A.W. Ellerman] *Region of Lutany* [poems], London: Chapman and Hall.

Bryher (1918) [as Winifred Bryher], *The Lament for Adonis*, from the Greek of Bion of Smyrna, London: A.L. Humphreys.

Bryher (1920a) [as W. Bryher], *Development: a Novel*, London: Constable/New York: Macmillan.

Bryher (1920b) [as W. Bryher], 'The Girl-Page in Elizabethan Literature', *The Fortnightly Review*, March: 442–52.

Bryher (1923) *Two Selves*, Paris: Contact Publishing.

Bryher (1925a) *West*, London: Jonathan Cape.

Bryher (1925b) 'South (from a book now being written)', *This Quarter* 1: 182–93.

Bryher (1952) *The Fourteenth of October*, New York: Pantheon 1952/London: Collins 1954.

Bryher (1954) *The Player's Boy*, New York: Pantheon, 1954/London: Collins, 1955.

Bryher (1954) *Roman Wall*, New York: Pantheon, 1954/London: Collins, 1955.

Bryher (1960) *Ruan*, New York: Pantheon, 1960/London: Collins, 1961.

Bryher (1962) *The Heart to Artemis: a Writer's Memoirs*, New York: Harcourt Brace, 1962/London: Collins, 1963.

Bryher (1972) *The Days of Mars: a Memoir, 1940–46*, New York: Harcourt Brace/London: Calder and Boyars.

Bryher (1990) 'Eros of the Sea', *H.D. Newsletter*, 3, 1: 7–14. With an afterword by Diana Collecott.

Butler, Judith (1990) *Gender Trouble: Feminism and the Subversion of Identity*, London and New York: Routledge.

Collecott, D. (1992) ' "What Is Not Said": A study in textual inversion', in J. Bristow (ed) *Sexual Sameness, Textual Differences in Lesbian and Gay Writing*, London and New York: Routledge.

Derrida, J. (1985) *The Ear of the Other: Ottobiography, Transference, Translation*, New York: Schocken Books.

DuPlessis, Rachel Blau (1985) *Writing Beyond the Ending: Narrative Strategies of Twentieth-Century Women Writers*, Bloomington: Indiana University Press.

Farwell, Marilyn R. 'Heterosexual Plots and Lesbian Subtexts: Toward a Theory of Lesbian Narrative Space', in Karla Jay and Joanne Glasgow (eds) (1990) *Lesbian Texts and Contexts: Radical Revisions*, New York and London: New York University Press.

Friedman, Susan Stanford (1986) 'H.D.', *Dictionary of Literary Biography: Modern American Poets, 1880–1945 First Series*, Peter Quartermain (ed), Detroit: Gale Research.

Friedman, Susan Stanford (1990) *Penelope's Web: Gender, Modernity, H.D.'s Fiction*, Cambridge: Cambridge University Press.

Friedman, Susan Stanford, and DuPlessis, Rachel Blau (eds) (1990) *Signets: Reading H.D.*, Madison: University of Wisconsin Press.

Fuss, Diana (ed) (1991) *Inside/Out: Lesbian Theories, Gay Theories*, London and New York: Routledge.

Guest, Barbara (1984) *Herself Defined: The Poet H.D. and Her World*, New York: Doubleday.

H.D. (1929) 'Confession – Answer to a Questionnaire', *The Little Review* 12, 2: 38–40 (May).

H.D. (1983) *Collected Poems, 1912–1944*, ed. Louis L. Martz, New York: New Directions, 1983/Manchester: Carcanet, 1984.

H.D. (1984) *Her*, London: Virago Press.

Hanscombe, Gillian E., and Smyers, Virginia L., (1987) *Writing for Their Lives: The Modernist Women, 1910–1940*, London: The Women's Press.

Lorde, Audre (1983) *Zami: A New Spelling of My Name*, New York: The Crossing Press.

Meese, Elizabeth, 'Theorizing Lesbian: Writing – A Love Letter', in Jay *et al, op cit.*

Rich, Adrienne, (1987) 'Compulsory Heterosexuality and Lesbian Existence', in *Blood, Bread and Poetry: Selected Prose, 1979–1985*, London: Virago Press.

Stimpson, Catharine R. (1988) *Where the Meanings Are: Feminism and Cultural Spaces*, New York and London: Routledge.

Woolf, Virginia (1980a) *The Diary of Virginia Woolf, Volume Three: (1925–1930)*, ed. Anne Oliver Bell and Andrew McNeillie, New York and London: Harcourt Brace Jovanovich.

Woolf, Virginia (1980b) *The Letters of Virginia Woolf, Volume Three: 1923–1928*, ed. Nigel Nicolson and Joanne Trautmann, New York and London: Harcourt Brace Jovanovich.

Safe and Sexy? Lesbian Erotica in the Age of AIDS

Gabriele Griffin

Lesbian erotica/porn,[1] in line with assorted conventions governing romance both with a small and with a large R,[2] frequently base the quest for the, or an, object of desire on precisely the combination of emotional attachment and sexuality problematized by Adrienne Rich in 'Compulsory Heterosexuality and Lesbian Existence' many moons ago (Rich, 1980). There Rich takes up the point endorsed by psychoanalysis, both classic and feminist, that a woman (the female carer) is women's first love object. For this reason 'heterosexuality is *not* a "preference" for women' because 'it fragments the erotic from the emotional in a way that women find impoverishing and painful' (p216). As a result, patriarchy has to enforce heterosexuality through, among other things, particular forms of heterosex-supportive legislation, 'the ideology of heterosexual romance' (p224) which fuses the male demand for the satisfaction of his sexual patrilineally procreative urge with the promise of emotional as well as sexual fulfilment for the woman. 'Internalizing the values of the colonizer and actively participating in carrying out the colonization of one's self and one's sex' (p225), many women submit to the enforcement of heterosexuality 'in the name of love', and even 'unto death'. They do so because heterosexuality is not presented as a *choice* but as 'compulsory', the 'natural' outcome of a 'normal' woman's psychosexual maturation process. Rich suggests that women are manipulated into heterosexuality through a discourse which exploits and re-directs their emotional needs away from the female and to the male.

In parallel with Rich's contentions, I would argue that much lesbian erotica/porn – contrary to the common suggestion (akin to the one made by Rich as regards heterosexuality) that such material, especially anything considered *pornographic*, fragments the erotic and the emotional – utilises the imbrication of the emotional in the sexual as part of its construction. This acts as a palliative for the more problematic aspects of the material. Typically, Pat Califia for instance, an in/famous American producer of sado-masochistic material, writes in one of her stories:

> Even when correcting serious misdeeds, Berenice [dominatrix and mother] was not brutal. She loved helplessness, she craved the sight of a female body abandoning all decency and self-control. These things are not granted save in loving trust. Dominance is not created without complicity. A well-trained slave is hopelessly in love with her mistress ... (Califia, 1988: 67).

This story, centring on a sadomasochistic mother-daughter relationship and recuperative of the primary love relationship between female carer and dependent postulated by psychoanalysis, presents a whole series of incest-taboo-breaking relations, in which the emotional ties between blood relations (sisters; mother and daughter; aunt and niece), and the notions that they (therefore?) *care for* and *take care of* each other, operate as the legitimating framework for their sadomasochistic activities.[3] Similarly, Califia's (1988) rather horrendous story, 'The Surprise Party', legitimates the sadomasochistic abuse of a lesbian by a group of men, supposedly 'cops', by indicating towards the end of the story that these men are friends of the lesbian protagonist giving her a surprise birthday party.

These are just two examples of what I perceive to be a common phenomenon in *written*[4] lesbian erotica/porn: the conjunction of the emotional with specific sexual practices. This phenomenon is shared with popular romance which, according to Radway (1987: 149), in its ideal version presents the heroine as 'emotionally complete and sexually satisfied'. This is one reason why lesbian erotica should be discussed in the context of 'romance'. Additionally, this conjunction raises issues concerning the impact of HIV/AIDS on erotica, and I shall consider some of these in the course of this chapter.

The Silence (?) of Lesbian Sex

I want to begin with a quotation from Marilyn Frye's essay 'Lesbian "Sex" '. Frye writes:

> Lesbian 'sex' as I have known it most of the time I have known it is utterly inarticulate. Most of my lifetime, most of my experience in the realms commonly designated as 'sexual' has been prelinguistic, noncognitive. I have, in effect, no linguistic community, no language, and therefore in one important sense, no knowledge. (Frye, 1991: 6)

The connections Frye makes between inarticulacy, absence of a linguistic community and lack of knowledge are crucial here;[5] they resurface in an interview between Sue O'Sullivan and Cindy Patton in which Patton links what she calls the 'paucity of sexual imagery for lesbians' (O'Sullivan, 1990: 132) to the difficulties of promoting safer sex among lesbians. I shall return to this point below. For now, I want to ask what Frye means when she talks of lesbian sex as 'utterly inarticulate' (Frye, 1991: 6). What interests me here is that these comments are made in the context of a *proliferation* of discourses[6] and texts on lesbian sexuality, many of these – if not most – written by lesbians. It is thus not exactly the case that lesbian sex is inarticulate. I am sure, for instance, that we can all think of texts depicting lesbian sex. Let me quote briefly from two such very different texts. One is a short poem by Suniti Namjoshi entitled 'I give her the rose':

> I give her the rose with unfurled petals.
> She smiles
>   and crosses her legs.
> I give her the shell with the swollen lip.
> She laughs.   I bite
>   and nuzzle her breasts.
> I tell her, 'Feed me on flowers
>   with wide open mouths,'
> and slowly,
>   she pulls my head down.
>
> (Namjoshi, 1991: 25)

The second quotation is from Ann Bannon's *I Am A Woman*:

> [Laura] only clung to Beebo, half tearing her pajamas off her back, groaning wordlessly, almost sobbing. Her hands explored, caressed, felt Beebo all over, while her own body responded with violent spasms – joyous, crazy, deep as her soul. She could no more have prevented her response than she could the tyrannic need that drove her to find it.
>
> (Bannon, 1986: 93)

Both texts depict lesbian sex and they do so in different, yet recognizably conventional, ways. Made famous by Gertrude Stein, the rose is a well-established euphemism for what Jeanette's mother, in *Oranges Are Not The Only Fruit*, calls 'down *there*' (Winterson, 1985). Such natural imagery is commonly employed in the depiction of lesbian sex; one of its effects is, of course, that it quite literally 'naturalizes' lesbian sex, thus offering overt resistance to the heterosexist notion that lesbian sex might be 'unnatural' while reinforcing the problematic notion that women are somehow closer to nature than men.[7] The scene from Bannon's novel presents sexuality as an irrational and irresistible force which renders the protagonist inarticulate: Laura groans 'wordlessly'. Fade-outs, not just, so to speak, of the visual, but also of the verbal, kind are very common in scenes depicting lesbian sex, creating a division between saying and doing, and suggesting that you cannot do it and talk at the same time.[8]

It seems not to be the case then, as Frye suggests, that lesbian sex is 'inarticulate' – there are, after all, plenty of depictions of lesbian sex available from good and not-so-good bookshops now. However, Frye talks of 'my *experiences* in the realms commonly designated as "sexual" ' (emphasis added); I take these to refer to her actual experiences in her personal life. In the face of the proliferation of discourses and texts on lesbian sex, Frye's assertion indicates not only a gap between the private and the public here (private inarticulacy *versus* public verbosity) but also a discrepancy between the two: the fact that lesbian sex is verbalised in cultural production for consumption by a general public does not as a matter of course enhance articulacy in the private sphere. Rather, to judge by the excerpt from *I Am A Woman*, for example, the public depiction of lesbian sex *reinforces* not only the divide between the public and the private in the realms of sexuality but also the notion of silence during sex in the private context.

As is made evident in the two texts depicting lesbian sex cited above, one reason for this division is that the depiction of lesbian sex operates within certain specific cultural and narrative conventions gleaned from romance which include, for instance, natural imagery and the 'speechlessness' of the lesbian protagonists when they engage in sex. The latter convention of constructing action and speech as divorced from each other is particularly important here because that division is one of the main concerns in discussions about erotica/porn *per se* and erotica and safer sex, specifically. As regards the former, the gap between articulation and action can surface, as it does in Sheba Collective's introduction to *Serious Pleasure* (1989: 11), in the assertion of a difference between what is presented as text and what 'real' people do in 'real' life, as well as in an intratextual construction of an articulate controlling 'doing' character whose sexual demands are made explicit and the passive, silent 'done to' other who services those sexual demands.

As regards the relation between erotica and safer sex, the gap between articulation and action is indicated by Patton in her interview with Sue O'Sullivan, when she suggests that it is difficult to establish safer sex practices if no discourse about lesbian sex is in circulation in the lesbian community. In discussing the difficulties of trying to create lesbian safe sex discussions, Patton explains:

> What it really felt like was that even lesbians didn't know what it was that lesbians did in sex, so there was no way that we could come up with a formula for figuring out what lesbian safe sex was. (O'Sullivan, 1990: 121)

Concerns about the presentations of lesbian sex and their relation to HIV/AIDS have surfaced in the context of lesbian erotica/porn because the latter depict sexual practices/behaviours that can heighten the risk of HIV infection. That such concerns have surfaced is not to say, however, that lesbians assume a unified position on this matter. In 'Fairy Tales, "Facts" and Gossip: Lesbians and AIDS', for example, Tessa Boffin (1990: 156) cites a variety of lesbians' views on the issue of lesbian and AIDS, one of which is: 'Lesbians worldwide are not a risk group. Lesbian sex is safe ... Only nuns show fewer cases of sexually transmitted diseases than lesbians.' In a parallel essay entitled 'Angelic Rebels: Lesbians and Safer Sex,' Boffin comments:

> These women [ie, lesbians who take that stance] also regard us as virgin angels, immune to infection by virtue of the fact that lesbian sex is somehow seen as purer, cleaner and safer than any other form of sexual practice. This view fails to acknowledge there are certain activities: rimming, fisting, cunnilingus, and so on, which cut across the fragile boundaries of sexual orientation, and could put anyone, regardless of their sexuality or gender, at risk. (Boffin, 1990: 57)

It has to be said that HIV and AIDS are still not understood very well; the parameters of their definitions keep shifting.[9] Two things that are pertinent here are: firstly, for a number of reasons, lesbians appear to represent a low-risk group in terms of the likelihood of getting infected with the HIV virus.[10] Secondly, the virus appears to be transmitted through bodily fluids, specifically blood, including menstrual blood and vaginal secretions. Being low risk does not, however, mean that you are immune, and publishers, writers and editors of lesbian erotica or porn have had to and are having to respond to the question of how to deal with the issue of HIV/AIDS in the context of representations of lesbian sex and whether or not to make the depiction of safer sex practices part of their presentations of lesbian sex. The responses are interesting.

A Question of Responsibility?

Alyson Publications, who publish Califia's writings, have, as Califia puts it, 'a policy against eroticizing high-risk sex' (Califia, 1988: 17), which means that Califia had to re-write any material which included the exchange of bodily fluids. Sheba, who published *Serious Pleasure* (1989) had no such policy. However, the Sheba Collective, who edited *Serious Pleasure*, felt as much impelled as Califia to discuss AIDS and safer sex in the introductions to their texts and to include 'Notes on AIDS and Safer Sex' at the back. Despite Sheba Collective maintaining that 'we do not believe that all fictional writing or visual representation of lesbian sex should immediately incorporate safer sex guide lines' (p12), ignoring HIV/AIDS is clearly no longer an option.

In their discussions on whether or not to include safer sex practices in representations of lesbian sex, both Califia and Sheba Collective make distinctions, already referred to above, between saying and doing, fantasy and reality. Both use this distinction to validate publishing erotica/porn in the same way that feminist critiques of romance have used it to address issues around the 'legitimacy' of popular romance as 'fantasy fodder' for women oppressed within heteropatriarchy.[11] Sheba writes:

> *Serious Pleasure* is in no way a lesbian sex manual. In the same way that fantasy is no indication necessarily of what any individual will do in 'real life', neither are the stories in *Serious Pleasure* what either the authors or the readers necessarily 'do'. Safer sex is a case in point. Interestingly none of the stories submitted to us include safer sex as an issue either to be addressed in the context of the story or built into a sexual encounter ... Do lesbians in general still believe that AIDS is not a significant reality for them in terms of sexual transmission? We would guess that this is so and may be the primary reason for the absence of any mention of safer sex in these stories. (Sheba Collective, 1989; 11–12)

Note Sheba Collective's own conflation of reality and fantasy here: first maintaining that there is no necessary relation between fantasy and reality, they then go on to suggest a direct connection between lesbians' practice outside and in the text. Similarly, and I would suggest without being aware of the ambiguity of her statement, Califia writes: 'Images and descriptions are forever getting confused with live acts' (p17). Precisely!

This leads me on to the issue of the consumer of lesbian erotica or porn, and her – and I shall just consider the lesbian consumer here – relation to that material. What does she want from it? Entertainment, escape, education? There does not seem to be a simple answer to this question but it appears to be the case that at least some lesbian readers some of the time go to lesbian erotica/porn for information, education, to gain knowledge about lesbian sex. I refer you to Jan Brown's 'Sex, lies, and penetration: a butch finally "fesses up",' in Joan Nestle's *The Persistent Desire: A Butch-Femme Reader* (1992). If it is the case that lesbian readers go to lesbian erotica or porn for information and knowledge, does this, or should this, mean that publishers and writers of such material have a responsibility to these members of the lesbian community to provide them with appropriate information concerning safer sex practices?

One could argue about this question in terms of the responsibility a publisher or writer has towards the community whom she serves and lives off, which moves the debate not only into the realm of the economic (to put it cynically and unceremoniously: what profit is there in promoting practices that will kill the consumers of your goods?), but also, more seriously and more importantly, into the realm of the ethical. In one of the few essays which I have read that address the latter, Jeffrey Weeks discusses 'values in the age of uncertainty' and suggests radical pluralism as the basis for a contemporary AIDS-conscious ethic (in Stanton, 1992: 389–411). Sheba Collective and Califia both engage with the question of responsibility and find themselves answering with a qualified 'yes'. As Sheba put it:

> We believe that all lesbians should think long and hard about HIV and AIDS and seriously take on the hows and whys of safer sex. For some, erotic stories consciously built around safer sex practices might be helpful. *Serious Pleasure* has not included that possibility in its brief. Even if unprotected lesbian sex was clearly a high risk behaviour we do not believe that all fictional writing or visual representation of lesbian sex should immediately incorporate safer sex guide lines. However, we feel it is important that the issue of safer sex is always acknowledged in some way. We have included some information which you will find at the back of the book. (Sheba Collective, 1989: 12)

What I want to highlight here is not so much the issue of the writer's/publisher's responsibilities as the fact that this issue, it seems to me, can *only* arise in a context where safer sex and the erotic/pornographic are seen as two discrete entities, uneasily coexisting as indeed they do in the texts under consideration. The fact that 'Notes on Safer Sex' are separated out from the erotic material that forms the main part of these texts suggests a split in cultural consciousness, reiterated in the introduction to *Macho Sluts* and *Serious Pleasure*, between safer sex and sexual practices which is reinforced by the fact that both are presented in very different forms of discourse, so that the erotic/pornographic texts are encoded in conventional narrative terms whereas the notes on safer sex display the characteristics typical of a discourse one would associate with information/instruction manuals but not with romance.

The Power of Conventions

I want to consider briefly some explanations of why Califia and the Sheba Collective exhibit such reluctance in facing HIV/AIDS and safer sex in their texts. One of these is associated with the earlier distinction between fantasy and reality and with the fact that depictions of lesbian sex are subject to cultural and narrative conventions. One of the sources of these conventions, romance, demands the construction of an object of love/desire which is perfect in a variety of ways including *perfectly healthy*. To project such an object as – at least potentially – the carrier of STDs (sexually transmitted diseases) raises all sorts of questions about that object's sexual behaviour which would explode the very sexual ideology underlying romance on which the latter is founded.

Additionally, the narrative structure of romance demands a closure which leaves the heroine intact and looking forward to a bright relational future.[12] In terms of specific literary definitions, romance conforms to the conventions of comedy rather than tragedy – it requires life, not death as its ending (Frye, 1957: 198).[13] In Western culture, and despite the conventions of Christian mythology which promise a great afterlife (though at the price of a horrible death – witness Jesus on the cross) death is not something to celebrate; it therefore cannot be a central part of comic or romance conventions. Not only does romance require life as its ending – it has to be unequivocal. Ambiguity in resolution would be the death of romance; the mere suggestion of safe sex therefore, which of course implies the possibility of death, would raise doubt, uncertainty, concerning the future of the heroine: what would happen if she or her partner was a carrier of HIV? Given the uncertainty of its incubation period, when could we, the readers, be certain that all was ok? One might thus argue that the inclusion of safer sex practices in lesbian erotica/porn would necessitate a radical revisioning of the construction of such material which could, after all, no longer utilize the formulae of romance as we know them. What is thus interestingly indexed is that on one level, at least, lesbian erotica/porn *are* fantasies, not *re*presentations of what lesbians do but presentations of imaginary scenarios into which the reality, namely that even lesbians can get HIV infected, is displaced in favour of a fantasy that either no matter what we do we cannot catch it, or no matter whether we catch it or not, we do not care.

Safer sex is 'not sexy' in two senses of that phrase: it has not – as yet – been conventionalized as part of erotic presentation, and it is not trendy to think of doing so. The latter may be because, as Gayle Rubin maintains, 'in times of great social stress ... Disputes over sexual behaviour often become the vehicles for displacing social anxieties, and discharging their attendant emotional intensity' (Rubin, 1989: 267). In other words, living as we do in dangerous times, riskier sex, meaning unsafe sex, becomes a way of displacing and discharging those anxieties for which we have no other obvious vent. It is also the case that in the 1990s we live in a society which displays an overt consciousness of violence, violence that can simultaneously be brought into our homes *and* is contained – inside the tv. The same is evident in other cultural forms such as cinema and books. Increasingly, we thus become inured to violence but are also offered the notion that while it occurs, it will not happen to us. A parallel can be drawn to HIV/AIDS. We are thus left with the problematic of how to engage with HIV/AIDS in the context of lesbian erotica/porn. This difficulty clearly surfaces in Califia's writing, which is fraught with contradictions about 'safe' *versus* 'risky' sex. It is also evident in Sheba Collective's stories where 'safe' *versus* 'risky' is frequently negotiated through making explicit that the events depicted are the narrator's fantasy.

Imaging HIV/AIDS

One other element which compounds the difficulty of presentation detailed above is concerned with the imaging of HIV/AIDS. Rejecting 'feminist erotica' Califia writes: 'This stuff reads as if it were written by dutiful daughters who are trying to persuade Mom that lesbian sex isn't dirty, and we really are good girls, after all' (1988: 13). Sheba in their notes on safer sex maintain: 'Learning about safer sex is a way of collectively talking about what we do sexually. It is also a way of confronting the notion that if you decide to practice safer sex you are "unclean" or suspect your partner of being so' (1989: 200). The words 'dirty' and 'unclean', by association, surface the idea of contamination, illness and social marginalization. Both Califia and Sheba seem to suggest that if, in doing lesbian sex, we are supposed to be 'dirty' in the eyes of the world/our partner, then at least we want to decide what the nature of the dirt is: Califia seeks to appropriate and re-value the term 'dirt' to index something positive; Sheba are looking to disarm it by questioning its appropriateness. Califia again: 'I don't believe "unsafe" porn causes AIDS … Nobody ever caught a disease from … a book' (1988: 17).

Lesbian erotica/porn, in Califia's book, are sexy (when unsafe) and safe (because *only* a text). Here we find, inversely expressed, the notion that by not incorporating – and note that word – safer sex practices, by not taking precautions into the body of writing, we might lay ourselves open to disease, that contamination may be the result of unsafe sex. Simultaneously, by taking it in, by incorporating safer sex practices in lesbian erotica/porn, we are taking it on – HIV/AIDS. Does 'taking it on' mean being contaminated by it? This, I would suggest, provides another reason why Califia and Sheba Collective are reluctant to include safer sex practices into their erotica/porn, indicating a persistent question and anxiety about how we get it – HIV/AIDS – and what we should do about it.

It might be argued that through the denial of HIV/AIDS, as much as through the incorporation of safer sex practices in lesbian erotica/porn, we are romancing death.[14] One thing seems clear to me: the emergence of HIV/AIDS has called for a revisioning of lesbian erotica/porn which is not evaded by avoiding the issue. Lesbian erotica/porn means something different now from what it meant before the early 1980s. The fact that lesbian erotica/porn has proliferated since that period makes a revisioning only all the more necessary. It is possible that the proliferation of this material constitutes an act of defiance, a refusal to be beaten by the public discourses around the disease not all of which are terribly accurate and many of which are homophobic.[15] It could also be a romancing of death which resembles that associated with the decadence of the 1890s when living for the moment supplanted the orientation towards a future many no longer believed was there.[16] Sarah Lucia Hoagland has called for a revaluing of lesbian desire which states that such desire need not be 'a matter of being "safe" or "in danger" ', but is 'a matter of connection' (1988: 169). She asserts: 'Thus, we can come to embrace more fully both desire and difference as biophilic, not necrophilic.' (1988: 169–70) The question, of course, is: who or what do we connect with? And how?

Notes

[1] I do not wish to re-hash arguments about distinctions or otherwise between erotica and pornography here, and am therefore going to use 'erotica/porn' throughout this chapter. Somehow the subtleties around mutuality/one-way, whole-body/bit-parts, etc. as argued over in essays such as Gloria Steinem's (1978) 'Erotica and Pornography: A Clear and Present Difference', or Audre Lorde's (1978) 'Uses of the Erotic: The Erotic as Power' have always escaped me. Basically, I agree with Gayle Rubin's assertion that 'Most people find it difficult to grasp that whatever they like to do sexually will be thoroughly

repulsive to someone else, and that whatever repels them sexually will be the most treasured delight of someone, somewhere ... Most people mistake their sexual preferences for a universal system that will or should work for everyone.' (Rubin, 1989: 283). I would argue further that those who do distinguish between erotica and porn frequently do so on the basis of what they find un/acceptable: the acceptable is erotic, the unacceptable is pornographic.

[2] For a discussion of conventions governing romance and Romance writings see Tania Modleski's (1982) *Loving with a Vengeance: Mass-Produced Fantasies for Women* (London: Methuen), esp. chapters two and three.

[3] The same legitimating framework is frequently at play in cases of sexual child abuse and other forms of domestic sexual abuse.

[4] I think that visual and written material needs to be distinguished here as visual material when it involves the presentation of more than one person, does not, as a matter of course, make explicit the relational connections between the people it depicts.

[5] For another version of this problematic see Kitty Tsui's 'Who says we don't talk about sex?', in which she considers the impact of her Chinese upbringing on her initial inarticulacy about sex, commenting, for instance: 'Chinese is my first language. But I was fluent only in the words my parents deemed it necessary for me to know. I was certainly not taught the words for breast, cunt, ass, or orgasm. There were no words for sex; therefore, sex did not exist.' (Tsui, 1992: 385)

[6] Linda Singer (1993) has explored this in *Erotic Welfare: Sexual Theory and Politics in the Age of Epidemic* (London: Routledge).

[7] For two different discussions of this problematic see Carol McMillan's (1982) *Women, Reason and Nature* (Oxford: Basil Blackwell), and Donna J. Haraway's (1991) *Simians, Cyborgs, and Women: The Reinvention of Nature* (London: Free Association Books).

[8] This is a convention much exploited in hetero romances such as those published by Mills & Boon, or Barbara Cartland's, which typically move from dialogue into euphemistic description at the point of actual sexual intercourse (e.g. ' "I love ... you! I love ... you!" she wanted to say, but the Earl was carrying her up on a shaft of moonlight into the sky.' (Cartland, 1987: 140)). The idea seems to be to establish sex as belonging to the realm of the pre-linguistic, a 'pre-social', instinctual phenomenon enacting an inherited 'natural' behaviour. It also suggests automatic sexual response and success, the partner always knowing what you want and fulfilling that desire. All of this is of course contradicted by the reports on sexuality which became in/famous from the late 1940s onwards and which chart heterosexual women's frustration

in heterosex (See S. Jeffreys (1990) *Anticlimax: A Feminist Perspective on the Sexual Revolution*, London: The Women's Press, esp. chapters two and three).

9 See Diane Richardson's (1987) *Women and the AIDS Crisis*, London: Pandora, esp. chapter one.

10 Chapter three in Richardson's *Women and the AIDS Crisis* is informative here, as is Zoe Leonard's (1990) 'Lesbians in the AIDS Crisis'.

11 See, for instance, Bridget Fowler (1991) *The Alienated Reader* (Hemel Hempstead: Harvester Wheatsheaf); Helen Taylor, 'Romantic Readers', in Helen Carr, (ed) (1989) *From My Guy to Sci-Fi* (London: Pandora), pp58–77; Jacqueline Sarsby (1983) *Romantic Love and Society* (Harmondsworth: Penguin); Jean Radford (ed) (1986) *The Progress of Romance* (London: Routledge & Kegan Paul).

12 In 'A Case of AIDS', Mandy Merck (1993) offers an account of the way in which AIDS and its victims can be assimilated and subjected to the conventions of hetero romance in order to affirm the latter.

13 The best known theorization of this is probably Northrop Frye's (1957, rpt. 1973) *Anatomy of Criticism*, Princeton: Princeton University Press. esp. his third essay therein. To quote the perhaps most relevant section here: 'Romance, like comedy, has six isolatable phases, and as it moves from the tragic to the comic area, the first three are parallel to the first three phases of tragedy and the second three to the second three phases of comedy …' (p198)

14 In 'Sexual Inversions' Judith Butler discusses the function of 'death' in current debates on the relationship of the politics of 'life and death' in the context of homosexuality and AIDS (in Stanton, 1992, pp344–61).

15 Though not in any way directly homophobic, I was surprised that the very recent *Working With Women and AIDS*, edited by Judy Bury *et al*, 'simply' stated in its introduction that 'although issues about AIDS for women from ethnic minorities and for lesbians are mentioned, they are not dealt with in depth.' (Bury, 1992: 3).

16 See E. Showalter's (1991) *Sexual Anarchy: Gender and Culture at the Fin de Siècle*, London: Bloomsbury, esp. chapters nine and ten.

Bibliography

Barrington, J. (ed) (1991) *An Intimate Wilderness: Lesbian Writers on Sexuality*, Portland: The Eighth Mountain Press.

Bannon, A. (1959; this ed. 1986) *I am a Woman*, Tallahassee: Naiad Press.

Boffin, T. (1990) 'Angelic Rebels: Lesbians and Safer Sex', in T. Boffin and S. Gupta (eds) *Ecstatic Antibodies: Resisting the AIDS Mythology*, London: Rivers Oram Press.

Boffin, T. (1990) 'Fairy Tales, "Facts" and Gossip: Lesbians and AIDS', in T. Boffin and S. Gupta (eds) *op cit.*

Brown, J. (1992) 'Sex, Lies, and Penetration: A Butch Finally "Fesses Up" ', in J. Nestle (ed) *The Persistent Desire: A Butch-Femme Reader*, Boston: Alyson Publications.

Bury, J., Morrison, V., and McLachlan, S. (eds) (1992) *Working With Women and AIDS*, London: Tavistock/Routledge.

Butler, J. (1992) 'Sexual Inversions', in D. C. Stanton (ed) *Discourses of Sexuality*, Ann Arbor: University of Michigan Press.

Califia, P. (1988) *Macho Sluts*, Boston: Alyson Publications.

Cartland, B. (1987) *A Circus for Love*, London: Pan Books.

Fowler, B. (1991), *The Alienated Reader: Women and Popular Romantic Literature in the Twentieth Century*, Hemel Hempstead: Harvester Wheatsheaf.

Frye, M. (1991) 'Lesbian "Sex" ', in J. Barrington (ed) *An Intimate Wilderness: Lesbian Writers on Sexuality*, Portland: The Eighth Mountain Press.

Frye, N. (1957; this ed. 1973) *Anatomy of Criticism: Four Essays*, Princeton: Princeton, University Press.

Hoagland, S.L. (1988) *Lesbian Ethics: Towards New Value*, Palo Alto, California: Institute of Lesbian Studies.

Leonard, Z. (1990) 'Lesbians in the AIDS Crisis', in The Act Up/NY Women & AIDS Book Group (eds) *Women, AIDS & Activism*, Boston: South End Press.

Lorde, A. (1978; this ed. 1980) 'Uses of the Erotic', in L. Lederer (ed) *Take Back the Night: Women and Pornography*, New York: William Morrow & Co.

Merck, M. (1993) 'A Case of AIDS', in *Perversions*, London: Virago Press.

Modleski, T. (1982) *Loving With a Vengeance: Mass-produced Fantasies for Women*, London: Methuen.

Namjoshi, S. (1991) 'I give her the rose', in J. Barrington (ed) *An Intimate Wilderness: Lesbian Writers on Sexuality*, Oregon: The Eighth Mountain Press.

Nestle, J. (ed) (1992) *The Persistent Desire: A Butch-Femme Reader*, Boston: Alyson Publications.

O'Sullivan, S. (1990) 'Mapping: Lesbianism, AIDS and Sexuality', in *Feminist Review* 34: 120–33.

Radway, J. (1987) *Reading the Romance: Women, Patriarchy and Popular Literature*, London: Verso.

Rich, A. (1980; this ed. 1984) 'Compulsory Heterosexuality and Lesbian Existence', in A. Snitow *et al* (eds) *Desire: The Politics of Sexuality*, London: Virago Press.

Rubin, G. (1989) 'Thinking Sex: Notes for a Radical Theory of the Politics of Sexuality', in C. S. Vance (ed) *Pleasure and Danger: Exploring Female Sexuality*, London: Pandora.

Sheba Collective (eds) (1989) *Serious Pleasure*, London: Sheba Feminist Publishers.

Showalter, E. (1991) *Sexual Anarchy: Gender and Culture at the 'Fin de Siècle'*, London: Bloomsbury.

Steinem, G. (1978; this ed. 1980) 'Erotica and Pornography: A Clear and Present Difference', in L. Lederer (ed) *op cit*.

Tsui, K. (1992) 'Who says we don't talk about sex?' in J. Nestle (ed), *op cit*.

Weeks, J. (1992) 'Values in the Age of Uncertainty', in D.C. Stanton (ed) *Discourses of Sexuality*, Ann Arbor: University of Michigan Press.

Winterson, J (1985) *Oranges Are Not The Only Fruit*, London: Pandora.

The Postmodern Romances of Feminist Science Fiction

Jenny Wolmark

Science fiction has become a key source of metaphors through which to examine the uncertainties of postmodern culture and society. Its narrative strategy of representing the present as the past of some imagined future is particularly appropriate in the context both of the shifting spatial and temporal relations that are characteristic of postmodernism, and of the 'incredulity toward metanarratives' in western culture proposed by Lyotard (Lyotard, 1984: xxiv). It is within feminist science fiction, however, that the erosion of critical and cultural boundaries is most convincingly and enthusiastically explored, boundaries such as those between high and popular culture, nature and culture, self and other. Recent feminist science fiction transforms postmodern anxieties about definitions of the subject into utopian possibilities for the redefinition of gender identity and gender relations. In this chapter I argue that feminist science fiction crosses the boundaries of both gender and genre in two ways: firstly, by drawing on the narrative fantasies of popular romance fiction to offer fantasies of female pleasure and power, and secondly by using the 'hard science' metaphor of the cyborg to redefine definitions of female subjectivity.

Feminist science fiction uses the codes and conventions of both science fiction and romance fiction, and as such it acquires that postmodern ambivalence described by Linda Hutcheon, whereby it is 'doubly coded' because it is 'both complicitous with and contesting of the cultural dominants within which it operates' (Hutcheon, 1989: 142). The feminist science fiction that has been written since the 1970s has negotiated the inherent contradictions of this double coding placing the desiring 'I' of romance fiction at the centre of SF narratives, and in so doing feminist SF has profoundly influenced this most masculinist of genres. The postmodern romances of feminist SF provided an opportunity for women writers to foreground gender relations and to explore the possibilities for redefining them. This was the case in Marge Piercy's *Woman on the Edge of Time* (1976), and Ursula Le Guin's *The Left Hand of Darkness* (1969) and *The Dispossessed* (1974). Women-only future societies were created by a number of feminist SF writers such as Joanna Russ with *The Female Man* (1975), Suzy McKee Charnas with *Walk to the End of the World* (1974) and *Motherlines* (1978), Sally Miller Gearhart with *The Wanderground* (1979), and Alice Sheldon, who used the male pseudonym of James Tiptree Jr. for her short story 'Houston, Houston, Do You Read?' (1976). Although none of the societies created by these writers were entirely utopian, they provided the fictional environment for the reworking of both gender identity and gender relations. Despite their ambiguous and sometimes embattled position within a genre that still appears to have a preponderance of white male authors and readers, these narratives have not only been able to make significant inroads into the dominant representations of gender, but they have also stretched the limits and definitions of the genre.

The women-only futures envisioned within feminist science fiction have been criticised, however, on the grounds that the social relations of science and technology which continue to inform the genre have been scrupulously avoided. Joan Gordon has argued that, not only are all feminist SF utopias dominated by images of a pastoral, organic world, but that most feminist SF 'incorporates a longing to go forward into the idealized past of earth's earlier matriarchal nature religions' (Gordon, 1991: 199). It is certainly the case that in the narratives of Sally Miller Gearhart and Suzy McKee Charnas, technology and the urban environment are associated with the repressive structures of patriarchy in a way that comes perilously close to a re-enactment of the duality of nature and culture. Sally Miller Gearhart's *The Wanderground*, for example, describes a community of women living outside the city in a complete and mystical harmony with nature. Such a communion is shown to be intrinsically impossible for men, for once they are outside the city, both they and 'their' technology become impotent and the earth itself rejects them. The emphasis on the essential qualities and differences of masculinity and femininity expressed in *The Wanderground* is also present in the two novels by Suzy McKee Charnas mentioned earlier: in the post-holocaust world of *Walk to the End of the World*, men fear and hate women for their gender, and keep them as dehumanised slaves in their cities. Only when women escape from the cities into the wilderness can they become free, and *Motherlines* focuses entirely on the separatist communities of women that have been established in the wilderness. The binarisms of masculine and feminine, nature and culture, are reproduced in these narratives so that they are as marked by essentialism as any romance text, despite the explicitly feminist intentions of the writers.

A shift of emphasis, however, can be discerned in feminist SF written from the 1980s on, as it confronts the question of gendered subjectivity more explicitly within the context of the masculinist hegemony of technology. Where romance has yet to find a set of metaphors that enables it to fully explore the socially and culturally constructed nature of gender, feminist science fiction has available to it the image of the cyborg, invoked by Donna Haraway in 'A Manifesto for Cyborgs' (Haraway, 1985). In this seminal discussion of the necessity to develop a new and non-essentialist politics of gender based on recognition of difference, Haraway argues that the cyborg, or cybernetic organism, is a metaphor that makes particular sense in the context of the postmodern breakdown of boundaries. The cyborg is a hybrid creature that transgresses and problematises binary oppositions and argues for the need for non-totalising and partial identities. Within feminist SF, the contradictory identities embodied by the cyborg provide a means of questioning existing definitions of gendered subjectivity. As Haraway suggests, 'The cyborgs populating feminist science fiction make very problematic the statuses of man or woman, human, artefact, member of a race, individual identity, or body' (Haraway, 1985: 97). The ambiguous postmodern romances of feminist SF are transgressive because they foreground female desire while evading closure around the binarisms of masculinity and femininity. The ironic 'cyborg monsters' (Haraway, 1985: 99) who inhabit these narratives move between and across the subject positions of masculinity and femininity and allow the relationship between identity and desire to be explored outside the confines of fixed subject positions. The cyborg can be regarded as a disruptive metaphor on a number of counts: by problematising the relationship between human and machine, the cyborg also problematises the relationship between self and other, nature and culture. By providing an opportunity for feminist SF to explore possibilities for the redefinition of gender identity in the context of cybernetic systems, the cyborg disrupts the gendered power relations of technology. Finally, by challenging the masculinist hegemony over technology, the cyborg disrupts the generic stability of science fiction itself, since the genre has largely been built around the unquestioned assumption of that hegemony.

The cyborg in feminist SF challenges the power relations that are embedded in postmodern cybernetic systems, but which are usually suppressed. The cyborg therefore stands in opposition to the kind of cultural pessimism that is a noticeable feature of the accounts of postmodern culture provided by both Fredric Jameson and Jean Baudrillard. Jameson has asserted that postmodern culture no longer has the capacity to imagine the future (Jameson, 1982), and from this perspective the utopian longings that infuse both romance fiction and science fiction are absent because the utopian imagination itself has atrophied. Baudrillard demonstrates a similar cultural pessimism in his definition of hyperreality as the point where the contradiction between the real and the imaginary is effaced, the result of which, he suggests, is 'the end of metaphysics, the end of fantasy, the end of SF' (Baudrillard, 1991: 311). Both Jameson and Baudrillard regard the penetration of social and cultural structures by information technology and cybernetic systems as the key to the fragmentation and depthlessness of the postmodern condition. Electronic imaging and the development of Virtual Reality are perhaps the clearest contemporary expressions of this, because of the way in which they give 'virtual' embodiment to an imagined space. The phrase that has been coined to describe the technologies of fantasy at Disneyland, for example, is 'imagineering'; Baudrillard has described it in terms of the hyperreal, that which is more real than the real. For Baudrillard, Disneyland is 'presented as imaginary in order to make us believe that the rest is real' (Baudrillard, 1988: 172). While the boundaries between the real and the imagined are becoming increasingly unstable, so too are the boundaries between the cultural categories of high and popular culture, and the cultural pessimism of both Jameson and Baudrillard is tied to some extent to a model in which those categories remain fixed. In his discussion of the relations between mass culture and modernism, in *After the Great Divide* (Huyssen, 1986), Andreas Huyssen has pointed out that the distinction between high and mass culture is a gendered one, and that historically mass culture has been feminized as modernism's Other. Anxieties about the way in which the boundaries between high and popular culture are being rendered unstable, both by the impact of technology and by the eclecticism of postmodern parody and pastiche, can also, therefore, be seen as gendered.

Far from being constrained by such anxieties, feminist science fiction exploits postmodern instabilities. Within the shifting parameters of cybernetic systems, the boundaries between body and machine, self and other, become increasingly uncertain. As a result, definitions of difference and otherness, and the discourses of power within which those differences are articulated, can be questioned. In the accounts of postmodernism already discussed, this uncertainty is regarded as a threat, both to the unitary categories of culture and, by extension, to unitary definitions of the self. This is certainly the case in science fiction's other notable encounter with the postmodern, 'cyberpunk', in which the virtual realities of cybernetic systems are constantly threatening to undermine the imagined stabilities of gender. The street-wise computer hackers or 'console cowboys' of William Gibson's cyberpunk novels, *Neuromancer* (1986), *Count Zero* (1987) and *Mona Lisa Overdrive* (1989), for example, are driven by the desire to abandon the body and to interface with the matrix, a situation that is surely replete with possibilities for the reconstruction of gender identity and of gender relations. Yet these cyberpunk texts draw back from the possibilities of the interface, in which both self and other could be redefined in non-essentialist terms. Not only are the masculine identities of the console cowboys carefully preserved, even in the virtual realities of cyberspace, but because the artificial intelligences that inhabit the matrix are also defined as masculine, the interface itself is made masculine.

Feminist SF, on the other hand, uses the imagery and metaphors of cybernetic systems to challenge unitary definitions of the self and to offer an alternative and oppositional account of gender identity in which provisionality and multiplicity are emphasised. Because cyborg identity is always in process, it thrives on ambiguity and destabilizes sexual difference. Cyborg imagery is present in the work of feminist SF writers such as Octavia Butler, Vonda McIntyre, Joanna Russ and C. J. Cherryh, all of whom have produced narratives in which the politics of female desire are negotiated through the problematising of female identity. Popular romance narratives also explore female desire through ambivalence and ambiguity, but because that desire is achieved only within the existing relations of dominance and subordination characterising contemporary gender relations, identity remains fixed rather than fluid. In the remainder of this chapter I shall be considering the ambiguity and fluidity of gender identity within the postmodern romances of feminist SF, concentrating on the work of two American writers, Emma Bull and Elizabeth Hand, and an English writer, Gwyneth Jones.

Emma Bull's novel *Bone Dance* (1991) is a post-catastrophe narrative in cyberpunk mode, in which street-wise hustlers do 'biz' in a decaying urban environment. Bull uses several motifs drawn from cyperbunk, such as genetic engineering and mind control, and reuses them to focus on gender identity. It is the cyborgs in the narrative, with their incomplete and partial identities, that call the whole framework of binary divisions into question. All the cyborg bodies in the narrative are genetically engineered, or constructed, as are their identities, and both bodies and identities are subject to change during the course of the novel. This produces a gender incoherence in the narrative, which is explored through the central character of Sparrow, a gender neutral cyborg who takes on the 'look' of masculinity or femininity according to the needs of the moment. Because it is gender neutral, and always other, Sparrow's body becomes unintelligible in terms of the binary definitions of gender. This unintelligibility is also present amongst the second group of cyborgs in the narrative, who are able to take over and control the minds and bodies of whichever 'host' they desire, in a literal embodiment of desire for the Other. The fantasies of power and submission that are central to popular romance are partially lived out in the narrative through the powers of these cyborgs. However, although the cyborgs began as gendered subjects, they also take on both the gender and desires of whichever host body they inhabit, and this multiplicity of sexual identities and desires fatally disrupts the unequal power relations that are embedded in popular romance fiction. The fluid identities of the cyborgs enable them to move between the subject positions of masculinity and femininity, and since gender identity can no longer be resolved in binary terms, both fantasy and desire can be reconstituted as heterogeneous. Sparrow's cyborg body is the literal expression of this fluidity, since it refuses categorization in terms of gender altogether. The cyborgs in *Bone Dance*, then, transform the binarisms which structure popular romance fiction into a transgressive fantasy of multiplicity.

The baroque science fiction novels of Elizabeth Hand, *Winterlong*

(1990) and *Aestival Tide* (1992), describe a post-catastrophe future world which includes artificial intelligence, genetic engineering, neurological control and germ warfare. The cyborgs within this environment are contradictory: they embody the dominant and hierarchical relations of control within cybernetic systems but also subvert them. There is an ambivalent relation between power and powerlessness in these novels which parallels that found in popular romance fiction, but in popular romance the subversive potential of this ambivalence is ultimately contained because the fantasies of female desire are structured around the fixed polarities of gender. In Hand's novels, the cyborg signifies an ambivalence and irresolution which calls those polarities into question, and as the boundary between self and other becomes increasingly ambiguous, desire can be differently configured. The novels are peopled with what Donna Haraway has called 'boundary creatures' (Haraway, 1991: 2), those transgressive cyborgs who exist disruptively outside the limits prescribed by the binarisms of gender, of nature and culture, of self and other. One such is Miss Scarlet, a talking ape that has been surgically altered to enable her to speak and to enhance her intellectual capacity, but whose physical embodiment has not changed so that she is neither wholly ape nor wholly human. The potential dissolution of boundaries between human and animal produces a cyborg identity in which the dualisms of nature and culture are thrown into disarray. The identity of a boundary creature like Miss Scarlet is enigmatic and unresolved, and as such it has the capacity to disrupt the binary order which cybernetic systems seek to impose.

In *Aestival Tide* the technologies of genetic engineering have advanced so far that the dead can be regenerated, to become a kind of mindless underclass, subject to the unmediated power relations of cybernetic systems. These are cyborgs without hope, incapable of offering any challenge to the gendered nature of those power relations. The significant challenge is offered instead through the potent combination of a doubly gendered hermaphrodite and a gendered android. These cyborg identities are neither unified nor coherent, and cannot be contained within the familiar constructions of gender identity. It is that incoherence which poses a threat to the already precarious stability of the hierarchical society described in the narrative, and both the android and the hermaphrodite are instrumental in its eventual collapse. The contradictory desires of these cyborgs are neither resolved within nor contained by the narrative, and the significance of their hybrid identities is that they disrupt what Judith Butler calls the 'regulatory fictions' (Butler, 1990: 33) of gender. The partial identities of 'boundary creatures' such as the hermaphrodite, the gendered android, and Miss Scarlet represent transgression against the limits of identity and subjectivity that are imposed by binary oppositions.

The novels of Gwyneth Jones present a more complex discussion of the transgressive potential of the cyborg's hybrid and partial identity. Her most recent novel, *White Queen* (1992), uses the familiar SF motif of an alien-human encounter to explore the collapse of stable boundaries between self and other, human and alien. The cultural construction of 'otherness' is a central concern of the novel, and the mutual incomprehension of gender relations and identities on the part of both humans and aliens is used to ironic effect to suggest that the binary framework is wholly inadequate for an understanding of difference. It is in the earlier novel, *Escape Plans*, however, that Jones engages more directly with the cyborg identities that emerge through the interface between human and machine. The penetration of social and cultural structures by cybernetic information systems noted by Jameson and Baudrillard provides the framework for the narrative, but it is the ability of such cyborg identities to transgress against the limits imposed by those systems that is of interest to Jones.

In *Escape Plans* (1986) Jones takes another familiar SF motif, that of the existence of an infinite universe, or universes, and ironically reverses it. It has been discovered that humanity is actually trapped in a 'bubble universe' that is possibly at the centre of the universe, if it had a centre, and has been since the beginning of the universe, if the universe had a beginning. Jones undermines the romanticised notion of an expansive future that is embedded in many science fiction narratives, and in the process she reveals the way in which the endless longing for an 'elsewhere' in such narratives reinforces an essentially conservative desire for transcendental otherness. In science fiction narratives which celebrate the transcendent otherness of infinitely expanding universes, the existing inequalities of power relations are never questioned. In contrast, Jones' self-reflexive narrative of containment makes the questioning of such relations central by refusing to subscribe to a definition of SF as the romance of the future. In describing a future that is about containment rather than expansion, the doubly coded narrative questions the power relations that produce, and are produced by, the binarisms of space and earth, inner and outer, nature and culture. It is a future in which the human-machine interface is both liberatory and repressive, and the cyborgs of this future both control and are controlled by the technology. Jones suggests that the interface contains not only possibilities for radical change but also possibilities for repression and exploitation, and the narrative refuses closure around either option.

The patterns of control that are embedded in cybernetic systems are scrutinised in the narrative, as are the relations of power that such systems embody. In the past of this future, the seemingly limitless possibilities of space exploration and total automation produced revolutionary changes. Women proved to be better suited to the interface than men and so, in space, they finally achieved equality with men, and as a result of these newly configured cyborg relations, heterosexuality no longer dominated social and sexual relations. However, the eventual discovery that space was finite undermined the utopian aspects of these dvelopments and cybernetic systems became instead a means of reproducing other unequal power relations based primarily on the distinction between the spacefaring elite, which controls the systems, and the 'Subs', those who have remained planet bound and who are ultimately subject to that control. In the present time of the narrative, cybernetic systems have become so ubiquitous that everyone has become 'plugged-in', but not with equal levels of access to the systems. Ironically, the most powerless of all the Subs are those who interface most completely with the central computer system: by means of brains sockets burned through the skull they process unimaginable amounts of information, but they are unable to access any of it. The Subs, however, regard the interface in almost mystical terms and the skull holes are valued as an indicator of both difference and status. Since the interface means one thing to the power elite and another to those who are subject to the needs of that elite, it is clear that the cyborg identities in this future are neither innocent nor free. The narrative indicates that, although women achieved social and political equality with men through the interface, unequal structures of power and control have continued to be embedded in the cybernetic systems: gender is, therefore, fully implicated in the perpetuation of those inequalities.

The 'pleasure of the interface' (Springer, 1991) is thus revealed as being somewhat ambiguous, and to emphasise this point, the self referential language of information systems is parodied throughout the narrative. Acronyms are used so extensively that they require a glossary, and personal names and acronyms are conflated as an ironic indication of the universality of the interface: the central character, for example, is known as both Alice and ALIC, depending on the formality of the address. The main focus of the narrative is ALIC's gradual realisation of the inequalities built into what seems to be a perfectly balanced cybernetic system. Her realisation, that it is precisely those inequalities that define definitions of identity and difference, enables the narrative to explore the pleasures and the pains, as well as the possibilities and the limitations, of cyborg identity.

The postmodern romances discussed in this chapter are concerned with the transgression of limits, and with the potential of the human-machine interface to define otherness outside the confines of binary oppositions. The cyborgs in these novels are made but not born, just as they are different but not 'other': it is not transcendence that they seek but rather the dissolution of the boundaries between inner and outer, self and other, nature and culture. The metaphor of the cyborg is a potent one because it is drawn from both the politics of information systems and the politics of gender. The binarisms inherent in the masculine hegemony of technology are also present in constructions of gender, and both sets of inequalities come together, in a very precise way, within cybernetic systems. Cyborg identities, however, are both imprecise and hybrid and as such they have the potential to re-order boundaries and demolish polarities. The doubly coded narratives of feminist science fiction do not propose the magical resolutions to the problem of female desire that are common to popular romance fiction, since the object of desire is differently defined within them. Equally, the idealisation of gender identity that occurs in popular romance is unsustainable within the postmodern romance of feminist SF, because the metaphor of the cyborg undermines the fixed polarities of gender on which such idealisations depend. The cyborg identities of feminist SF emphasise the ambiguities and contradictions of subjectivity, and in the context of such a redefined subjectivity, femininity and female desire are subjected to extensive interrogation.

Bibliography

Baudrillard, J. (1988) *Selected Writings*, M. Poster (ed), Cambridge: Polity Press.

Baudrillard, J. (1991) 'Simulacra and Science Fiction', trans. A. B. Evans, *Science Fiction Studies*, 18, Part 3, 309–13.

Bull, E. (1991) *Bone Dance*, New York: Ace.
Butler, J. (1990) *Gender Trouble*, New York and London: Routledge.
Charnas, S. M. (1974) *Walk to the End of the World*, New York: Ballantine.
Charnas, M. (1978) *Motherlines*, New York: Berkley.
Gearhart, S. M. (1979) *The Wanderground*, Watertown: Persephone Press.
Gibson, W. (1986) *Neuromancer*, London: Grafton.
Gibson, W. (1987) *Count Zero*, London: Grafton.
Gibson, W. (1989) *Mona Lisa Overdrive*, London: Grafton.
Gordon, J. (1991) 'Yin and Yang Duke it Out: is Cyberpunk Feminism's New Age?', in L. McCaffery (ed) *Storming The Reality Studio*, Durham: Duke University Press.
Hand, E. (1990) *Winterlong*, New York: Bantam.
Hand, E. (1992) *Aestival Tide*, New York: Bantam.
Haraway, D. (1985) 'A Manifesto for Cyborgs: Science, Technology, and Socialist Feminism in the 1980s', *Socialist Review*, 80, 65–107.
Haraway, D. (1991) *Simians, Cyborgs, and Women*, London: Free Press.
Hutcheon, L. (1989) *The Politics of Postmodernism*, London: Methuen.
Huyssen, A. (1986) *After the Great Divide: Modernism, Mass Culture, Postmodernism*, Bloomington: Indiana University Press.
Jameson, F. (1982) 'Progress versus Utopia; or, Can We Imagine the Future?', *Science Fiction Studies*, 9, Part 2, 147–58.
Jameson, F. (1991) *Postmodernism, or, The Cultural Logic of Late Capitalism*, London and New York: Verso.
Jones, G. (1986) *Escape Plans*, London: Unwin.
Jones, G. (1992) *White Queen*, London: VGSF.
Le Guin, U. (1969) *The Left Hand of Darkness*, New York: Ace.
Le Guin, U. (1974) *The Dispossessed*, New York: Harper & Row.
Lyotard, J.-F. (1984) *The Postmodern Condition: A Report on Knowledge*, trans. G. Bennington and B. Massumi, Manchester: Manchester University Press.
Piercy, M. (1976) *Woman on the Edge of Time*, New York: Knopf.
Russ, J. (1975) *The Female Man*, New York: Bantam.
Springer, C. (1991) 'The Pleasure of the Interface', *Screen*, 32, no. 3, 303–23.
Tiptree, J. Jr. (1978) 'Houston, Houston, Do You Read?', in *Star Songs of an Old Primate*, New York: Ballantine.

Negotiations: Love Across the Tracks – Interracial Romance

The Heart of Whiteness: White Subjectivity and Interracial Relationships

Kathryn Perry

> White people in this country will have quite enough to do in learning how to accept and love themselves and each other, and when they have achieved this – which will not be tomorrow and may very well be never – the Negro problem will no longer exist, for it will no longer be needed. (Baldwin, 1963:27)

Among the questions raised by James Baldwin's eloquent polemical essay, *The Fire Next Time* (1963), is the conundrum of how white people are to love black people, subsumed as they are in a history that has so coloured desire. His reply is that white self knowledge is the first step; the means of release from the tensions of narcissism which comprise the unacknowledged fears and longings that white people project on to black people. For James Baldwin, love is a 'state of grace' (Baldwin, 1963: 82) that yields no easy explanation. He intends it to carry little of the superficiality of happiness, but to exist in a sterner sense of 'quest and daring and growth' (Baldwin, 1963: 82). Through this love, he suggests a redirection of the white quest away from the supposed problem of black people and towards an exploration of how white identity has problematised blackness as a counterpoint to white supremacy.

Like much else in *The Fire Next Time* (1963), James Baldwin's framing of this question points to a means of considering what whiteness may be. Vron Ware clarifies whiteness as an ideology, refering to race as a 'socially constructed category with absolutely no basis in biology' (Ware, 1992: xii). Although most white people remain complicit in their ignorance of white racial identity, in interracial relationships white people do have to encounter the racialization of a private relationship and their own identities as white. Up until then, many will have assumed that, unlike black people, they do not have a race; that they do not comprise an ethnic group. They will have simply considered their whiteness to be universal and race-free. Many will have disguised their racial convictions through the assertion of nation, thinking it more acceptable to be a patriot rather than a racist. Yet in Britain, ideologies of whiteness are everywhere, the legacy of a vast colonialist project that legitimised the economic and military demands of an empire based on racial supremacy. Within this overreaching context, white responses to a black and white love affair are just one configuration of how white people create or participate in their whiteness. These responses are historically specific; the racial preoccupations of the 1990s are not those of the 1890s. Yet as ideologies of whiteness they possess a fluidity of image and fantasy that reveals cumulative echoes of decades before. They are governed by many of the familiar dualities of racism: the tensions of longing and anxiety, supremacy and submission, the fear of alienation and the desire for transformation. Projected as 'common sense' white views about blackness, these dualities more properly describe the drama of the racialized white self.

Ultimately, it is paradoxical to consider whiteness within the context of an interracial relationship if, through the strategy of projection, white racial identity is refering back to itself rather than to blackness, and thus might be disclosed equally well through the relationship of a white couple. Richard Dyer has pointed to some of the difficulties in achieving this, 'It seemed from our discussion of the film [*Brief Encounter*] as if white identities are ineluctably dependent on non-white for their existence, so that even a film with only white characters in it has to have recourse to non-white reference to convey the boundaries of whiteness' (Dyer, 1993: 65). However, since projection structurally mirrors the dualisms of white thought, examining these dualities in an interracial context may suggest how they reappear even when they are not determined by a dialogue between black and white people. Finally, although these dualities are oppositional, it should not be inferred that interracial relationships are uniquely driven by conflict. In reality, interracial couples engage with racialized difference just as, for instance, heterosexual couples engage with gender – with greater or lesser success depending on the couple and their environment.

Like Nkweto Simmonds, I will be drawing upon the collection of interviews, *The Colour of Love: Mixed Race Relationships* (Alibhai-Brown & Montague, 1992), in which white and black men and women talk about their relationships with each other, I will focus on the revelation of white racial identity. As white people rarely discuss their racial attitudes with any sense of real exploration or frankness, it is exciting that these interviews capture their powerful conjunction of private and public emotions. Although the book does not interpret the interviews, it is particularly valuable in offering a more complete portrait of interracial relationships than it is possible to do justice to here. Although the editors interviewed only heterosexual couples, justifying that the lesbian and gay experience merited a book in itself, I assume that readers here are of all sexual orientations, and that they will successfully reinterpret any genders referred to here with gay abandon.[1]

Forbidden Love

Interracial love has a complex relationship with romance, being in a sense still forbidden love, even if it is no longer prohibited. Unlike romance, this forbidden love promises no guiding fantasy of integrating sexuality into a socially sanctioned relationship. The mythologies of racism anticipate a 'perverse' erotic encounter: a thrilling excursion into the landscape of inter-racial desire, or they permit a doomed relationship clinging to the edges of society; ever marginal and destined to end. More sexual perversion than social institution, forbidden love is seen to be a twilight neighbourhood visited in secret. However, although their forays into the dominant discourses of romance are necessarily episodic, those people who cross the tracks do construct a story of emerging coherence. Encountering taboo, they describe a journey of descent into the territory of transgression, the betrayal of family and culture, and of obstacles overcome in the attainment of enduring love. More epic than romance in that it concerns exile and alienation, it is a domestic story, but it is also very much a public story. Unlike romance, the interracial relationship is rarely publicly sanctioned, yet it will borrow from romance the narrative of how elusive desire becomes a happy union.

Written on the Body

Romance begins with desire. It is almost inevitable that the white person who desires a black partner must step into an arena choked with the lusts of their white ancestors and the history of their violent retributions. Whether they seek out 'perverse' encounters or the commitments of love, their desire is likely to be cloaked in this racist mythology. Many white people are wary of discovering that the myths of black sexuality have spilt over into their own imaginations. Uncomfortable to be seen to have 'a thing' about black people, they deny that their desire may also encompass their partner's blackness. Others unashamedly desire the 'forbidden fruit' of racist mythology. They like to 'screw black but marry white', and if the encounter does not live up to the myth, they move on.

Whether exoticized as compliant or brutal, blackness is constructed through racialized desire in the form of white obsessions:

> If I desire someone, why can I not have a Black or Asian or Chinese woman? They are all prettier than those English women who have lost their femininity ... They are real women, not bloody feminists burning their bras and all that. Rani is soft to touch and soft as a person. I know she will be faithful to me and not run around. She will have a lovely meal ready when I come home, and sexually too she doesn't try and make me feel inadequate, or compete with me. She appreciates me. (Alibhai-Brown & Montague, 1992: 291)

> He had a lovely voice and although he wasn't handsome, he was really strong, big and masculine. My boyfriend, who was white and in the army, really seemed a weakling. I went to the bar and bought him a drink. He came home with me that night, laughed at the picture of Len on the coffee table, made love to me all night whether I wanted to or not – I could hardly walk the next day – and made me breakfast in bed, which no one has ever done. (Alibhai-Brown & Montague, 1992: 138)

These white people are living out familiar fantasies that create an image of blackness which extends all the way from the soft illumination of a vision to the muscular bestiality of lust. As a counterpoint to blackness, both enjoy their partners against a backdrop of whiteness, whether characterised as 'bloody feminists burning their bras' or poor Len who could only look on from the coffee table. In a drama of control, the complex exchange of dominance and submission, present to some degree in most sexual encounters, and represented here as an exaggerated masculinity and femininity, is additionally charged with the weight of the racialized exchange between black and white. Although it does not necessarily mean that this exchange of power is non-consensual or that it is reproduced verbatim outside of a sexual context, fantasy does echo social realities. It is the white partner who potentially derives immense sexual potency from their control of the black partner, whether through dominance or submission. In symbolic terms, where whiteness is the pimp, it is blackness that becomes the whore.

The strategy of projection ensures that white people maintain control, bestowing upon black sexuality the secret topography of white desire. Typically whiteness identifies with the mental and is often seen as alienated from its own sexual and embodied self, and yet it craves the glamour of sexuality and the warmth of the body with which it invests black people. But the strategy of projection entails that this is a longing destined to endless repetitions, never possessing those qualities with which it endows blackness, and casting a shadow of impotence across white sexuality. When, for instance, white men compete with the sexuality of black men, it is their own myths of potent black sexuality – created for the functioning of the slave system – that has left them with what they fear to be the limp counterpoint of their own sexuality. Ultimately, as the extract below demonstrates, the strategy of projection entails that the black partner become an icon or receptacle for the white person's fears and longings. Thus, white racialized sexuality is written onto the black body.

> She had the most amazing skin and this enormously huge sensuous mouth, but at the time she looked very innocent. She had a big red Hindu tilak mark and she was wearing a yellow sari. It was the most incredible image, and I stared open-mouthed at this apparition, I followed it down the platform and waited while it got into a taxi. It wasn't even a person, it was like a kind of icon. (Alibhai-Brown & Montague, 1992: 141)

The Colour White

In many senses we carry the history of racism in our bodies. White people, however, still assume the invisibility of their own colour, despite evidence, for instance, that white notions of beauty specifically celebrate an Aryan ideal, or that some people wear their colour white as a badge of pride in their racial superiority. Gradations of shade in the skin colour of white people in Britain carry little of the corresponding significance that slavery attached to the range of colour in black people. So it is with some shock that white people confront the visibility of the white body when it is seen alongside the black body. The blunt iconography of a black man's fingers interlaced with those of a white woman on the poster for the film *Jungle Fever* (Lee, 1991), surprised with its simple message of sexual intimacy between black and white. The visual impact demonstrated the power of colour as a racialized metaphor, which functions all the more powerfully as a symbol for being grounded in the physical language of the body. Anxiety about the visual evidence of the transgressive interracial relationship may lead white people to distance themselves from the racialized meanings of colour. In the extracts below, the black and white body are firstly distanced as through a photographic image, with the camera representing the scrutinising dominant discourse of whiteness that polices adherence to its racial codes. Secondly, charm functions as a denial of blackness, reinvesting the interracial relationship with the same normalising invisibility of colour that white people believe their own whiteness to represent:

> When I see photographs of us together I get a shock because I think he's so Black and I'm so white, but I don't think about it from day-to-day ... I don't see the colour. (Alibhai-Brown & Montague, 1992: 131)

> Once they get over the fact that he is a foreigner, he has olive skin and a slight accent, they like him, he's charming ... In fact I have friends today who say they forget he is foreign. (Alibhai-Brown & Montague, 1992: 214)

Some white people in *The Colour of Love* take a denial of blackness even further. One Indian partner was accepted only when the family decided that she looked Hungarian (Alibhai-Brown & Montague, 1992: 82), and there is a fascinating story told by a woman who had recently discovered that her deceased husband was black (Alibhai-Brown & Montague, 1992: 206–207).

Blood Thicker Than Water

A black and white love affair has a complex relationship with the conventions of romance that invest a dark hero with dominant masculine qualities and a fair heroine with submissive feminine qualities. To the extent that these conventions may override gender (viz, the film *Desert Hearts* (Deitch, 1985), which applies these codes to two lesbian women), they may also override race. However, the discourse of racism will not readily permit a black hero, invested with dominant qualities, to take the lead. The impossibility of black dominating white entails that black must be disinvested of its potency and feminized. Here, the denial of blackness also represents a more diffuse anxiety about the merging of white and black. It is feared that a vigorous, predatory black sexuality will engulf and annihilate a white self that is weak and easily overwhelmed. Black will dilute the purity of white; and the outcome of this alchemy? The racist nightmare of progeny whose very beings are evidence of the pollution of blood, the weakening of the race; a treacherous disavowal that blood is always thicker than water:

> One time I took the twins out for lunch and my father had one too many drinks and said how upset he was with me and how I had let him down because I had contaminated my Anglo-Saxon blood by marrying an Iranian and having half-breed children. He referred to it as though I were a pedigree bitch who would never be able to go with another pedigree again. (Alibhai-Brown & Montague, 1992: 217)

> I would never marry anyone who wasn't from my class or race. I wouldn't contaminate my genes in that way, down-grade them. They are all promiscuous and dirty, and even physically I would be revolted by it. I have friends who are Black but no physical contact, no way. These mongrel children you see around you these days, it is disgusting. (Alibhai-Brown & Montague, 1992: 293)

In these extracts, blood functions metaphorically as the vehicle of contamination in much the same way as the fear of AIDS employs body fluids. Their racist inflection speaks of these white people's horror of contamination in terms that could belong just as easily to a previous century. Historically, since the mingling of blood implied degeneracy, racist conviction deemed it 'natural selection' that white people should not choose as partners those 'lower' and 'less mentally developed'. Darwin's theory of mutability was widely interpreted to describe how the mixing of white with black would begin the drift back to the primitive, echoing present-day racist attitudes to mixed race children who are considered to be less well adjusted than either white or black children. Although the racial application of mutability suggests that whiteness is subject to change and transformation, at the same time whiteness is most commonly represented as a fixed and essential identity, having evolved to a pinnacle of 'natural' superiority.

Culture Clash

At the point in romantic fantasy when two people are supposed to live happily ever after, white people enter the culture clash of the interracial relationship. One white woman describes the assumptions of her white visitors:

> They come into your house and if they know you're married to a foreigner they expect you to have funny decorations – like purple gloss paint and orange shag-pile carpet – and they're relieved; 'Oh good, they have taste too.' And sometimes they actually say it – 'Oh, this is a nice house' – with amazement. And food – they all expected my house to stink of curry: 'I bet you have a lot of curries, don't you? Don't you cook them for him?' (Alibhai-Brown & Montague, 1992: 220)

The white partners in *The Colour of Love* reveal a culture under threat. Smells, noise, people everywhere, clashing colours and textiles: this assault on the senses is experienced with an alarming physicality. One white woman is afraid of her partner's forceful manner appearing overbearing and rude. Her reaction is to intervene to protect white cultural norms:

> I have thought he is often very brusque with people. I had to be a spokesperson for him sometimes because he wasn't being 'nice' enough. That, I think, is cultural. (Alibhai-Brown & Montague, 1992: 111)

White people worry that white culture will be swamped, and because black and white will not speak the same language, the white voice will be silenced. Hot and spicy food may overwhelm the delicacy of white taste, as if blackness itself were taken into the white body in a rather gothic subversion of the Eucharist. As the experience below testifies, the fantasy of love luring white women towards an alien culture is an expression of acute anxiety about the loss of white identity:

> Lots of people – particularly men – tried to warn me that if you marry Iranians, Turks, they take you back and once they're out of the country everything is different, they change once they're married to you. They even brought newspaper cuttings to show me incidents that had happened to girls who'd married those people. (Alibhai-Brown & Montague, 1992: 213–214)

White people may also welcome engulfment in an alien culture. Many find their white culture restrictive, cerebral and lifeless. They crave the supposed glamour, vitality, and originality of black culture. They long for a renewal of enthusiasm and vigour, as if to be magically awakened from a spellbound sleep. Many white people are excited about the discovery of an internationalism that challenges the limitations and distortions of white European culture. The white mother in the extract below was initially angered by her daughter's conversion to the Ahmadi Muslim faith, but has come to value the cultural diversity of her family:

> What's so nice is the cultural exchange which you can give and receive – something we've lost in England. Most people are interested in what Nicola's doing and what's happening with the two of them. I've passed on information about Islam and quite a few of my hairdressing clients don't want to convert, but they want to understand. (Alibhai-Brown & Montague, 1992: 202)

Privilege and Punishment

A sense of privileged insight often permeates the white partner's first-hand experience of racism. Whereas they might have noticed only the most overt forms of racism before, now the white person begins to observe it in all its subtlety. Although they know that what they see they can never again deny, many do try to deny racism:

> Prejudice surprises me and when we come across it I tend not to believe it, which irritates Patti. I tend to find some other reason, which of course it could be. (Alibhai-Brown & Montague, 1992: 41)

White people may feel the initial zeal of the convert, but at the same time they have become aware of their whiteness as privileged, and this sets them in a troubled relationship with white culture and society:

> It has been a shock to experience firsthand what life is really like for a lot of Black people in this country. For me, I am just another white, middle-class lady; people listen to what I have to say and behave respectfully towards me. What is so horrifying is that these great British institutions that I have been nurtured on – and I suppose must have believed in – are this corrupt and this vindictive. Most white people don't have that insight. (Alibhai-Brown & Montague, 1992: 29)

White people experience the shock of their white skin acting as a talisman, whilst their black partner is abused. They also experience for the first time a sense of being implicated in racism. They see the racism in other white people, and they wonder about the racism in themselves. Sometimes they feel paralysed with guilt, and sometimes they go on to use their whiteness to the advantage of their partner or children. They know that it is easier from their position to challenge racism and prejudice:

> I know that I feel as strongly as any of the Black mothers I've spoken to about racial stereotyping at school. The only difference is that sometimes, being white, I find it easier to challenge the school about it. Black friends have said, 'You go and talk to them about it, because then they can't say that you've got a chip on your shoulder.' (Alibhai-Brown & Montague, 1992: 229)

In the encounter with racism, white people cannot avoid self reflection and the uneasy acknowledgment of a privileged racial identity. Nevertheless, a good deal of privilege is lost through association, and the transgressive white person is invariably punished:

> The reactions of Terry's Black friends are something else. I feel frightened at the strength of that anger with me because I am white, and typically white I suppose – blonde, and so on ... We all grow up together and nothing changes. (Alibhai-Brown & Montague, 1992: 135 136)

> This chap had been chatting to Sayeed, who thought he was marvellous, and I said I'd go and introduce myself. This man stood up, looked at me with such disdain and said, 'I don't understand girls

> who betray their race', then walked away. (Alibhai-Brown & Montague, 1992: 215)

Many white people feel betrayed by the black community and are made to feel that they themselves have betrayed their white community. Although money, class and occupation may shield some of the worst experiences, racism ensures that the white partner may no longer be able to live wherever and however they choose in 'their own' country. With white friends and colleagues, they may encounter the frustration of experiences that can no longer be shared:

> I haven't lost friends, but there were people who I thought were quite close who I purposely distanced myself from over probably quite obscure remarks that they have made. I remember having a general discussion about race with a friend and she said something about Indian people that just made me realise she was on a different wavelength. (Alibhai-Brown & Montague, 1992: 228)

The white anti-racist agenda may appear especially perplexing. When white people rush to acquire a black friend with tokenistic haste, but are unaccepting of their white partner, they reveal a subtly disconcerting form of racism:

> I had a number of colleagues and friends who seemed, intellectually, to be contributing far more to the race scene, writing learned books and 'right-on' articles, than I was. At first I was taken in by all this, until I realised that their human relationships with Black people were all wrong, they couldn't extend it to their emotional lives. (Alibhai-Brown & Montague, 1992: 64)

No-person's Land

The experience of being white but with black allegiances situates the white person differently. They are deemed to have crossed the tracks, and yet this expression is inexact. They have not travelled from one territory to another by crossing the boundary between them. They are permitted to inhabit neither, as this extract describes:

> You are in a no-person's land. You are not part of the white community and you are not part of the Black community. You are caught in the middle. I know there are many white women who do

> find that difficult, especially if there is a politically aware Black group around, or people who are very angry with the white establishment. (Alibhai-Brown & Montague, 1992: 30)

Yet the white people who find themselves in 'no-person's-land' manage to borrow from both sides of the tracks. They have something of a pioneering spirit, celebrating a world of diversity, creativity and challenge:

> I have a real dream for the world that everyone accepts everyone for the person they are inside and what they can give. People are always looking for differences – too fat, too thin, too dark – always looking for some reason why they shouldn't accept somebody instead of trying to find the reasons why they should and what they can learn from them. (Alibhai-Brown & Montague, 1992: 221)

For those who daily engage with the burden of racism, it is essential to be able to dream of racial harmony. But how resilient is this ideal, and how well does it serve those who look for direction in resolving the questions and conflicts of interracial relationships? The plea to accept everyone 'for the person they are inside' is a heartfelt response from within a white supremacist culture. Yet as this extract ironically shows, whatever white people may be 'inside', they will never be anything other than white on the outside in a society that remains significantly racist:

> There were some skinheads the other day – scum, you know – and one of them kicked my little boy Matthew and when I screamed they just laughed and said, 'Look, one white wog and three bloody Black wogs.' (Alibhai-Brown & Montague, 1992: 221–222)

The ideal of harmony accepts white and black people as racially distinct, but constructs identities such that race is no longer conflated with racism. But an ahistorical idealisation of difference that takes no account of how whiteness has been racialized is easily confused with the widely held belief that the identities of white people are universal and race-free. Racialized identities can scarcely be abandoned before their existence has been acknowledged and adequately defined.

The white response to many of the significant trajectories of interracial romance – desire, culture, racism – reveals the preoccupations of whiteness itself. Anxieties about engulfment and longing for renewal are central to a litany of desire and fear that white people experience as their identities: that which is craved is perceived as the lack; that which is feared is perceived as imminent: Through sensual metaphors the black body is conjured in a language almost alchemic in its fixation on the elements of blood, colour, smell, taste and sound. Its mental and spiritual counterpoint is considered white, yet it is the tension between both that structures the white imagination. Humanistic philosophies have accustomed us to considering that such polarisations of light and dark, mind and body, spirit and matter, God and the Devil, good and evil are necessary structures of thought. In fact they are historically specific, being Judeo-Christian in origin and dominating Eurocentric thought since the Renaissance. The expansionist ambitions of empire found in these dualities a model convenient to the legitimisation of racism. Their legacy is an oppositional impetus whose language of conquest is enshrined within the discourses of racism. But there is also a further dimension to conquest. At the same time as whiteness fears blackness, it also views it as a resource to be plundered. The culture of the plantation persists, in which white people still expect to be weaned, worked for, entertained and sexually serviced by black people.

Whiteness appears like a hungry ghost, the intellect disembodied in its Eurocentric duality. A pale shadow of the vitality of blackness, it craves substance and rejuvenation. This desire could become a powerful drive for transformation if the endless cultural and psychic repetitions of dualism would be abandoned and Eurocentric symbolic divisions reinterpreted. To begin this, James Baldwin believes that the white person must consent, in effect, to becoming black:

> The white man's unadmitted – and apparently, to him, unspeakable – private fears and longings are projected on to the Negro. The only way he can be released from the Negro's tyrannical power over him is to consent, in effect, to become black himself, to become a part of that suffering and dancing country that he now watches wistfully from the heights of his lonely power and, armed with spiritual traveller's cheques, visits surreptitiously after dark. (Baldwin, 1963: 82)

James Baldwin's call for the white person to abandon the heights of their lonely power and become, in his beautiful phrase, part of 'this suffering and dancing country' is a recognition of how power at the heart of whiteness shapes the white person's fears and longings, and how desire compels the surreptitious strategy of projection. To challenge this, he does not ask for the white person to take on black identity as such; his plea is for them to abandon the alienating power of white supremacy, and to acknowledge in the white portrait of blackness those very qualities of whiteness that have been so denied. The call for white self knowledge and critical self acceptance is not a call for white separatism, it is a quest for reconciliation, within the white self and with the wider community of races. Then, from the 'very same depths as those from which love springs' (Baldwin, 1963: 82), white people may experience that renewal of enthusiasm for which romance is so resonant a metaphor.

Notes

[1] Helen (charles) and Inge Blackman discuss lesbian and gay issues in interracial relationships in *(Not) Compromising: Inter-skin Colour Relations* and *White Girls are Easy, Black Girls are Studs* in this collection.

Bibliography

Amin, Samir (1989) *Eurocentrism*, London: Zed Books.

Alibhai-Brown & Montague (1992) *The Colour of Love: Mixed Race Relationships*, London: Virago.

Baldwin, J. (1963) *The Fire Next Time*, Harmondsworth: Penguin.

Dyer, Richard (1993) *Brief Encounter*, London: BFI Publishing.

Fanon, Frantz (1986) *Black Skin, White Masks*, London: Pluto.

Morrison, Toni (1992) *Playing in the Dark: Whiteness and Literary Imagination*, Cambridge: Harvard University Press.

Said, Edward (1978), *Orientalism: Western Conceptions of the Orient*, Harmondsworth: Penguin Books.

Tizard, Barbara and Phoenix, Ann (1993): *Black, White or Mixed Race? Race and Racism in the Lives of Young People of Mixed Parentage*, London: Routledge.

Ware, Vron (1992): *Beyond the Pale: White Women, Racism and History*, London: Verso.

White Girls Are Easy, Black Girls Are Studs

Inge Blackman

Girl Meets Girl

When anyone falls in love, how much of the object of their desire do they really see? The intense excitement of romantic fever is largely fuelled by imagination and fantasy. All cultures maintain sexual myths about Black and White women[1]. If a Black woman and White woman were to fall in love, it is inevitable that their sexual desires will be coloured by gendered racial fantasies.

On a crowded dance floor women cruise each other. Some surreptitiously, others with naked lust. Eyes dart expectantly from face to face, hoping to make some connection. Suspended above them in cages, half-naked nymphets writhe to throbbing love anthems. In the flash of the strobe a Black woman's eyes freeze into those of a White woman. The White woman does not look away and lowers her eyes to the Black woman's gyrating hips. Does she just see an attractive woman having a good time, or does she read into the swivelling hips the promise of a hot fuck, the fulfilment of her most torrid sexual fantasies? Is this the first time she has allowed herself to surrender to the desire for a Black woman? Or can she only come hard and fast when a Black woman's face is buried deep between her alabaster thighs? Does she believe she is not good enough for another White woman?

> I was attracted to her ultra-femininity more than anything else, and her colour added to that. Her skin tones are a very soft brown. I love

> the texture of her skin; it feels so very soft.[2]

> I like Black women's voices because they are full of emotion. Their hard round bottoms look very sexy. Dreadlocks look powerful and sexual and wild. Smooth dark skin is thrilling. It makes me shiver all over.

Her eyes feast on the Black woman's skin, so different from her own. Her eyes devour the Black woman's breasts as they strain against the tight white T-shirt tucked into her black leather trousers. Black is beautiful to this White woman because she is in love. Can she make the first move? Will she say something that will make her seem foolish or a racist? If the Black woman spurns her advances, will it be because she is White, or because she is just not cute enough?

The Black woman looks away, suddenly coy under the intense gaze of the White woman. Or is she playing hard to get? She spots another Black woman, a gorgeous babe. Should she do the Black thing and chat *her* up? Will the Black woman think she is too Black or not Black enough? If they get it together will it be an affirming experience, or will they annihilate each other, unable to face who they see in each other. Maybe Black women don't turn her on. Her gaze returns to the White woman. Does this Black woman believe the hype that the White woman is a goddess, that any man or woman who possesses her has the ultimate prize? Does she think the White woman is sexy because she tosses her mane like those White starlets in the movies? Does she think she is stunning because she reminds her of kd, Jodie, Martina, Gabriella? Does she go for the White woman because there are more of them? Can she only come when a White woman kneels before her fellating her dildo? Or does the Black woman just see another dyke she fancies, who fancies her?

> I'm attracted to White women because my White lover is Other to me and that turns me on. It just is easier coming on to a White woman. I don't feel scared. I'm also attracted to Black women but I've been rejected by Black women so many times. I think they feel I'm not Black enough for them. I'm usually attracted to White women or men who want to be submissive. I like SM sex and White women are more willing to act out roles. Usually the Black women I know won't even try it, won't even allow themselves to get pleasure from it, because they think SM sex degrades them as a Black woman.

> I love piercing blue or hazel eyes. But I wouldn't go out with a no-lip White woman, I like nice full lips. I haven't seen any Black woman that does anything for me. Your typical Black lesbian who is into Blackness with locks, does not turn me on. I think there is a block for me with Black women because they are another Black woman and I am one, and know what it's like. I know what their hair feels like. There is no mystery. Though I did think the Black women in the Whitney Houston video were stonkin'!

The night-club scenario is familiar to some women who are on the lesbian 'scene'. It is one of the ways that lesbians meet prospective lovers, along with introductions through friends or encounters in other gay environments. All lesbians daydream about meeting Ms Right, by chance, anywhere. This may be an everyday occurrence for the confident and brazen dyke; however most women are reluctant to make a pass at women in spaces that are not homo-friendly.

How Was It For You?

The Black woman zooms off on her Harley with the White woman riding pillion, clinging tightly to her with one hand, while caressing her thigh with the other. They arrive at the Black woman's home. Hungry hands tear at clothes, eager to touch. They make love – all night. The morning after they have breakfast in a little café, and go for a long walk, arms intertwined.

This experience of seduction is retold repeatedly in an effort to recapture the heightened desire of that 'first moment' – ripe with excitement and eroticism. The act of conquest provides the climax for countless narratives in lesbian lives. It is the driving force for all lesbian romantic films and novels. The two women (usually White) have mind-blowing sex; they come effortlessly and often. These books and movies feed on lesbian fantasies about love and sex. In the golden haze of the fairy tale, homophobia and awkwardness are banished. 'Reel life' lesbian love smoothes artfully over painful cracks.

Real life, however, can be rough. One woman may not be able to come, the other may be worried about how her naked body looks. One lover may be worried about how she tastes or smells, the other may want desperately to be spanked, but is afraid to risk asking for it. The two lovers may be spat at because they walk hand in hand in public. They may be thrown out of the café for smooching. Their parents may forbid them to see each other again. The first night for many interracial lovers can be intoxicating, but it may also be distressing.

> At the beginning of the relationship it was a bit tense because I was afraid of putting a foot wrong. My lover was anxious to know if I'd been with an Asian woman before. Because I hadn't, I felt that she was thinking that I was with her as part of experimenting with an exotic woman. But if I'd said that I'd been with an Asian woman before, she would have thought that I was only after her because she is Asian. I couldn't win.
>
> In sex the body for me becomes fetishised. I get off on the contrast of colour. I find difference incredibly erotic. If I'm with a Black woman I see the differences in tonality and colour between her skin and mine and eroticize that. My girlfriend is very smooth and hairless, and has very even, very white skin like china. I find her very beautiful.
>
> Sometimes when my girlfriend is crouching over me when she is fucking me, and she seems so powerful and black, her body is so taut and perfect. At other times she seems so vulnerable, her eyes are deep brown and her features are so soft. I love the fact that I look at her and she doesn't look like me.
>
> I'm into bodies. I'm not into colours. I'm into really athletic bodies. I like women with small but firm tits, strong well-defined stomach muscles and a nice back. Sometimes when my girlfriend is asleep, I peel back the sheets and just look at her.

Lesbian Serial Monogamist Strangles Cupid!

Lesbian women and their sexuality are pathologised and demonised by homophobic and sexist ideology. Lesbians are sick. The children of lesbians will be corrupted by the presence of their mothers as well as by the absence of fathers. The word 'lesbian' is an effective weapon, hurled at women to prevent them from loving other women, and to keep them in their place. Lesbian sex is widely presented as illicit, kinky and deviant, but intensely alluring to the curious and adventurous. The message from straight society is that lesbians can have their sex, but only if straights can watch.

Lesbian identity is grounded in frequent and intense sexual activity, complicated by the urgent desire for women to settle down. Consummation constitutes foreplay for cohabitation amongst lesbians. But there is also a frantic quest for more sex, to be gratified by the next beautiful Amazon with well-hung hands. After about two years each dyke feels she knows her lover inside out, there is no longer any mystery. The drug-like state associated with intense passion and lust has worn off. The honeymoon is over. In urban areas of Britain where the lesbian sub-culture is highly commercialised and club oriented, the 90s decade has heralded the breaking of taboos and the voicing of once-forbidden fantasies. These days words like 'dildo', and 'fist-fuck' slip easily into casual conversation. Muse on fantasies about domestic bliss, however, and you will be met with discomfort. In the cities talent 'to die for' is freely available and abundant. Serious coupledom is strictly for those deprived gals in the provinces.

> The scene is very singles oriented. There is no room to go out on the scene and be couply on the dance floor. It's almost as if people are thinking, if you're a couple why are you here?
>
> If I found a man attractive and heard that all his relationships lasted only about two years, I'd run a mile. I'd think here is someone with some serious intimacy problems. The bonding phase with women is very compulsive and fun, but there is no dialogue about how you deepen intimacy and prolong relationships. With heterosexuals I think a lot of their relationships would also not survive if they did not have the acceptance of society, marriage and the bond having children can give to a relationship.
>
> Being in a lesbian relationship is the most isolating experience. There is no support. Because so few achieve lasting relationships, those that do are seen as exhibits in a museum. People are reluctant to see the contradictions of the building of a sexualised identity and building a lasting relationship.

The experience of intense and dizzy emotions that come with short-lived and frequent relationships may be the only way some women can numb their terror of their lesbianism and cope with hatred from society. If a woman has a healthy long-term committed sexual relationship with another woman, she is less likely to be afraid of her lesbianism. However, most lesbians unwittingly collude with the dominant belief that lesbian *sex* is exciting but *to be* a lesbian, unless you're rich and famous, is boring.

Sleeping With the Enemy

Britain is a segregated country. In so-called racially mixed neighbourhoods, adults generally socialise with members of their own cultural and racial backgrounds. Anti-racists and multiculturalists campaign for the day when all cultures and races mix freely – the romanticism of racial politics. A compelling myth exists that the lesbian community is a sub-culture where Black and White women mix easily under the banner of sisterhood to form unproblematic romantic and social liaisons. It is assumed that when women enter the bars and clubs, they leave behind all the prejudices they have acquired from the outside (straight) world.

The lesbian interracial couple is used as a visual symbol to uphold this racially harmonious fantasy. The interracial image is used in publicity photographs, demonstrating that events are welcoming to women of all races. It may be used in a film to illustrate the diversity of lesbian women. Images of White couples, however, still dominate, as this image is read as the 'universal' lesbian. Images of Black couples are rare, and are assumed to address Black women only. They are seldom used to demonstrate diversity in the lesbian community, because White lesbians who cannot see their Whiteness reflected back at them do not relate to these images. A Black lesbian without a White lesbian is invisible to, avoided and feared by White lesbians.

> I know as I'm with a White woman White people accept me more. If I was with another Asian woman, they would see me as Other.

> I seem to be more validated if there's a White woman on my arm, than if there is a Black woman. One Black woman is fine. Two Black women together are a threat. White women do not talk to me if I'm on my own, but when I'm with my White girlfriend they approach me.

It is feared that the White partner in an interracial relationship has now become party to the Black experience and will expose the racism of her White friends. Black people fear she is privy to those aspects of Black culture they are ashamed about. It is often assumed that the Black partner has been racially neutered: that she has accepted the values of White culture.

> Black women and White women are shocked that I have a WASP girlfriend. They look at my dreadlocks, and listen to my views on racism and assume that someone with my strong identity of Blackness, must be with another Black woman.

> Some of my White friends were astounded that I was fucking my girlfriend. They thought I wasn't PC enough for a Black woman.

> Right at the beginning I thought they were envious of me because my lover is good looking and also someone that gave me credibility in their eyes. If I was with another White woman, I'm sure I would be able to integrate into the lesbian community much more easily. I think my friends wouldn't feel they have the anxieties of dealing with race, and would feel they can just get on with socialising.

Black lesbians who choose to centre their erotic experiences around other Black women for ideological reasons are openly hostile to interracial lesbian relationships. They feel that the Black woman in an interracial relationship is not prioritising race and wasting her time by sleeping with the enemy. White lesbians uncomfortable with interracial liaisons choose a passive form of hostility: they socialise with White women only, or put limits on intimate relations with Black women. This creates an isolating and unpleasant atmosphere for both partners in a lesbian interracial couple. Most women involved in interracial relationships end up inhabiting a social ghetto consisting of other interracial lesbian couples.

> My Black friends who are not in interracial relationships usually have a clever way of not bringing up the fact that I've got a White lover, or even a lover at all. In most of their minds I think they think that I'm single because I'm not with a Black woman. Sometimes I think they're thinking that it's because I've got a White grandmother, and I haven't quite come to terms with my Blackness.

> I was told to my face that I was a coconut because of always going out with White women. Asian lesbians who go out with other Asian lesbians belong to a close knit group, and I'm not included because I'm with a White woman. If I was with another Asian woman I would immediately be approved of and have more Asian friends.

> I feel threatened because I feel that there are forces larger than the two of us trying to break us up. I also feel scrutinised by some Black lesbians. The effect makes me silent and makes me not want to participate in lesbian things. It is a relief to be with those Black lesbians who are not political. I feel they are looking at the reality of the relationship, rather than at the ideology.

> Some of my girlfriend's Black friends ... [think] my girlfriend has a little problem about White girls, which they should try to be sympathetic to. Others don't even acknowledge me.

> When I broke up with one of my Black girlfriends, my White friends told me that I shouldn't bother going out with a Black woman. They said it was too much trouble.

White and Black lesbians who oppose mixed race relationships apply pressure on an interracial couple to choose between their racial allegiances and loyalty to their partners. Both women are therefore constantly questioning where they belong, and wondering if they have let 'their' side down. Both Black and White lovers are forced to re-enact the 'tragic mulatto' drama; the turmoil mixed-race children are assumed to experience.

Black and White Unite and Fight!

We meet up with that Black and White lesbian couple one year later. In romantic lesbian films this stage is never reached; one partner would have been killed off by death or by heterosexuality. The couple is now living together, and have made several long trips to Habitat agonizing over carpets and curtains. But this idyll has been marred for the White woman. She felt she was walking around with a selective amplifier that highlighted racist remarks and attitudes of White people. She became sensitized to how White people treated her partner in department stores, in restaurants and on the streets. The choice of neighbourhoods where she could live with her Black lover was restricted. The countries they wanted to go to for holidays had to be selected with care. Visits to the countryside were filled with apprehension – entering a country pub was always met with a brief stunned silence as everyone froze, then blinked to absorb her lover's presence.

> I notice the small ways in which Black people are marginalized as well as the more dramatic ways. If I go into a shop and the White person maintains eye contact with me even though my lover is doing all the talking I notice it, whereas I didn't before.
>
> I feel more sensitised to racism. I find all that stuff around the BNP really scary, because now I feel that it is not distant. They may want to hurt my girlfriend.

The White woman tried to talk to her Black and White friends about her feelings. The Black ones would smile wryly and share anecdotes of their own. Her White friends would just smile wryly, and offer nothing but an uncomfortable silence. She never knew if it was embarrassment or guilt that silenced them.

> I think most White lesbians who are aware of the politics around race are excruciatingly PC. They are afraid to say anything in case they put a foot wrong.
>
> My White friends do not say anything. Given that they are old friends and know the relationship, nobody has asked what it is like, if the sex is different, if there are special problems. I find it easier to talk to Black friends more than to other White women even if they are involved in interracial relationships.

Guess Who's Coming To Dinner?

One romantic daydream is that you will take your lover to meet your parents and they will be bowled over by your new found love. This is a tricky process for lesbians. If women are not 'out' to their families, the lover may be introduced as a friend. Some women may be 'out' to parents who are homophobic, in which case taking the lover home is out of the question. If they dislike her lover, she is never too sure if it is because they see the girlfriend as the person who corrupted their innocent daughter, or because they pick up on something that she is too much in love to notice. If she is having an interracial affair it may provide potential for further anxiety when going home.

> Until recently my family were like anything goes. My father relates to lesbianism as a *concept*. It is academic to him. My mother is now incredibly homophobic. But this has made my relationship with my girlfriend stronger. It will be difficult to visit because she doesn't like my girlfriend. I've always gravitated towards White people, and I feel this makes them feel as if they blame their upbringing of me. Maybe they feel I'd have a job if I was going out with someone Black.
>
> I think getting approval from my family is important to the survival of my relationships. Although I am out to my sister, when we go to stay, she gives us two single beds. She treats us as if we are friends. We are not acknowledged as a sexual partnership.
>
> My family is careful what they say when my girlfriend is around. When I'm on my own with them all the Paki things come out. My sister makes comments about people, calling them Paki-lovers. I challenge them, and they say that I'm too sensitive.
>
> It's very important what my family thinks about my partner whether they are male or female, Black or White. I'm from the South West which is very White. My parents are very laid back. They took a shine to my girlfriend. My father however kept making jokes about colour at first. I think he was nervous.
>
> My family is much more welcoming to my Black lover than all my previous White lovers. Maybe they think it doesn't count. Maybe she's nicer. Maybe it's because they're liberal and see it as part of the challenge of dealing with racism.

Happily Ever After ...

It is difficult for lesbians to maintain interracial relationships in a lesbian culture that does not value long term relationships, and a racially divided society that actively discourages interracial union, and a homophobic culture that does not want you to be lesbian in the first place.

The lovers attempted to communicate their anxieties and hurts to each other. How could the Black woman explain lovingly to her White lover that she was being racist? Could the White woman be open about her fear of losing her Black lover to a Black woman? If they are to have SM sex, is it less threatening for the White woman to be submissive?

Public dialogue between races has been informed by identity politics which is framed by ideas of hierarchy of oppression, socio-economic status, and history. However, lovers operate in a private space where intimate conversations are not publicly studied. Power hierarchies of identity politics are considered to be irrelevant in love affairs between two women even though power relationships are constantly shifting in any lesbian relationship. In a mixed-race relationship the White woman is not always in control, nor the Black woman always powerless. An essential ingredient of loving anyone and having sex with them is that each lover submits to the loved one.

In order to attain an enduring healthy relationship the lovers need to be patient, caring and trusting of each other. Each will have to let go of racialized identities based on fear, loathing and distrust of the Other. The Black and White woman will each have to let go of ideologies upholding racial superiority of their own race. Black people and White people collectively dread this transformation, for different historical and social reasons. They both experience this as a threat to their mythologized racialized identities. It shatters their simplistic world view and so they react with hostility: Black people will accuse the Black woman of being a self-loathing coconut; the White people will curse the White woman as a sick nigger-/Paki-lover.

If the Black lover is strong in her Black identity, a good relationship with a White lover can only enhance her positive feelings about the possibility of dialogue between Black and White women. The Black lesbian will know that she can be a self-loving Black woman involved in an enriching relationship either with a White or Black woman. The White lesbian will develop a sense of herself as a White person who is free of guilt, and is not paralysed when confronted with the racism of other White people and the anger and prejudice of Black people.

> If I'm aware of someone's racism, in a strange way I feel they are being racist to me because I don't separate from my lover. But I'm

> White and they're White and I feel an obligation to challenge them. If I don't I feel terrible.
>
> Being with my girlfriend has changed my idea of Whiteness. It has given me a colour identity. It has made me understand Black separatism. When Black people say it's nice to see a reflection of themselves in the world I can understand it now.
>
> My lover can check out the racist vibe with White people, even in ways I cannot know. She tells me they are her people, so she knows them better than me. She won't stand for it, because she knows they could be hurting me. She now sees the world through Black eyes.

All lesbians fantasise about meeting the perfect woman. They buy into the whole romantic package fed through television, movies and books. However the reality for most women especially those in interracial relationships is that the journey is often thwarted by forces that actively seek to undermine any lasting union. The lesbian interracial couple is always considered to be public property and is always scrutinised and judged. They cannot take refuge in the relative anonymity of a same-race couple. But if the couple survive they are making a radical statement which flies in the face of the received wisdom that like should stick with like – unless they are of the same sex, of course.

I would like to thank all the women who shared their experiences with me.

Notes

[1] I use capitals to refer to politicised racial identification, rather than to the colour of skin.
[2] All quotes taken from interviews with Black and White women involved in lesbian interracial relationships.

(Not) Compromising: Inter-Skin Colour Relations

Helen (charles)

> I've got you under my skin
> I've got you deep in the heart of me
> So deep in my heart, you're really a part of me
> I've got you under my skin,
>
> Ella Fitzgerald, from her album, *Lover*

What are the implications of a straight woman of African descent singing a plethora of songs, written by a white gay man, that go down in history as the epitome of assumed white heterosexual romance? Her assimilation into a dominant white culture would make harsh compromises: her fame and fortune established as well as his, but her skin colour and his homosexuality undisclosed in the honeysuckle lyrics. As a double crossing of the tracks and an indemnity against any overt racism and homophobia from the wider community, the question is, what compromises should or should not be made in the name of romance?

Questioning romance and its affiliation to relationships, especially those of an interskin-colour nature, was the theme of the opening session at the *Romance Revisited* conference. This set a new agenda for race-awareness as these were presentations in a predominantly white arena by four race-conscious women, one of whom was white and three Black, all of us from different cultural backgrounds. A crossing of the tracks was evident here in the construction of the agenda, and also within the content of our papers – which circumscribed the compromises that we were, and were not, prepared to make in terms of the dominant cultural ethos of relationships: Black with Black, white with white and heterosexual, of course.

Our skin colours visible and our sexualities up front, the subject of romance was challenged by our visibility. Thus, the issue of compromise, which I use to thread this chapter together, suggests a method of intermediacy – not so much a way '*between* conflicting opinions' (*Concise Oxford Dictionary*) – but a way of passing *through* different cultural opinions that may or may not conflict. Opinions about the way we construct our partnerships have been fed by dominant discourses which have relied on the conflict of opposites. Binary oppositions dyads and dualities have been used to keep transgressive behaviour at bay and to maintain traditional taboos in our society.

In this chapter, I look at inter-skin colour relations in the television programme *Taboo* (1993) along with Barbara Burford's novella, *The Threshing Floor* (1986) and Ann Allen Shockley's *The Mistress and the Slave Girl* (1987). In looking at these examples I discuss the internal dichotomies of racial self-denial and the positioning of the Black author. This authorship and ownership dyad is explored with the aim of highlighting the methods that some Black writers use in attempts to counter homogeneity in an assumed heterogeneous white culture. I also indicate the impossibility of the 'non-raced' author/speaker if their identity is already perceived as sub-cultural.

A Compromising Position

Looking at the topic of romance homogeneously has obvious difficulties and, like the binary opposition, requires dismantling. Any traditional western reference point from which romance *per se* can be said to evolve (Adam and Eve, Romeo and Juliet, Jane Eyre and Mr Rochester) bears prescriptive notions which necessarily break down when viewed heterogeneously: Beauty and the Beast; Othello and Desdemona; Vita and Violet. The challenge to the status quo creates conflict in the binary opposition, which can be said to transpose itself across the tracks into a mutiny against censorship.

With the potential success of such a mutiny comes the potential failure of self-awareness. What emerges when a race-conscious speaker or writer re-presents (in practice) aspects of, say, 'the romantic self' becomes a comment on the interlinkage and breakdown of two separate binaries: the Self (person/'I') and the subject (romance/race). Clear-cut definitions of romance are then seen to be insufficient when viewed from the myriad positions held by a) the speaker/writer, b) the subject, and c) the content. If you have a critical awareness of your white identity in relation to your privilege in dominant culture, then your identifications and allegiances (speaker/writer, subject, content) might be compromised in order to occupy the sub-cultural spaces that are slowly edging towards centres of their own: marginal minorities that are creating their own shade of culture from which independent foci emanate. To talk about romance from a white and/or heterosexual position, can be interesting in its own right, but in terms of western development, it would be more interesting to further problematize two (op)positions that the dominant culture relies on: i.e. 'whiteness' and heterosexuality.[1]

Academic Romance

Changing the colour of the great white pillars of traditional academia is challenging to say the least. To speak of romance can suggest a formula for white classical discussion: the lives and love(r)s of eminent writers in the literary canon; the passion of verse or sonnet; the ardour held in the pens of nineteenth-century women writers, cloaked in that era's etiquette; the posthumously published scandalous letters of one famous woman to her female lover; the serialisation of an upper-class lesbian affair. But how is 'romance' constructed within the context of the (sub)cultures of race and sexuality? This is my concern here.

Eager to speak on a multitude of issues surrounding race and romance, I compromised by speaking in general terms on the subject(s). My position lay frustratingly in the fixity of the binary opposition: personal/academic. A standard guess was that most of the speakers at the conference would be presenting papers on white desires: romances gleaned and theorised from the western annals of cinematic and literary convention – the same conventions within which I had been educated. But my slot was 'Race, Ethnicity and Romance' and it was at the opening session. It needed to refer to themes of race as well as romance. It transpired that the need to speak of the sub-cultural was integral to maintaining positive friction upon those great white pillars of tradition.[2] With few traditional references to romance and Blackness, it was a matter of either researching someone like Baudelaire's 'dark lady mistress' or accepting the limitations of such a presentation by reducing the subject content to a reflection on the Black Self.

The conference presented an opportunity for race-conscious women to speak. But there was a restriction in having to tackle the doubling of race and sexuality without making a 'display'. It seems to me that the problems encountered when there is an opportunity to do something positive for 'the Cause' make promises of visibilization ambiguous, compromised by the very words, acts and deeds of the activist. It could be asserted that these are the necessary steps towards awareness, and the merging or developing of positive marginal spaces (feminist, Black, dyke and so on), but at what subjective cost?

My paper presented a list of suggestions on how romance subdivides into sex, desire, attraction, loss and fantasy. I had an awareness that I was setting myself up as the object of the (perhaps unwitting) white and/or straight voyeur. The paper did not specifically attach itself to the racial economy. This was the choice I made with the knowledge that my three co-speakers (Felly Nkweto Simmonds, Kathryn Perry and Inge Blackman, in this volume) would be speaking about race, in terms of Blackness and whiteness, 'across the tracks' in inter-racial relationships, both straight and gay. We shared race-consciousness as a personal and political common denominator, but we were cutting across the tracks in different ways, not only according to our individual skin colours, sexualities and so on, but also according to what we were saying about 'race, ethnicity and romance' in the context of a conference arena that could be construed as mostly 'non-raced'. My attempt to cross the tracks was by counter-acting the assumption of subject-matter with my own body-colour in order to speak about the discourse of romance generally. Thus, any inappropriate voyeurism on the audience's part would be limited and/or returned to the listener's gaze. An extract from my paper follows:

> The subject of romance lends itself to a form and a display that neither relinquishes past ideologies, nor embraces them. In the time of the 'now' I flirt with notions of desire, as and how they have seemed in the heat of many moments. Moments that may or may not consciously subscribe to political development in the neo-feminist arena. I am talking of the concentration of power in those first or knowing looks when sexual fantasy takes a seat in the mind's front row. Or the expectation and arousal that accompanies the knowledge that someone fancies you. Or the consensual experiment of a staged seduction in a supermarket. The sexual resistance (or

> not, as the case may be) in a sudden phonecall. Or the mutual excitement in a courtship that leads to (un)inhibited performance.
>
> Romance can be revisited through the arrested gaze of another, conjuring up impulse and suspense. Through having dinner with your ex. Through thoughts of a one-night stand that linger. In romance you can imagine having sex with someone without letting on. And you can throw up a plethora of possible scenarios in gay abandon. The questions are, who dominates who? Who submits to whom? Do you fancy someone because they fancy you? Is there an underlying agenda going on that can safely be labelled 'chemistry' – no more questions asked, for what you do in bed is none of anybody else's business. Do you re-enact special scenes of seduction in every relationship that you have? And is there a familiarity, a similarity between all or most of the people that attract you? Do you exchange submissive and dominant roles with your lover – even though there are aspects of the two of you that are equal – even though there are aspects of the two of you that are different?

The absence of any specific reference to colour would have been negotiated by the fact that I, as a Black person, was doing the speaking. The extract could be said to be 'non-raced', but was I?

James Baldwin's novel *Giovanni's Room* (1963) is interesting in terms of the way in which authorship and ownership of character/fictional identities reach a place where writers from the sub-cultural negotiate a twilight visibility. The absence of the racial economy as related to Baldwin's own colour (black) is striking in his novel. His protagonists are not described as black, leaving the reader to assume the homosexuality, but not the blackness, of the author.[3] For me, Baldwin's attempt to cross the racial boundaries (or restrictions) in romance was facilitated by entering into the literary sub-culture of Parisian gayness, accessing the dominant culture without necessarily 'losing' his race, by playing an author's hand that was not 'raced'.[4]

How could we talk about sex openly and positively and not be compromised by the stereotypes that not only white people, but also Black people, have encountered through their acculturation? Protection of the self is an all important aspect of self-presentation and the risks that accompany the possibility of making yourself into a token representative (of a 'Black Community') at best, and sub-cultural entertainment at worst, are risks that you take if you have an investment to make in creating positive images of yourself in cultures that have been demonized, moralized, exoticized and condemned. To speak of romance should be a simple matter of selecting the right theme for the right moment. But if the chosen theme is to be related to not only a sub-cultural order, but also *by* someone who is visibly sub-cultural, how can the 'personal', and therefore the person, maintain a sense of self-preservation by the usual dyad: author/subject? The answer: they cannot. Thus, the self-conscious object of an inevitable voyeurism drops her handkerchief in the hope that it will be found by someone who empathises.

Taboo Culture

With the advent of a new tri-part series on Channel 4, *Doing It With You Is Taboo* (October, 1993), there was a chance for (British) Black cultures to view a representation of attraction and desire within the so-called Black Community.[5] In the programme, Black individuals presented a pioneering but disappointing display of the 'race and sexuality' debate. Dealing with white partners in the lives of the Black studio guests, it was a shattering experience to watch, as the reinforcement of the old stereotypical equation – Black woman = over-sexed and Black man = bigger dick – unfolded before my very eyes. Shrinking further and further into the sofa, the old colonial stereotypes of the lascivious black libido came at me, loud and clear, from the television screen. It seemed that the perpetuation of centuries-old white fantasies of the Other had travelled long-distance and reached a place of bizarre sanctuary in the minds of Black television producers. The programme's over-emphasis on the way Black people engaged in *sexual* activity was far too reminiscent of traditional anthropological research into kinship and reproduction in 'other cultures' (read: Black).

In the third and final week of the programme, zamis,[6] lesbians and gay men talked about their past and present relationships with white people. Perhaps because of the doubling and tripling of minority status, they had more verbal control and understanding of the issues affecting them and, as such, did not fall into too many of the traps set up by colonialist discourse. They spoke about power and the problems of compromising in inter-racial relationships. Romance appeared to be answerable to the taboo culture that tried to dictate partnerships. As a result, it could not be enjoyed by cross-colour couples exclusive of the power of race and racism, unless perhaps both partners ignored their

racial identities together. Most, if not every, Black pe Black/white relationships would agree that one of the mos aspects about having a white lover is being compelled to ec explain, elucidate and verify the way racism actually works in pr (women, conscious of sexism, would have similar experiences wit men in their lives). The process is long and the white partner wo have to be 'exceptional', as Oscar Watson put it, in Part 3 of *Ta* (October 1993).

In taboo culture, then, how would the label 'exceptional', applied a white person who occupies a space in the dominant culture, b viewed in terms of the power relations in Black/white partnerships? Would the white partner be in a compromising position by having to live up to the expectations of exceptional behaviour (it is no easy thing having to prove yourself all the time)? Or would the white partner have to *learn* how to be exceptional, like learning how to rap, or cook curry? If this is the case, then, the white partner as part of the dominant culture, shifts position in order to accommodate new influences from the now independent margins. The subsequent changes of position can sometimes be met with disapproval; for instance, the Black partner might find this difficult when remembering the historical tendencies of white people to emulate, copy and dominate cultural positions which are not their own. The 'white' move towards 'exceptionality', even if compromised, manages to somehow subsume those changes (different cultural affiliations) into its own central body – ejecting them at a later date in its own name ('white' rap: Homepride curry). Credit where credit is due, but it is often at the great expense and energies of the race-conscious (sub)cultures who are usually not white and are constantly trying to redress the (im)balance.

Awareness of how dominant culture controls and interferes with romance between people who do not share the same skin colour can be devastating. All subsequent positions for both partners are examined in microscopic detail (race-rows), and can be suppressed through denial. Whichever way, the power dynamics in romance are more complex when skin-colour is overshadowed and controlled by the dominant other (read: white culture). Being 'exceptional' is part of romantic discourse anyway, but the cross-racial couple is under more pressure to attain and sustain exceptionality. It was positive to see in the programme that exceptional white people did exist in the love-lives of Black women and men, and some (if not all) rejected the notion that 'inter-racial' relationships do not work.

Denial of the Dyad: Black/White

At the start of an interskin colour relationship, the issue of political colour and difference (as in Black/white) is foregrounded. It may be taboo, but difference translates as love – or lust. Using flashback, Barbara Burford's *The Threshing Floor* (1986) traces the long-term relationship between a Black ('mixed-race') woman, Hannah, and a white woman, Jenny.[7] Here, Hannah talks to a friend about the first time she meets Jenny:

> 'Elaine,' she had started ... 'I'm in love. Her name is Jenny ...'
> 'Is she Black?' Elaine had asked.
> 'No,' Hannah had replied impatiently. 'Elaine aren't you listening? I'm in love with a *woman*. Aren't you surprised? I am.'
> 'I'm only surprised that she isn't Black.' (Burford, 1986: 103–104)

The onset of romance is immediately compromised by race. Hannah needs prompting into dealing with her denial of the dyad, Black/white, and the protection of Black-confidence is suppressed. Whiteness, by the same token, does not have to compromise itself in the same way. As the dominant identity, white is the control 'colour' from which all 'others' are sub-determined. How the so-called Others (in this case, Hannah) position *themselves* in white society is vital in understanding the choices made between assimilation, self-denial and confrontation. What are the results of the manifestations of colonial stereotypes within the Black psyche? The binary Black/white, and the forthcoming romance, is useless to Hannah if she thinks of her and Jenny's, cultural position as being non-racial. Burford highlights this: 'And from there she had begun an examination for the first time of her love for this white woman. She had believed ... that love was something uncontrolled, outside even personal politics' (Burford, 1986: 104). In so doing, she attempts to bring together white and Black as racial identities, into the politics of romance.

Out of Control?

That love is controlled, and not the neutral bond between two individuals that the discourse of romance would have us believe, puts into question the power relations involved. When one partner belongs to a sub-culture and the other to a dominant, does the inter-play

between them include the sharing or giving up of power? Is it logically possible? Can power be used playfully – or will it always end in tears? Romance, according to the *C.O.D.* dictionary, is a 'love-affair viewed as resembling (a) tale of romance' (1982: 905). The suggestion of fiction here highlights the way that fantasy is imbibed in romance. The self that controls those fantasies (inevitably) also carries with it the images and stereotypes created by the dominant culture.

In Ann Allen Shockley's short story '*The Mistress and the Slave Girl*' (1987), overt power dynamics are at play when a white woman plantation owner buys a slave woman who eventually becomes her (consenting) lover. In the story, Heather, the mistress, has fallen for Delia, the slave. It is no surprise when Heather makes the first move when Delia is bedridden after an accident, where a 'horse reared up and plunged wildly across the field, knocking Delia down while she gathered flowers for Heather' (p111). Now, whether Delia has been ordered to pick flowers for her mistress or whether it is her choice is not clear. Nonetheless, who is and who is *not* in control of the 'courtship' appears to be the author/narrator's choice. Shockley, as a Black writer, makes the subject content of her story controversial. Between her third-person narrative, and the way that the mistress holds dual domination (white female power over black slave girl), the story offers a provocative twist to the dominant discourse of romance. Shockley uses the concept of the slave/master discourse[8] in order to tell a version of the classic white fantasy.[9] The couple, being both women, cross the traditional track of the white master fucking the female slave. So does this make the inter-skin colour relationship more acceptable? A compromising position ensues, via any discomfort in reading Shockley's story. This position need not be condemned and censored, but can be discussed and explored in the light of consensual acts, by 'sex-conscious' partners who recognize the variations and differences within those acts. Here, Heather (mistress) makes her approach:

> That night when darkness fell, Heather went to her, a shadow seen moving across the room in the lamp's glow. 'Would you like to sleep with me?' … She couldn't order, demand, for it wouldn't be the same.
>
> The girl's face first showed surprise … 'Yes –' A quiet response that said so much.
>
> *The fantasy in Heather's dreams had come true.*
>
> '*My* Delia –' Heather breathed hoarsely … (pp111–112 [my italics]).

To engage in fantasies of 'master' and 'slave' mirrors another binary opposition: 'top' and 'bottom' (as in Cole Porter's song, 'You're the Top') – which suggests a play of subject positions that are performed, conscious of them being 'acts'. The dictionary definition of romance attributes it to be an 'exaggeration' or a 'picturesque falsehood'. If applied to Shockley's story, would it become more of a fiction or would the continuum between fantasy and reality become more focused? Or, has the biggest colonial fantasy of all time now developed to bridge across the tracks to a display of submission: from a Black woman to a white woman?

Dominance and submission can be seen as states of play: the consenting practices of those who are aware of acting out roles in sexual liaisons and relationships. In gay culture, there is controversy surrounding the binary opposition of submission and domination, with its relation to Sado-Masochism (SM), but there has been little published on British Black people's engagement with the themes through choice. The book *Lesbians Talk: Making Black Waves* (Mason-John & Khambatta: 1993) makes an attempt against a background assumption in lesbian circles, that all Black lesbians are 'naturally' against any sex-play to do with submission and domination; the evidence to disprove this is slowly emerging.[10] Such choices about sex-play do exist in Black women's lives and form a substantial part of fantasy and 'scene' enactment. And perhaps, because of the historical proximity of 'post'-colonialism to this era, some Black women may fall into the 'dominant' category, if only to patronize, uphold or contradict the 'Strong Black Woman' or 'Passive Asian Woman' labels. 'The Mistress and the Slave Girl' is a unique augmentation to taboo culture. Shockley is, of course, in control of her story/fantasy. What perhaps exceeds her control is the original colonial discourse on white exploitation of the black (slave) body. It is a legacy from which contemporary Black writers originate and there is the unsettling fact that slave history inevitably and necessarily manifests itself as part of modern society. The development of 'singular sexualities' (Foucault, 1979: 47) since the nineteenth century in western societies has given rise to methods of understanding repression, exploitation and taboo: what they are and the differences between them; how they are understood, and how their negativities can be re-developed positively. Shockley's story can be seen as a testament to this, as well as being a bit of a teaser. Its nine pages culminate in a simultaneous orgasm between Delia and Heather (the happy ending of the romance narrative) and a prologue illustrating that the outside world could only see a white woman and a black woman, 'who lived together, [and] were terribly devoted to each other' (Shockley, 1987: 113). The figure of the white mistress represents a forbidden crossing of the tracks but the colonial fantasy is maintained without the horror of the white master who rapes.

To conclude, it can be said that even though the personal does not enter the work of most academics greatly, traces of it can be found in the choice of material that academics make when writing. When Black academics write, nine times times of ten (if not more) the personal as well as the political emerges in the writing as 'race'. It is not rare. It is common. Similarly, and particularly in the first couple of decades of the feminist movement, the genderized 'personal as the political' bled through the words of white women writers. The Black writer's 'choice' of subject matter falls within the boundaries of the racial economy first, and other subject matters subsequently. When musicians or writers discover a way across these boundaries it is with the ability to reject ghettoization and to confront assimilation.

Do the great white pillars of academia have to be smashed down, or are they to be partitioned in the vein of the 'European scramble for Africa'? There are sections of the British Black population that have helped build the pillars in the first place, but as they have been hidden from our general history lessons, the raised Black hand is still struggling to be seen at the front of the class.[11]

The fictionalized fantasies that emanate from all those romantic songs, films and novels make their way into a cultural system that refuses to acknowledge not only its dominant status as 'white' but also its need for the sub-cultural entities that give those pillars their strength. When romance and race meet across the tracks they are faced with a whole set of binary oppositions (self/other, Black/white; subject/object; and so on) which jostle for attention at a time when the gay abandon of courtship is usually uppermost in the mind. The consequent examination of subject positionings finds a place where the only option may be to compromise, in the name of romance; but such compromise, even if conciliatory, may make simultaneous moves towards self-denial and self-awareness. Thus, 'across the tracks' becomes 'between the tracks', or even 'outside the tracks'. (Self-) confidence and the ownership of power dynamics (being 'different') provides a more alluring base for romance to come together with race, where binary oppositions can finally begin to be dismantled. To compromise in race and romance may offer the dubious benefits of assimilation, but between the honeysuckle lines, there is always another story, where the author is not compromising the ownership of language.

Thanks are due to Jackie Stacey for her editorial suggestions and encouragement; to Inge, Felly and Kathryn for their co-visibility. Also, to Tiz Cartwright and Tina Papoulias for their unfailing support.

Notes

[1] For examples, see Dyer, 1988; Jeater, 1992; (charles), 1992; Rich, 1983; Wilkinson and Kitzinger, 1993.

[2] See Frankenburg, 1993.

[3] I am using the word 'black' without the politicized upper-case 'B' because this has not applied to African-Americans (or 'Afro-Americans' as would have been the phrase in Baldwin's day) in the past.

[4] See Bergman, 1992, for a discussion of the homophobia meted out to Baldwin.

[5] The phrase 'Black Community' propounds a homogeneity which is unrealistic considering the enormous diversity in community, race and culture. Compare to the 'white community': what would this mean? The term 'Black' is used in its political sense but still remains restrictive in its homogeneity.

[6] The term 'zami' is the preferred term for many Black women in relationships with other women. See, Lorde, 1982 and Rudet, 1987.

[7] The term 'mixed race' is problematic as it suggests impurity. The London-based group for Black lesbians and gay men of 'mixed racial heritage' recognize this by naming the group *MOSAIC*.

[8] See, Fanon 1986, and the fourth premise of Hegel (1977) which pertains to the master/slave discourse.

[9] Refer to Griffith's film *Birth of a Nation* (1915) for examples of this, and for a visual critique of tragedy in the construction of racial mixed-ness, see also Avalos and Small 1991.

[10] In *Quim*, an alternative British magazine, 'for dykes of all sexual persuasions', there is coverage of Black lesbians who are against SM censorship.

[11] For example, see Edwards and Walving, 1983.

Bibliography

Avalos, D. and Small, D. (1991) *Romona: Birth of Mis-ce-ge-NATION*, video: USA.

Baldwin, J. (1963) *Giovanni's Room*, London: Transworld.

Bergman, D. (1992) 'The African and the pagan in gay Black literature', in J. Bristow (ed) *Sexual Sameness*, London: Routledge.

Burford, B. (1986) *The Threshing Floor*, London: Sheba.

(charles), H. (1992) ' "Whiteness" – the Relevance of Politically Colouring the "Non",' in H. Hinds *et al* (eds) *Working Out: New Directions for Women's Studies*, London: Falmer Press.

Dyer, R. (1988) 'White', *Screen* 29,4: 44–64.

Edwards, P. and Walvin, J. (1983) *Black Personalities in the Era of the Slave Trade*, London: Macmillan.

Fanon, F. (1986) *Black Skin, White Masks*, London: Pluto.

Foucault, M. (1979) *The History of Sexuality: an Introduction*, London: Penguin.

Frankenberg, R. (1993) 'Growing Up White: Feminism, Racism and the Social Geography of Childhood', *Feminist Review* 45: 51–84.

Hegel, G. W. F. (1977) *Phenomenology of Spirit*, trans. A.V. Miller, Oxford: Oxford University Press.

Jeater, D. (1992) 'Roast Beef and Reggae Music: The Passing of Whiteness', *New Formations* 18: 107–121.

Kojève, A. (1969) *Introduction to the Reading of Hegel*, New York: Basic Books.

Lorde, A. (1982) *Zami: a new spelling of my name*, London: Sheba.

Mason-John, V. and Khambatta, A. (1993) *Lesbians Talk: Making Black Waves*, London: Scarlet Press.

Norman, R. (1976) *Hegel's Phenomenology: A Philosophical Introduction*, Brighton: Sussex University Press.

Rich, A. (1983) 'Compulsory Heterosexuality and Lesbian Existence', in E. Abel and E. K. Abel (eds) *The Signs Reader: Women, Gender & Scholarship*, London: University of Chicago Press.

Rudet, J. (1987) 'Basin', in Brewster, Y. (ed) *Black Plays*, London: Methuen.

Shockley, A. A. (1987) 'The Mistress and the Slave Girl', in *The Black and White of It*, USA: Naiad.

Wilkinson, S. and Kitzinger, C. (eds) (1993) *Heterosexuality*, London: Sage.

Love in Black and White

Felly Nkweto Simmonds

Prologue

Under the Tyne Bridge
I fell in love ...
With a Blue Eyed Boy.
As he reached for me
His friends called out
Why aye man,
Isn't she just a little too black ...?

Newcastle-Upon-Tyne is a very romantic city for me ... full of surprises. This is the closest I've come to having a romance with a town. Parts of the city, by the river for example, are quite romantic and ideal for seduction. In such a place it is all too easy to fall in love. Newcastle also has a smaller Black population than many British cities. As a heterosexual woman it is almost inevitable that any romantic encounters I have in Newcastle will be with white men.

In the city I have a particular romance with the Tyne bridge. I love that bridge. It has its own magic. I wrote the poem for the bridge.

I use the moment under the bridge to represent the core of romantic encounters between Black women and white men. This is the contradiction of experiencing an interracial romance in a racist society. I suggest that this makes it an almost impossible reality to articulate ... and sometimes, to sustain. The underlying question for me as a Black woman is, am I selling out? And, can I separate my personal experience of romance with a white man, from the racism I experience from other white men (and women)?

A Black/white relationship is easy to explain and articulate in the privacy of the bedroom. I love him ... He loves me. But what explanations are offered in the real world? It is the racism that confronts us as Black people (and as Black *women*) in society that exposes the contradiction. In public, a white lover becomes another white person. He is one of them. The trick, for that is what it is, is to separate *him* from *them*. *They* could be racists, but surely *he* can't be, *he* is different. Could a Black woman love a racist? What would that say about her?

Many couples in interracial relationships survive such contradictions by separating their private lives from their public lives. It is not uncommon that the partners in such relationships lead separate public lives, *literally* relegating their romantic lives to the 'private', in every sense.

In this chapter I will focus *only* on relationships between Black women and white men. The dynamics and history of this particular interracial combination are different from other interracial experiences, some of which will be dealt with in the other essays on ethnicity (see Blackman, (charles), and Perry). Like Perry I will, however, be drawing extensively upon the recent collection of interviews with individuals involved in mixed-race relationships, *The Colour of Love* (Alibhai-Brown and Montague, 1992).

This chapter is also likely to disrupt the romantic discourse of the other chapters in this book. It has been difficult to believe that I can go with the theme *Romance Revisited*, without fully recognizing the specific issues of interracial romances, some of which would be dangerous to *revisit*. This chapter will, therefore, disrupt even the idea of love itself ... especially that of romantic love.

Romantic love has often been defined and theorized at such a personal level that any idea that the lovers could be of very different 'racial' backgrounds cannot be accommodated. If, for example, one of the 'psychological needs that romantic love satisfies ... is our need for human companionship: for someone with whom we share values, feelings, interests, and goals ... (and) the burdens and joys of existence' (Branden in Sternberg and Barnes, 1988: 224) it becomes problematic to deal with the idea of romantic love across the 'racial' tracks. I have yet to find an academic text on love that incorporates interracial relationships in theories of romantic love. I want to argue that romance across 'colour' cannot be left to the private arena: the issue, therefore, becomes one of linking the personal with the political.

Black Bodies/White Bodies

First, I want to deal very briefly with the linguistic definitions used in this paper: not as justification for using ideas and terms that are at best questionable and at worst offensive and meaningless, but to suggest that since we still have very limited conceptual tools to define words such as 'race', 'interracial', 'Black' and even 'white', there is still a level at which we are forced to use such terms because they *do* have socially constructed ideological meanings.

I will work from the basic premise that 'race' as an idea and an ideology produces racialized people (Banton, 1987: Fanon, 1967; Fredrickson, 1988). I also acknowledge that racist discourse and the naming of 'racialized' people has its own history, which is not possible to go into in any detail in this paper. But as racialised people our experience of life reflects political, economic and social realities, both in history and in the present. Thirdly I acknowledge that my use of the term 'Black', has its own ideological problems and has been questioned, for example, for its apparent essentialism and 'the ascriptive characteristic of "blackness" ' (Anthias and Yuval-Davis, in Lovell, 1990: 105). There have also been questions around 'the hegemonic claims of the category' (Donald and Rattansi, 1992: 8) by those who 'do not see themselves in terms of colour and do not want a public identity that emphasises colour' (Modood, 1992: 273). I want to argue, however, that in any theorising of romantic relationships across 'racial' boundaries the issue of 'colour', in fact, *becomes* a critical one for *ideological reasons*. In such romantic encounters it is impossible to ignore the *embodied* experience and its implications. We have to take on the body because it is through the body that the desires/pleasures/pain of romance are, literally, experienced. The need to 'write the body' (Game, 1991: xi) into theories of romance becomes imperative, and by implication the actual 'colour of the body' (Scott and Morgan, 1993: 16) becomes significant. In doing so there is a possibility of deconstructing the social reality of 'race' by re-examining the social construction of colour ... both Black and white. The 'fact of blackness' (Fanon, 1986) and that of 'whiteness' (Helen (charles), 1992) has to be seen as a relational one, and in doing this a new reading of these constructions becomes possible. This is the point at which 'race' becomes literally embodied.

For the black body, this is often a negative experience because historically 'blackness' has been constructed not only in opposition to whiteness (ie, Black = non white and not vice-versa), but also as occupying an inferior position to whiteness. What is also being articulated in the social formations of 'blackness' and 'whiteness' are the power relations of the dominance of *white* over *Black*. This consequently raises questions around how a romantic encounter can be negotiated within these social realities of 'race', in which 'whiteness' always carries power over 'blackness', and 'blackness' is constructed as a sexual threat to 'whiteness' (Young, in Rutherford, 1990). Basically, can the sharing of the 'joys and the burdens of existence', that romantic love demands, be achieved?

One of the problems for Black people is that contact with whiteness has demanded the ability to have an external view of oneself *on some one else's terms*. As Fanon articulates in *Black Skin, White Masks* (1986) this can be a difficult and painful experience. For example, Fanon's own awareness of his body as a *Black* body, is sparked off by a remark ... overheard:

> 'Look, a Negro!' It was an external stimulus that flicked over me as I passed by. I made a tight smile. 'Look, a Negro!' It was true. It amused me. 'Look a Negro!' The circle was drawing a bit tighter. I made no secret of my amusement. 'Mama, see the Negro! I'm frightened!' Frightened! ... Now they are beginning to be afraid of me. I made up my mind to laugh myself to tears, but laughter had become impossible. I could no longer laugh, because I already knew that there were legends, stories, history, and above all historicity, which I had learned about from Jaspers. Then, assailed at various points, the corporeal schema crumbled, its place taken over by *a racial epidermal schema* ... In the train I was given not one but two, three places ... I was at the same time responsible for my body, for my race, for my ancestors. I subjected myself to an objective examination, I discovered my blackness, my ethnic characteristics; and I was battered down by tom-toms, cannibalism, intellectual deficiency, racial defects, slave-ships ... [my emphasis] (Fanon, 1991: 111–12).

Every Black person who comes into contact with whiteness arrives at this point sooner or later and continues to carry (yes ... as a burden of existence!) this reality with them with varying levels of consciousness. As Fanon argues:

> In the white world the man of color encounters difficulties in the development of his body schema. Consciousness of the body is solely a negating activity. It is a third person consciousness. The body is surrounded by an atmosphere of certain uncertainty ... A slow composition of my *self* as a body in the middle of a spatial and temporal world – such seems to be the schema ... Below the corporeal schema I had sketched a historico-racial schema. The elements that I used had been provided for me ... by the other, the white man, who had woven me out of a thousand details, anecdotes, stories. I thought that what I had in hand was to construct a physiological self, to balance space, and here I was called on for more ... (Fanon, 1991: 110–111).

A Black person therefore enters a romantic relationship with a white lover carrying an embodied self that has been constructed by whiteness ... After all, aren't Black women *supposed* to be more sexy than white women! I want to argue that at the root of some of what is seen as *the* problem of cross- 'racial' romance are deep seated (mis)understandings of ourselves at physical and psychic levels, which inform not only our expectations of ourselves but, also, our lovers' expectations of us.

At a personal level this can be an uncomfortable and confusing reality. Romantic encounters between Black and white remain *invisible* as an experience because, to put it simply, they are not part of the plan ... And yet when such encounters do take place they are immediately *visible* to society and therefore available for public scrutiny. The personal experience becomes simultaneously a public experience. Yet the public space and private space are not of equal value. And if, as Robert Nozick suggests, in romantic love two people unite 'to form and constitute a new entity in the world, what might be called a *we*' (Nozick, 1993: 153), the 'we' that is formed by an interracial romance is a rather fragmented one. The reality is that even the internal understanding of the relationship can also be a fragmented one, as one white man explains:

> My image of brown people were (sic) that they were very attractive, although my images of Africa were the usual ones and I must admit that I'm still nervous when I meet groups of teenage boys ... But

> colour never occurs to me when I'm looking at relationships, just whether the person is attractive or not. P ... was the first Black woman I had a relationship with, but for me she was just a very attractive woman, nothing at all with her being Black ... Her being Black was not a problem ... Men find her terribly attractive, especially white men. I know it is there ... (Alibhai-Brown and Montague, 1992: 39–40)

This example shows how some people in interracial romances choose to limit their experience to one of 'interpersonal interaction' (Wetherell and Potter, 1992), separating it from the wider social realities. Those who do have an explanation which takes into account the wider social realities see their own personal/private relationship as inevitably bound up with other wider political/public realities. One Black woman sees this as fundamental to the relationship and argues that

> the relationship could not survive, and will not survive, unless we are totally honest with each other on all the really fundamental things. First of all, we talk about racism together – not as something 'out there' which negatively affects my people but also as something 'in here' inside the relationship ... (Alibhai-Brown and Montague, 1992: 57)

The Politics of 'Race' + Sex

For Black women and white men, the history of the sexual exploitation of Black women by white men gives this particular interracial coupling a context that overshadows any personal ideas of the relationship. One particular feature is the very fact that because historically white men have been able to '*have*' Black women as sex toys, concubines, and as commodities, this assumed right is part of most white men's sexuality. One white man talks of his lover in these terms:

> As a Black woman maybe she evokes some folk memories in white men; of slavery, of Black women being available, being forced. I think that, maybe, is what makes a lot of white men sexually attracted to Black women – they were slaves; you could do what you liked with them ... (Alibhai-Brown and Montague, 1992: 40)

Any Black woman/white man encounter has to negotiate with this fact. Sometimes it can be a painful personal experience.

> David and I went out for years. Then he went away to India and when he came back, he was only interested in owning me. And at that stage I really started to question things. I had a gut reaction about the Black-white thing ... If I was a passive person I could choose to blank out issues associated with being Black, but I don't choose to do that because the repercussions are so dangerous. When I was with David people used to say to me, 'What are you doing with this white guy?' I think he did actually love me, but it was this exotic thing too. He wanted to possess me ... It's always the same thing, always to do with possession ... It's something that is happening more and more – for example, lots of Italian men want Black women. If you go into lots of European cities, you see these fat dumpy white men with beautiful Black women. It's the sexual thing, they have this idea about Black women, they think you're going to be a rampant sex maniac. I think English men think that too ... So now I'm wary when I meet a white guy ... (Alibhai-Brown and Montague, 1992: 156–157)

Are all white man/Black woman romances compromised by this kind of explanation? And if so, what are we to make of the now commonplace adverts for Black women put in newspapers, such as the 'Heart to Heart' page of one of Britain's best selling Black newspapers, *The Voice*? These advertisements have a very explicit agenda which needs to be addressed.

> Attractive, white guy, 30's, 5′8″, muscular, smart, good job, house, car, seeks an attractive, curvaceous, black lady, for a serious 1-2-1. (*The Voice* 10.8.93)

> Geoff, 29, 5′11″, Croydon, White, warm, wicked and slightly wacky, seeks lady with rhythm and no blues for sharing busy nights and mellow moments. (*The Voice* 10.8.93)

What, in fact, is going on here? There are no sociological explanations available to us yet. Our understanding, therefore, can only be gleaned from societal attitudes to interracial romances.

Private and Public Lives

In order to be able to theorise interracial romances adequately, we need to deal explicitly with what such romances signify both privately *and* publicly. In order to make sense of interracial romances there is a need to understand the concrete material ways in which such relationships are viewed. For example, many public readings of such relationships pathologise them at an individual level. In Black terms this usually is understood as an incorrect *choice* over other possible (more politically correct?) partners. What is raised are issues of 'racial' betrayal as argued in the letter below:

> As a member of the Nation of Islam, I find the news that broke this weekend of the forthcoming marriage of supposed super model Naomi Campbell hard to bear. More like super collaborator. After appearing in the amoral Madonna sex book, Ms Campbell has already let down the Black race by showing such loose political morals. Now like all the other black superstars, who get too much too soon, she has decided that our black men are not good enough. She has followed in the footsteps of Iman, a true African who has settled for an ageing rock-star, and Whoopie Goldberg, a proud African American who is also living in sin with a white man. When will our successful sisters take pride in their history and choose men from their own race? (*The Weekly Journal*, 6.5. 93)

This is not an extreme/isolated example. It is quite common. The central issue is the linking of a romantic relationship to some perceived individual (female?) (a)morality and the apparent lack of self knowledge.

One of the complicating factors is that as Black people we have no means of separating experiences of white racism at a societal level from that of personal relationships with white people through which the racism of society is articulated. There is also the added dimension of the (sexual) relationship between Black and white in which the white body is ascribed the status of consumer ... of Black bodies. Black women, for example, have been placed on many historical and contemporary markets ... slave markets, colonial markets, tourist markets and consumer markets. Dusky maidens can sell anything from airline tickets to coffee and rum, and can be a real 'Southern Comfort' to whiteness.

As Black people and as Black women we carry too much of this sexual history for it not to affect how we experience our sexual selves with white lovers. This is what makes it impossible to deal with an interracial romance as a purely individual and personal experience. Inevitably the central contradiction remains and the Black/white relationship becomes manageable *only* if explained in very personal terms. And, indeed, what is it that separates a white lover from other white people (ie, those who are racist) when he has not only the power of whiteness on his side, but also all its privileges? At worst the white lover can use his Black lover as a badge that proclaims 'I'm not racist' ... Or as one white man puts it:

> Lots of white fellows want to go out with a Black girl just so they can say what great liberals they are ... They don't care about the girl individually. All she has to be is Black ... (Alibhai-Brown and Montague, 1992: 190)

For a Black woman there is nothing overtly politically correct about having a white lover!

To cope with such conflicting personal and public experiences we rationalise the romantic experience in *very* personal terms and adopt a process of separation ... of the personal from the political. It becomes almost imperative that such romantic encounters are relegated to the private, and remain a private affair, because, in fact, what other choice is there? Romantic encounters between Black and white, as a result, remain invisible in terms of cultural discourse (in literature, film etc) *yet* are highly visible as a cultural fact and a reality in society. Currently (the summer of 1993) Richard Benjamin's film *Made in America* has hit our screens. This is a romantic comedy in which Whoopie Goldberg and Ted Danson are the lovers. As Derek Malcolm states, 'Time was when a romantic comedy featuring a black woman and a white man would have been thought impossible to present as popular entertainment ... *Made in America* takes the bit between its teeth without quite biting the bullet. Bed scenes are out ...' (*The Guardian* 12.8.93). The irony, of course, is that we are all acutely aware of the fact that Whoopie Goldberg and Ted Danson have become lovers (in real life) while making the film. So presumably in the privacy of their bedroom ... bed scenes are in! But we seem only to cope with this reality if it remains a private affair.

Crossing The Tracks in Search of Love

Everyday, against all the odds, women and men, cross 'racial' boundaries in search of love. Why do people seek out partners who, according to many theories of love and romance, could hardly be seen as an ideal type? After all, one of the apparent reasons we fall in love has to do with finding someone who shares our beliefs, values, experience of life, etc. What other meanings can we give to interracial romance? Or, do we need to give any meanings beyond that of 'falling in love'? Consider, for example, the following advertisements from *The Voice*:

> Free and single white guy, young looking 37 year old, very caring and loving, interested in meeting a warm and slim black woman to love.

> Sweet and sexy black beauty, 23, 5′6″, delicious, wild and addicted to cuddles, desires fulfilling relationship with cute, sensitive, handsome, white guy under 6′. London. (*The Voice*, 23.2.93)

And from *The Guardian*'s 'Lonely Hearts' column:

> Attractive, white, solvent, lunatic (31); into music, bikes, travel, kids; seeks gorgeous black princess with SOH for lovin' good times. Your photo gets mine! (*The Guardian*, 13.2.93.)

For some, having a partner from a different 'race', in fact gives them what they see as *the* positive dimension: that is, *difference itself*. The answer is clearly that it is the *difference* (more visibly emphatic than all the other differences which mediate our relationships) that becomes the attraction. And as one partner in an interracial relationship has candidly observed:

> I don't think I could have found a companion like Stephen if I had married someone from my background, although I don't know what could have been, so maybe it is unfair to say. I couldn't have found such a friend, someone I feel totally at ease with ... With Stephen, the real me, the hidden me, has come out. The fact that we are different has enhanced our relationship. (Alibhai-Brown and Montague, 1992–36)

What is being suggested here is that a person outside one's own 'culture' apparently enables the partners to choose what aspects of themselves they want to bring to a relationship, so that at one level there are no expectations. There is the illusion, perhaps, that the relationship has to be built from scratch. But can it be? Can *any* romantic relationship be built from scratch? After all, we know about love even if we don't experience it ourselves … from films, books … other people (see Jackson, this volume).

'Difference' as Racism

The idea of 'difference' as a positive dimension to interracial romance can be contested. The perceived difference is one that arises out of the socially constructed idea of 'race' in which 'Blackness' carries negative white meanings. The construction of 'racial' difference has always had an explicit agenda, one in which difference is articulated in terms of the 'good' *white* self and the 'bad' *Black* 'other'. As Lola Young has argued: 'Having structured the differences into the Other, sexual intermixing becomes an unthinkable, unspeakable act …' (Young, 1990: 197). Some white partners, for example, having internalized the negative stereotypes associated with 'blackness', proceed to separate their Black lovers from 'blackness' itself. It is not uncommon to hear liberals declare, 'I don't see you as black' … leaving one to wonder what exactly they do see when they look at a Black person! They also used pained expressions, for example, 'We just don't think in terms of Black and white, but everyone around does, so you are forced to remember all the time. And you feel hemmed in …' (Alibhai-Brown and Montague 1992: 135) – this once again reinforces the contradiction of the private experience and the public reality. The question that arises time and time again remains: can there ever be a purely personal experience of love and romance in an interracial relationship?

To theorise interracial relationships there is a need to confront the racism that frames them and allows silences to build up around them. In all societies, what frames such relationships are the historical realities of the fear of Black sexuality, on one hand, and the (s)exploitation of Black women by white men on the other. The particular Black woman/white man combination also exposes the impossibility of separating the individual experience of an interracial romance, from the history of oppression, racism and sexism.

It also becomes imperative that if interracial romances are to have a place in society and in cultural discourse, they have to be theorised at both the private/personal level and at the public/political level. This is the only way that interracial relationships will come out of the closet and become part of the feminist agenda on love and romance.

And maybe, one day, I will be able to re-write the poem with which I began this chapter.

Bibliography

Alibhai-Brown, Y. and Montague, A. (1992) *The Colour of Love: Mixed Race Relationships*, London: Virago.

Anthias, F. and Yuval-Davis,N. (1990) 'Contextualising Feminism-Gender, Ethnic and Class Divisions', in T. Lovell (ed) *British Feminist Thought: A Reader*, Oxford: Basil Blackwell.

Banton, M. (1987) *Racial Theories*, Cambridge: Cambridge University Press.

Branden, N. (1988) 'A Vision of Romantic Love', in R. J. Sternberg and M. L. Barnes (eds) *The Psychology of Love*, New Haven: Yale University Press.

(charles), H. (1992) 'Whiteness – The Relevance of Politically Colouring the "Non", in H. Hinds, A. Phoenix and J. Stacey, *Working Out: New Directions for Women's Studies*, London: The Falmer Press.

Donald, J. and Rattansi, A. (1992) *'Race', Culture and Difference*, London: Sage Publications in association with The Open University.

Fanon, F. (1991) *Black Skin, White Masks*, London: Pluto.

Fredrickson, G.M. (1988) *The Arrogance of Race: Historical Perspectives on Slavery, Racism, and Social Inequality*, Middletown, Connecticut: Wesleyan University Press.

Game, A. (1991) *Undoing The Social*, Buckingham: Open University Press.

Modood, T. (1992) 'British Asian Muslims and the Rushdie Affair', in J. Donald and A. Rattansi *'Race' Culture and Difference*, London: Sage.

Nozick, R. (1993) 'Love's Bond', in A. Minas (ed), *Gender Basics: Feminist Perspectives on Women and Men*, Belmont, California: Wadsworth Publishing Company.

Scott, S. and Morgan, D. (eds) (1993) *Body Matters: Essays on the Sociology of the Body*, London: The Falmer Press.

Wetherell, M. and Potter, J. (1992) *Mapping The Language of Racism: Discourse and The Legitimization of Exploitation*, London: Harvester/Wheatsheaf.

Young, L (1990) 'A Nasty Piece of Work: A Psychoanalytic Study of Sexual and Racial Difference in "Mona Lisa" ' in J. Rutherford (ed) *Identity, Community, Culture and Difference*, London: Lawrence and Wishart.

Newspapers

The Guardian, Guardian Newspapers Limited, London.
The Weekly Journal, Voice Communications Limited, London.
The Voice, Voice Communications Limited, London.

Refusals:
Resisting Romance

A Public Romance: 'The Charles and Di Story'

Celia Lury

> Diana, however, had only started. As she and Prince Charles went walk-about, it soon became apparent that everyone wanted to see her. (Campbell, 1992: 186)

In this chapter, I want to explore the ways in which the use of the conventions of popular genres in the presentation of public life are refiguring contemporary politics. This study in the convergence between cultural and political representation takes as its focus the Charles and Di story. It argues, on the one hand, that romance as a popular genre is being rewritten through media representations of the relationship between Prince Charles and Princess Diana. On the other hand, it suggests that the adoption of the genre of romance in interpretations of the royal family is reworking contemporary understandings of national culture and political life.

Before I proceed with the argument itself, however, I want to make it clear that I am not trying to uncover the truth about the state of the royal relationship or judge who should take the blame. I do not mean to privilege some representations as more accurate, objective or authentic than others.[1] Nor do I want to bring the story they seek to tell to an end by providing an interpretive framework, whose techniques can be applied to reveal the inevitable outcome of the story so far. This would be to miss the point. It is clear that much of the fascination to be derived from such representations arises from their provisional nature and the endless deferral of resolution they make possible.[2] Indeed, to evaluate these representations in terms of adequacy to reality, fixity or closure is to ignore the defining characteristic of the promotional discourse they inhabit (Wernick, 1991), and the central and contested role of the audience in the representations themselves. It assumes that the representations have their effect only in so far as they can be shown to be true, rather than in so far as they mobilise particular sections of the public as an audience. This second view, adopted here, implies that the media representations are an integral element of the romance as a public genre, not outside it; they are part of the phenomenon under investigation, not a commentary on it.

Perhaps the most striking fact about these representations is their number: there seems to be no end to the media fascination with the Royal marriage (as I revise this paper for publication, Diana has declared her desire to withdraw from the public gaze, but the media debate about why she has made such a statement indicates that this will not be easily achieved). Clearly, it is not possible here to review such representations systematically; however, many fall into a recognisable narrative. Early representations of the courtship and marriage of our hero and heroine presented the union between the world's most eligible bachelor and shy Di, an ordinary commoner, as 'the stuff of which fairytales are made', a story of how love overcame the barriers of class and status, a living exemplification of the textual conventions of the genre of romance. That this fairytale romance was to come to grief over that most predictable obstacle to true love, the other woman, is now, however, typically presented as no surprise.

The suitor Charles, the then future King of England, is seen by Andrew Morton (1992), perhaps the most notorious of recent public commentators, to have overwhelmed Diana, who was 'flattered, flustered and bewildered by the passion she had aroused in a man twelve years her senior' (p70); she was 'his willing puppy who came to heel when he whistled ... He called her Diana, she addressed him as 'Sir' (p77). And Diana is now presented as too young, too naive to have understood the threat to her happiness posed by the hidden presence of another woman, but even she is said to have had an inkling: 'She was in love, she thought he was in love with her and yet she was aware that there was another woman, Camilla Parker Bowles, hovering in the background' (p79). But it is not simply the 'other woman' who is held to blame: it is also the public itself, understood as an active participant in what was necessarily a public romance.

In an illuminating anecdote, Morton recounts Diana's anxiety before the wedding, expressed during a visit to her sisters while Charles was absent giving Camilla a gift of a bracelet displaying the initials 'F' and 'G' entwined (Fred and Gladys are said to be their pet names for each other); he writes:

> She was confused, upset and bewildered by the train of events. At that moment, as she seriously considered calling off the wedding, they [her sisters] made light of her fears and premonitions of the disaster that lay ahead. 'Bad luck Duch,' they said, using the family nickname for their younger sister, 'your face is on the tea-towels so you're too late to chicken out now.' (p91)

In retrospect, then, Diana is presented as a virgin sacrificed on the altar of the public's expectations: our desire for a fairytale romance, made material in tea-towels and other souvenirs, is presented as the imperative underlying what is now revealed, in a rewriting of the romance narrative, as an arranged marriage, which resulted in impossible pressures being placed on its central protagonists.

What is significant about this anecdote, then, is not its revelation of the accuracy of Diana's fortune-telling ability, but that it is the force of the public's expectations which is now given as the reason for the marriage (and the ultimate cause of its demise). The significance of this is two-fold. On the one hand, it suggests that the demands of the public, like the other woman, have come to be seen as an obstacle to true love. Clearly, the challenge of overturning social expectation has been an element in the appeal of most, if not all, romances, although the royal romance outdid the fantastic nature of most romantic make-believe. What becomes clear, however, in recent interpretations of the marriage of Charles and Di is that public expectation can be implicated in the very character of love itself, and conversely that the value and significance of love and romantic partnership can now be explored by means of a consideration of the publics it makes possible. At the same time, the adoption of the genre of romance in representations of royal life brings traditional conventions of national culture and political life into question. The public has clearly been seen to have the right to express a view regarding royal marriages before; what is increasingly visible is a mediatized reflexivity in such representations, a reflexivity in which cultural (rather than political) representations of the public themselves are the site at which issues of governmentality are contested.

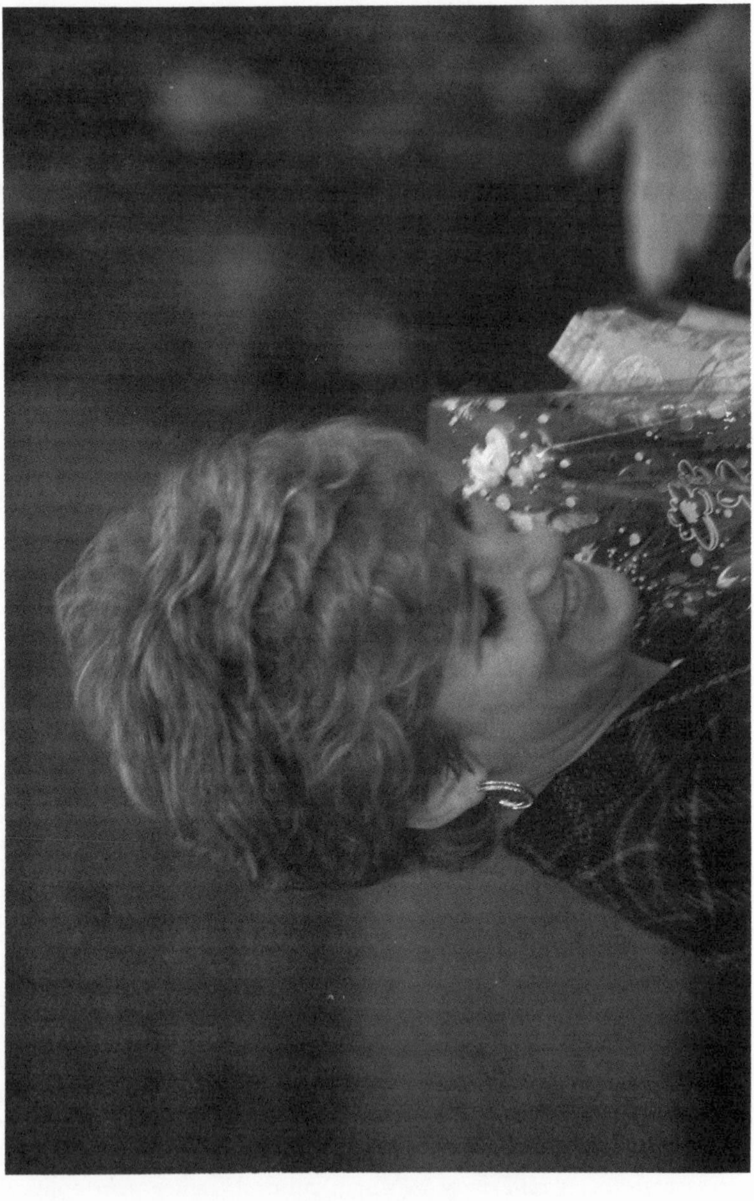

Figures 3 and 4: Princess Diana at Southwark in London in March 1993 © Steve Eason. Courtesy Hulton Deutsch Collection.

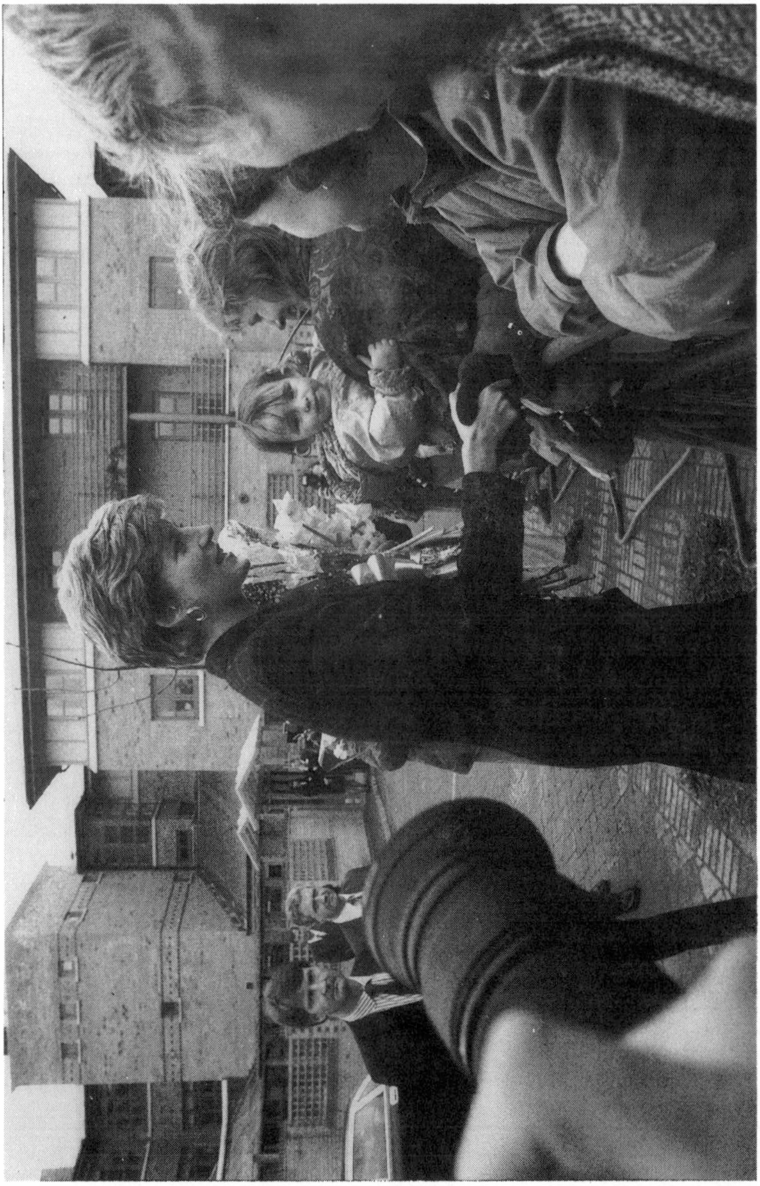

In a remark which is untypically sympathetic to Charles, Morton writes that by the 1970s the Prince's quest for a wife had developed into a national pastime which had gotten out of hand: 'The Prince, then nearly 33, had already made himself a hostage to fortune by declaring that 30 was a suitable age to settle down (p69) ... The difficulty, the Prince declared, was that marriage was a partnership where his wife was not simply marrying the man but a way of life. As he said: "If I'm deciding on whom I want to live with for fifty years – well, that's the last decision I want my head to be ruled by my heart".' Morton draws out the now ominous implications of this remark:

> Thus marriage in his eyes was primarily the discharge of an obligation to his family and the nation, a task made all the more difficult by the immutable nature of the contract.

The contract referred to here is simultaneously the marriage contract and the contract of governmentality between the monarch and its subjects. It is not surprising, then, that in recent interpretations of the end of the royal marriage, the question of the legitimacy of that other contract has also been raised since the two are intimately linked in the history of British national identity.

I want to show how the contemporary media representation of the Charles and Di story makes that link newly visible. During most of the twentieth century, the monarchy has symbolised the nation through its self-representation as a family: the imagery of the British nation has drawn on that of the family, while the ideal of the family has been depicted as the natural unity from which the nation was built. The Royal family has been the condensation of this mutually enabling analogy. Clearly the failure of the marriage of not only Charles and Diana but also of other Royal couples calls into question the effectiveness of this analogy. But more than this, the importance attached to constructions of the public in interpretations of the fate of such marriages makes the very terms, both of contemporary romantic partnership and the constitution of the public as a collective, more open to scrutiny.

In many interpretations of the lives of the royal couple today, Diana's overwhelming popularity is identified as a primary source of conflict between the royal spouses. For example, Morton writes about their first major public appearance as a couple (which, incidentally, is often presented as if it were the consummation of the marriage[3]), that

> the crowds made it painfully obvious who was the new star of the show – the Princess of Wales. Charles was left apologizing for not having enough wives to go round. If he took one side of the street during a walkabout the crowd collectively groaned: it was his wife they had come to see. 'I seem to do nothing but collect flowers these days,' he said. 'I know my role.' (p106)

More recently, discussions of their separation draw on the same theme (and they too sexualize this conflict, with Charles' defeat by his wife depicted as a kind of symbolic castration):

> Charles is fed up with having his wife steal his spotlight; he is also weary of having their bad marital vibes drown out his worthy speeches. A future Queen more popular and respected than the future King – the status quo for the foreseeable future – poses an open-ended nightmare for the British monarchy. (Holden, 1993: 52–3)

In a characteristically self-concerned way, current media discussion of the relative popularity of Charles and Diana is now frequently set up in terms of an evaluation of their ability in managing the media, and thus indirectly, the public. Photographic images of Diana are frequently subject to analysis by amateur and professional semioticians who detect a flirtatious deflection of the onlooker's gaze in her typical sideways glance and lowered head, and what appears to be a self-conscious display of her body for an audience. Amateur photos from the Spencer family album are scrutinized for early indications of the media-consciousness of this pop princess. The effects of Diana's training in speech-giving are also noted:

> The Princess of Wales communicates her appeals for public understanding and tolerance through the speeches she writes herself, identifying aspects of her own predicament with the victims she seeks to help. She works for weeks to get the emphasis and intonation right, practising the delivery. Listen, and you often hear the personal note. (Howell, 1993: 50)

Alternatively, both Charles and Diana are judged in terms of their culpability in undermining the publicity put out by their rival. Morton remarks:

> It would be a mistake to assume that the contest between the Prince and Princess of Wales is fought on even terms. The Princess may be the bigger draw to the press and the public but inside the palace walls she is reliant upon revenues from the Duchy of Cornwall, controlled by her husband, to fund her private office while her junior status within the royal hierarchy means that Prince Charles always has the final say. Everything from her attendance at his planning meetings, the composition of joint overseas tours and the office structure is ultimately decided by the Prince of Wales. When she suggested she start a 'Princess of Wales Trust' to raise money for her various charities he refused to countenance the idea, knowing that it would take away kudos and cash from his own Prince's Trust charity. (p193)

In all these ways, the rivalry for popularity in their marriage becomes a site of contest for the evaluation of both the terms of love itself and the legitimacy of royal rule.

> Since the announcement of the end of her marriage on December 9, Diana, Princess of Wales, has been visibly reborn ... For Diana it was a moment of triumph. For Prince Charles it was a crushing defeat, which could eventually cost him the throne. At this low point in the history of the House of Windsor, Diana is the new Britannia, who very much rules the waves. (Holden, 1993: 50)

This scrutiny of the terms of governmentality is further facilitated by the fact that there are important differences in the publics which media representations of the personas of Charles and Diana invoke. The contents of their professed interests are not so very different, but their route into such interests is seen to be divergent: Charles is said to be concerned about 'issues', while Diana is a 'people' person. But it is in their mode of self-presentation and address to a public that they differ most widely. Charles is verbal – moreover, he doesn't simply speak, he lectures and people, we are told, listen; Diana is visual: as Morton writes,

> The girl who would only appear in school plays if she had a non-speaking part was now centre stage ... the camera had ... fallen in love with the new royal cover girl. (p109)

Charles is cerebral, rational if a little eccentric, while Diana is emotional, tactile and outgoing: Morton again:

> [Diana] is tactile, emotional, gently irreverent and spontaneous. For a white gloved, stiff-upper-lip institution with a large 'Do not touch' sign hanging from its crown, the Princess of Wales is a threat. (pp198–9)

To Lord Rees-Mogg, Diana is,

> 'not academically clever, but she has an intuitive understanding of human nature that is of more use to the world.' ... Very shrewd says another man who knows [her]. Diana has an intuitive grasp of other people's problems, and how to respond to them – more so than any other royal. (Holden, 1993: 54)

Charles maintains the distinction between public and private, front-stage and back-stage, while Diana blurs them and is confused by them.

> Diana was deeply confused. Her face graced the cover of a million magazines and the public sang her praises, yet her husband and his family rarely gave her a word of encouragement, congratulation or advice. (Morton, 1992: 134)

However, in a recent twist in the public romance, the distinction between private and public is brought to the surface, and self-consciously problematised by Diana:

> At an international conference, Eating Disorders '93, in London this April, her colour rose and she took a deep breath before standing up to speak.
>
> 'I have it on very good authority that the quest for perfection our society demands can leave the individual gasping for breath,' she began, pausing for the full significance of the 'very good authority' to sink in. 'Eating disorders, whether it be anorexia or bulimia, show how individuals can turn the nourishment of the body into a painful attack on themselves ... By focusing their energies on controlling their bodies, they have found a refuge from having to face the more painful issues at the centre of their lives.' She sat down afterwards as if unburdened. (Howell, 1993: 50)

In her persona as pop princess, Diana has, as many commentat have noted, set up an alternative court in which the literal metaphorical importance of 'hugging' is stressed, not only betw husband and wife, parents and children, but also between royalty subjects. This stands in stark contrast to the distanced formality relations embodied by Charles and expressed in media representati of his view of marriage, family life and royal ritual. Diana's breach the private and public boundary, her girl-next-door-made-good-n her liking for popular rather than high culture, her association w dance, the music and fashion industries and most of all, the central of the media to her self-presentation, allow her to call upon the pub not as a nation, but as an audience, an audience which does not resp national boundaries but rather is simultaneously individual and glob

> While maintaining an unassailable glamour, she has gone beyo cover girl and star. She is a force to be reckoned with ... She revealed herself as genuinely committed to humanity. (How 1993: 50)

> It has taken a decade of public triumph and private suffering Diana to reach the unprecedented position in which she finds hers today. To the British people, their cruelly wronged Princess is m than ever an object of sympathy and admiration. To global victi from AIDS patients to deprived children, she is a saint, a genuin loved guardian angel with the perfect bedside manner. (Hold 1993: 54)

However, while the public which Diana makes possible is n exclusively British, neither, despite her association with such wo figures as Mother Teresa, is it uniformly inclusive. Rather, it is British popular audience refigured in relation to a global panhuma ty.[4] As such, it retains many of the exclusive and excludi characteristics which had defined the earlier public: it is, for examp saturated in whiteness.

This line of argument suggests that the rewriting of the roy romance to acknowledge the audience as an active participant h implications not only for individual but also for collective identiti On the one hand, it is a form of romance in which the difficult facing women in the quest for self-esteem (and what Winship (198 has called 'feminine individuality') is seen to be linked to

> family; family wealth; dynastic fertility; sexual promiscuity; outsiders/rivals/lower orders. The on reality only adds to its fascinati

She argues that, as a soap opera, 'The R of dilemmas which feature in many wo romantic storyline of uncertainty, self-realisation'. However, she further ar

> 'The Royals' addresses choices fa that it does so from a peculiarly 't of the 'Royals', there aren't really there any issue of female independ there's not a moment's hesitatio heroine even though she mar twenty-one, and never had any (1985: 170)

In short, she suggests that 'The Ro independence. That was in 1985, and w recently seen the return of the r self-realisation in representations of the me, as it does to Camille Paglia, that D feminism at the end of the twentieth-c self-expression made visible in repre somewhat limited. Although some fem the recent representation of single p Britain's most popular Royal, other ima their equation of femininity with a Nevertheless, the question of female in sidestepped.

[3] This sexualized representation of Dian in other arenas, such as this account o professional make-up artist:

> I was introduced to Lady Diana S ... a day that foreshadowed great those moments I shared with powdered her face for the scrutin steps in her appointment with des

> On that occasion she was still a mere slip of a girl and what has become the most photographed face in the world was flushed with excitement when I first touched it. Lady Diana's skin was clear and fresh, though. A joy. I could tell from the look and its softness that this was a face that had never bothered much with make-up. Yet she was so nervous, and obviously worried about confronting a professional make-up artist for the first time, that I realized I would have to lead her very carefully into my own world. (Howard, 1992: 10).

[4] The term 'panhumanity' was first suggested to me by Sarah Franklin in our many discussions of global culture with Jackie Stacey.
[5] Moreover, it is clear that the political impact of the collectivity made possible by the media telling of Di's true story depends upon the continuation of her marriage to Charles and her role as mother of the future King.

Bibliography

Blundell, N. and Blackhall, S. (1992) *Fall of the House of Windsor*, London: Blake Paperbacks.
Campbell, Lady C. (1992) *Diana in Private: The Princess Nobody Knows*, New York: St Martin's Paperbacks.
Coward, R. (1985) *Female Desire*, London: Pan Books.
Holden, A. (1993) 'Diana's revenge', *Vanity Fair*, February: 48–57, 98–102.
Howard, C. (1992) *Look Like a Princess: The Beauty Secrets of a Make-up Artist*, London: Anaya Publishers.
Howell, G. (1993) 'Diana, princess of charities', *Reader's Digest*, September: 49–53.
Lacey, R. 'Next in line', *Tatler*, April: 82–87.
Morton, A. (1992) *Diana: Her True Story*, New York: Pocket Books.
Paglia, C. (1992) 'Diana, myth and media', *Guardian*, July 30, 23.
Wernick, A. (1991) *Promotional Culture: Advertising, Ideology and Symbolic Expression*, London: Sage.
Winship, J. (1983) ' "*Options* for the way you want to live now" or a magazine for Superwoman', *Theory, Culture and Society*, vol. 3, no. 1.

Can Men Love? – 'Reading', 'Staging' and 'Resisting' the Romance

Jean Duncombe and Dennis Marsden

Cultural studies and sociology share an interest in the relationship between culture and individual identity and subjectivity. But pioneering work on 'reading the romance' (Radway, 1987) has not been matched by sociological exploration of the impact of such reading on individuals' everyday lives (Jackson, 1993). In this chapter we draw on our research to show how – according to gender and the history and current state of their intimate personal relationships – people not only 'read', they also 'stage' and 'resist' romantic narratives.[1]

The cultural narratives of romance are well-known: lovers on moonlit shores, candlelit dinners, 'our tune', Valentine's Day cards and red roses. And to understand their links with individual subjectivity, Stevi Jackson suggests:

> We create for ourselves a sense of what ... being 'in love' is ... by ... positioning ourselves within discourses, constructing narratives of self ... through these discourses [of love] we have learnt what love means ... [Brunt's description of 'getting to star in your own movie'] is not a passive internalisation of these scripts but an active sense of locating ourselves within them ... manifest ... in the half-conscious self-dramatisation so acutely observed by Barthes. (Jackson, 1993: 212, 213)

By actively reading romance narratives, the reader develops the 'emotional literacy' to understand and label 'romantic' feelings, but with a degree of role-distance and sophistication in spotting clichés. However, this process is multi-layered, with some layers more accessible, and, 'it is much easier to refuse to participate in romantic rituals … to resist pressures towards conventional marriage, to be cynical about "happy ever after" endings than it is to avoid falling in love' (Jackson, 1993).

There is disagreement concerning the relationship between media representations of romance and the everyday experience of readers, who are predominantly women. Radway (1987) argues that, unlike most husbands, fictional heroes are 'manly' and passionate but also tender, caring and supportive, so women read romantic novels as escapist 'emotional servicing', to compensate for the emotional demands of husbands and children and make emotionally unfulfilling marriages bearable. Other writers, however, see romantic narratives as potentially much more disruptive:

> In these deeply unsound [Mills and Boon] fantasies men 'sweep us off our feet', wrap us in their 'strong tanned arms' and, of course, adore us … These dreams … accompany us through our daily lives … making us feel disappointed and cheated by the humdrum reality of our actual relationships with men. (Gill and Walker 1993: 69)

These contrasting pictures can be reconciled if we recognise that Radway's account of romance conflates a felt need for nurturance and 'romantic desire experienced as overwhelming and insatiable. Stevi Jackson argues that the 'happily ever after' conclusion of romance papers over the contradictions between these two forms of love (Jackson 1993: 217).

There is a babble of discourses arguing that Western Anglo-Saxon men shun displays of tender emotion (Duncombe and Marsden, 1993), resisting romance and avoiding 'commitment' because they fear entrapment by emotionally needy women (Hollway, 1983), to a degree where we might ask whether, or how, they love. Women make allowances ('all men are little boys') and hope to bring about change (Jackson, 1993; Radway, 1987): through their love, the frog may turn into a handsome prince. But clearly, such contrasting orientations to romance may bring considerable disruption between heterosexual couples.

Our study shows how (in Jackson's terms) individuals 'position themselves' and 'construct narratives' in relation to romance; how women and men in long-term couples perceive love and romance, and how they negotiate the contradictions between real-life experience and the culturally-expected transition from 'being in love' to 'living happily every after'. We found that women especially do talk about love and use romantic imagery to describe their deepest emotions and motives: as one woman explained, 'I don't love him "love" him, if you know what I mean. But I do *love* him'. However, we needed to listen carefully to catch the range of meanings encapsulated in phrases delivered subliminally because 'everybody knows' too well the conventions of romance.

Our interviews confirmed men's and women's profoundly differing orientations to romantic narrative:

> I think my husband would like a good, sort of, *sexy* sort of romance ... or the odd sort of *porno* film, but something more *romantic*, sort of, more feeling, more upsets ... No, he says, 'I've got to go and do some work' ... I *love* all that emotional stuff. The more it makes me cry, I feel sort of in touch with something here (her solar plexus).

Most of our women respondents appreciated 'a good love story', but almost all the men seemed to regard romantic fiction as 'unreal', 'soft' and 'a waste of time', and while they might guardedly watch TV soaps, they became uncomfortable or fell asleep during romantic films.

'Getting to Star in Your Own Movie': Performing and Staging Romance

Our respondents described love in terms of sequential phases which differed in erotic or 'visceral' excitement (Goodison, 1983), and sense of intimacy, security and companionship. Most people, but particularly women, knew about 'falling in love' from personal experience – not necessarily with their husband. Some described a 'stomach churning' insecurity fed by uncertainty about the response of the unknown other, when fear of 'losing control' had led to 'playing cool' or 'hard to get'. But at best, 'being in love' was described as 'like being in a film', an almost hallucinatory 'performance' where everyday experience was heightened and transformed:

> If you weren't in love, making love on the beach would be an extremely uncomfortable experience … well, it is! The sand gets … kind of, everywhere … The number of women I've known who've finished up with cystitis, it's the normal experience! But somehow … when you look back … you just remember the romantic … being there, and the crashing of the waves.

Even uncomfortable experiences became suffused with romance (*From Here to Eternity*!), as did mundane occasions like getting caught in the rain, or riding on a bus. Such moments were romantic because they were shared with someone perceived as 'being there for you' and 'wanting you alone'.

People's narratives often involved natural settings, for example 'moonshots', where romantic feelings had been enhanced by chancing upon moonlit waters. However, the line was thinly drawn between finding oneself in a romantic scene, and one partner being aware and setting the scene for 'staging' romance.

It was usually women respondents who felt they had had to make the *emotional* running during courtship, and (perhaps only in retrospect) some described attempts to stage romantic moments to gain an admission from the man that he loved and wanted them (male fears of entrapment may have some basis!). Even with more 'romantically resistant' male partners, careful staging could sometimes be made to pay off:

> I knew he liked me without make-up in, sort of, long flowing dresses, kind of pre-Raphaelite … but I had to be very careful not to overdo it or he'd have … cottoned on … He couldn't *stand* anything artificial. There'd been times before when we got to a romantic bit and he'd said, 'Well, I suppose this is the moment when I'm supposed to say I love you … Well, I ain't!' … He thought I didn't wear any make-up but I did …, only very carefully. And this time I got ready, I put on my silk dressing gown, like, as if I always wear that when I'm not expecting anyone … I put the cushions in front of the log fire, so I was … lying reading this book that I knew he'd be impressed … And I put a record on … as if that was how I always was and he just happened to have found me. I must have played that record about ten times! … But then … he just stopped at the door and looked … 'You look *wonderful*'. He never guessed a thing!

Staging romance might be a part of courtship to encourage a partner who is 'playing hard to get'. Yet to say this implies too great a self-consciousness: the distinction between 'happening upon' and 'staging' the romance becomes hopelessly blurred.

In staging romance, women needed subtlety so as not to arouse male self-consciousness or suspicion by appearing too forward, and there were a number of 'failed moonshots':

> She suggested we should go round the corner to look at the moon ... I think she'd spotted ... the tide was up ... I'm not much of a one for romance but I'm a sucker for moonlit water! So pissed as I was, I got a sense of over-the-top romantic ... But then she sprang the trap! She kind of, manoeuvred me to face the moon and ... put her arms round my neck and said, 'D'you love me?' I felt somehow ... 'dropped on' ... Anyway, I made the mistake of trying ... to tell her I didn't know. I said, 'You shouldn't keep asking. Love's not like that, it's something that grows slowly. You shouldn't keep pulling it up by the roots to examine it.' Well ... all hell broke loose ... We had the biggest row we'd ever had!

> He would never say 'I love you', and he would never admit ... to anything being ... other than just what it was, a bit of scenery or whatever. But I was in love with him and when I went for a walk round this moonlit lake I thought it was most wonderfully romantic ... But then when we got back and I was trying to talk about it, he wouldn't have it ... It was just a walk by a lake with the moon out ... I always remember that as the biggest ... 'betrayal' ever.

Not all men were quite so resistant to romance, and one of the more susceptible described such heightened moments of time-out-of-life as 'idylls'. But clearly, romantic moments such as moonshots must be *shared* if they were to contribute to the ongoing romantic narrative of 'our relationship'.

Ironically, *men* are expected to play the lead and stage romantic moments during courtship, which may partly explain a myth that men are more 'romantic' than women. And, indeed, early in relationships men seemed more likely to give flowers or arrange dinners in romantic restaurants without prompting – although for men romance had more to do with deploying material resources than recognising and exploiting romantic moments, and being able to say sincerely 'I love you'. Unfortunately for men who might wish to make sincere gestures, the *conspicuous* male staging of romance in real life has become devalued by its extensive use in sitcoms – where men invariably come humiliatingly unstuck – or associations with infidelity and cynical seduction:

> He pinched some red roses off a dining table ... and then every woman he, sort of ... danced with he'd produce one ... 'I've just plucked this and I want to give it to you because you're so beautiful' ... We couldn't believe it, it was so corny! But it was amazing ... of the women he tried it on with, one went outside with him and did it with him up against a wall ... and another went home with him and moved in with him! And these women weren't dopes, but they lapped it up! Mind you, he was ever so handsome ... Other men think men like that are ever so corny ... creeps.

This typically male mode of staging romance makes many men uncertain how to make romantic gestures which will feel at once sincere, valid and not corny.

Our interviews suggest that major gender differences in orientations to romantic narrative appear in relation to the staging of romance. While 'in love' both women and men feel sexual desire, but for most women the experience of desire seems greatly enhanced by living the romantic narrative, and recognition of a degree of staging does not devalue the heightened experience itself. Nor will the moment necessarily be spoilt by sex 'going wrong'. However, for men sexual performance is of itself more important, and romantic imagery and staging are not only less necessary but may all too easily intrude because the very currency of staging the romance seems to them devalued.

'Finding Someone I Could Talk To': The Development of Emotional Intimacy

Some people said that what they valued most about 'being in love' was 'finding someone I could talk to', the endless talking ('we lay in bed naked and we talked all night'), to explore who the other person was and what they were feeling. Confidences were exchanged, where the narrative of the current relationship was worked out and those of the past rewritten as they must 'really' have been: 'I was too young'; 'I don't think I was ever in love in the first place'; 'It was just infatuation' or 'sex', and so on.

Compared with romantic desire and passion, the discourse of intimacy seems less developed: 'intimacy' may serve as a euphemism for sex, verbal openness and disclosure, or being emotionally on the same wavelength. And this confusion mirrors lived experience where some respondents (particularly women) described how they had mistaken sex or talk for deeper emotional communication. But as one man explained:

> When I first met my wife, we talked excessively, about our previous dates and about ourselves and 'the third' – you, me and 'the relationship' ... (But) I'm not sure it *is* disclosure, it's more testing each other out, what I call '*dangerous*' talk. Your bodies have interacted 'dangerously' and now you *talk* to each other 'dangerously' ... you might be committing yourself too much. It requires a lot of alcohol and dope!

'Telling all' entails trust and the taking of risks – giving hostages to fortune – which may inhibit disclosure.

Disclosure also demands emotional sophistication, the absence of everyday responsibilities and distractions, and opportunity and time for talk. Relatively few therefore seem to achieve or maintain the kind of emotional intimacy described by one woman:

> There was always something missing. But since I've met David, I mean, it's just totally different ... We had ... obviously, at the beginning, but now I feel, he only has to, sort of, hold me, and I really feel content and whole ... It sounds a bit corny, but I feel we're so 'as one' ... once we're in bed, we might cuddle, and we might talk about, really sort of, deep emotions as well ... It's just complete ... We treat each other as equals. There's no demands on one another ... He feels that he can expose himself that much to me, because I'm not going to judge him as being weak ... We're living together but as individuals ... we're, like supporting each other ... (but) I'm encouraged to be the person I want to be.

With its stress on calm togetherness, emotional intimacy and communication, and mutual support and equality, this description contrasts markedly with the heady excitement and emotional insecurity of 'falling in love'.

But ironically, in contrast to the romance narrative where passion and intimacy coexist, intimate disclosure brings familiarity (corresponding degrees of physical disclosure might be appearing without make-up, wearing glasses, revealing you have false teeth, washing less and farting). And there is a trade-off where familiarity strips away any sense of intrigue and mystery, and undermines the very basis of romance and eroticism.

'Living Happily Ever After'? The Decay of Eroticism and Intimacy

There was general agreement that 'being in love' could normally last no more than six months to a year, after which 'the flame' of erotic love 'died down' to an 'affectionate', 'caring' and more secure love: as one respondent put it, a 'massive companionship' with 'a major friend who is easy to be with'. Yet, as with the absence of attractive media depictions of romance in middle age, our respondents lacked a common discourse for 'living happily ever after'. Perhaps during busy family life the couple relationship becomes submerged by 'the crap of everyday living' (Rubin, 1991). But also respondents perceived 'living happily ever after' as increasingly hard to attain and hardly to be expected.

Women approaching middle age now tended to feel that perhaps their partners had never fully 'been there' for them emotionally or had 'psychically deserted' early by becoming workaholic (Duncombe and Marsden, 1993). Certainly romance appears often to have been a fairly early casualty:

> We went through the romantic bit to start with ... (But) he loved his *work* and that was the problem ... He still loved me in the sense of, you know, the *picture* was right ... a successful businessman with a wife who could entertain and nice little children, always lots of presents, lots of money spent on 'em because the emotional wasn't spent on 'em, so he thought as long as he was spending money, everything must be all right ...

Some women had occasionally experienced almost subliminal flashbacks to the excitement of earlier romantic feelings, what one woman called *déja vu*. But over time these moments seemed to fade:

> To me the biggest ... probably the one where I say, 'Oh stop it!', – is

> when I'm washing up and I get a cuddle. That's the most important because it's spontaneous, it's much better.

Even such small gestures were enormously valued by women as indicating that men were not merely taking them for granted.

Overall, these relationships exhibited a 'gender assymetry' of emotional behaviour, with women feeling but hardly able to express a need for emotional intimacy and support – perhaps to recapture something of being in love – which men resisted or even failed to perceive:

> I went through quite a rough time about not feeling *special*, not feeling my needs were being met. OK, there's the matter of him earning, there's him helping me ... But somehow there was something missing ... and it came hard for him, and he couldn't understand what I meant when I said I didn't feel *special* like I used to ... (If he gave me) just a *cuddle* now and again, and nothing more, just a cuddle of reassurance, just a sort of, 'There, there, it'll be all right', sort of thing.

In the longer-term, couples might emerge after a struggle with a sort of companionship and mutual support which must not be undervalued. But this had only been achieved through women accepting that they could not change men emotionally, redefining themselves as at fault for 'loving too much' (Norwood, 1985), and shifting their life interest to their children, friends or a paid job. And among these women some gain emotional sustenance from reading romantic novels.

Re-reading and Restaging the Romance

The fact that women in emotionally unsatisfactory relationships continued to read romantic fiction did not prevent (and indeed may have stimulated) a re-reading and reassessment of the romantic narrative of their own lives. And in some instances the outcome was a marked resistance to any further attempts at romantic gestures by their male partners. These women now saw romance as associated only transiently with falling in love, when it could be treacherous: 'I was the *usual*, sort of "looking-for-love-and-being-married" '; 'It was, "Am I in love or not, I suppose I must be" '. (In contrast, men seemed more prone to complain that their partners had become less responsive sexually, or that they had been taken to the cleaners by calculating women only interested in security and children.)

Looking back, some women were baffled as to how they had fallen in love with men who had changed so drastically after their early promise – like the story of the frog prince run backwards:

> I feel so stupid now ... but I think we all, well, not all of us, but a lot of us set out with the idea that you, you fall in love with this person and you think you can change them, or you think you can, you think things will be perfect. You think, 'Oh, when we get together, he won't do this, he won't do that'.

> I was really sort of living on my own and finding life a struggle, and this wonderful man came along and listened to all my problems, and brought me bottles of brandy. He was wonderful. *Until* he moved in. And then it, it was like a monster! This monster seemed to come out of the skin of this lovely man ... I mean, for a start, he's got some revolting habits ... things like passing wind and freely doing it ... I can't understand why I fell for it when I did. That's the bit that puzzles me ... I guess it was the ideal, because he was like, honestly, it was like the 'knight in shining armour' job ... this man who, who, you know, with this lovely sort of soft-spoken voice and a nice smile ... I literally fell into his arms ... and everything just said, 'Yes!', you know, 'This is the one' ... I feel *done*! I really do! I feel really *had* over it!

These women now reluctantly associated their partners' romantic gestures with soft-soap, an all-too-predictable substitute for support, an excuse for arriving home late and drunk from the office, or an attempt to patch up a shaky relationship:

> If there was some sort of problem where I was complaining or upset, it was a bunch of flowers, pat on the head, leave her alone, she'll get over it ... (He) used to bring me flowers every Thursday and it meant nothing! Because the flower seller happened to be outside the station on Thursday night!

> He tries very hard to keep the romantic side going ... When we have a row or bust-up, then he'll suddenly think, 'Oh God! I haven't bought her flowers', or 'I haven't done this or that', and then he starts trying again. But it, it goes in cycles. Like he'll try, and then it all wears off, and then we have a row, and then it starts all over again.

> I was shaved ready for an abortion ... (when) he sent this wonderful bouquet of flowers to the hospital, but he wouldn't turn up himself. And I felt totally shattered, and I thought, 'There's no way this is going to work, but if he wants to ...' I think ... part of me died over this abortion thing ... He's not been married to me emotionally. He's a very, very caring man, and he gives the impression that he's a very, very, family committed man ... But when the chips are down, when I really needed him ... not anybody else, just him, he couldn't be there for me ... Now ... I've got a sort of, a brick wall round, well, my sexual feelings ... I can't turn the clock back. Too much, you know ... I love him, but not in love with him. You know, I love him as a friend ...

Yet some men still did not realise what women wanted, and one complained bitterly that his partner now behaved like a member of the 'emotional Gestapo' and wouldn't *allow* him to be romantic when he tried.

However, women's resistance to romance in decayed relationships did not necessarily confer a more general invulnerability, and a number described how their equanimity had been shattered by entering or encountering other, more passionate relationships. Some women had rediscovered desire through affairs: 'I used to think it was me, that I had no feelings left'. The woman who no longer 'felt special' had experienced violent envy when her eldest son (with whom she had become a 'sort of couple') fell very demonstratively in love: 'I wish I had it!' Another woman described how the husband of a newly-remarried friend had rung to say he had some time to spare:

> She said, 'Ooh good, come home!' They were so happy together. That's what started the row. I couldn't imagine either of *us* saying that!

Both these women had been so upset that they had persuaded their partners to accompany them for marital counselling.

In Conclusion

We may begin to answer the question, 'Can men love?', by recognising that in their everyday lives people draw upon the media narratives of romance in heavily gendered ways which are more complicated than our opening discussion indicated. 'Gender' should be seen as a process of constant (re)production where gender 'roles' and identities are sustained or subtly changed through selection, combination and *performance* from culturally-available scripts. And media images encourage females (much more than males) to believe that they exist fully only in a romantic relationship (Giddens, 1992; Rubin, 1991); and women will stage and perform romantic roles ('madonna' or 'whore') for the loved one but also *for themselves*. In contrast, men resist the cultural scripts of romance, which they interpret as sex and romantic deeds rather than feelings (indeed one option is to do 'nothing', to remain remote or brutal and await women's transforming love – Mr Darcy or the frog prince).

Romantic performances may be sustained whilst in love or in short-term relationships like affairs. But the real-life irony – or tragedy – is that with time the performance or appreciation of romantic roles becomes less possible and even distasteful and passion decays: the narrative of romantic intimacy contains the seeds of its own destruction through over-familiarity.

A still greater irony of romance is that, even (or above all?) at what may fell like the most spontaneous and authentic moments in their lives – 'being in love' – people are 'performing' or staging romance. Yet to realise this is not to invalidate their feelings of heightened everyday experience, for 'love' cannot be expressed completely outside the cultural forms of society. The real difficulty is to know whether one is authentically *feeling* the emotions associated with the role of lover: 'Am I acting now? How do I know?' (Hochschild 1983; Cohen and Taylor 1992).[2]

Notes

[1] Our ESRC-funded study (ROOO 23 2737) covered 38 couples in 15 yr-old marriages (Duncombe and Marsden 1993).

[2] Hochschild (1983), and Cohen and Taylor (1992), pose the problem of how to be authentically oneself under the tyranny of discourse. Hochschild describes emotion as 'managed' according to culturally-prescribed 'feeling rules', distinguishing 'shallow' from 'deep' (method) acting, where a person's own (authentic) feelings are displaced.

Bibliography

Cohen, S., and Taylor, L. (1992) *Escape Attempts*, (2nd edn.) London: Routledge.

Duncombe, J. A., and Marsden, D. (1993) 'Love and Intimacy: The Gender Division of Emotion and "Emotion Work" ', *Sociology*, May, 27, No. 2.

Giddens, A. (1992) *The Transformation of Intimacy: Sexuality, Love and Eroticism in Modern Societies*, Cambridge: Polity.

Gill, R. and Walker, R. (1993) 'Heterosexuality, Feminism, Contradiction: On Being Young, White, Heterosexual Feminists in the 1990s', in S. Wilkinson and C. Kitzinger (eds), *Heterosexuality*, London: Sage.

Goodison, L. (1983) in Cartledge, S. and Ryan, J. (eds) *Sex and Love*, London: The Women's Press.

Jackson, S. (1993) 'Even Sociologists Fall in Love', *Sociology*, May, 27, No. 2.

Hochschild, A. R. (1983) *The Managed Heart*, London: University of California Press.

Hollway, W. (1983) in S. Cartledge and J. Ryan (eds) *op cit*.

Mansfield, P. and Collard, J. (1988) *The Beginning of the Rest of Your Life?* London: Macmillan.

Norwood, R. (1985) *Women Who Love Too Much*, Los Angeles: Tarcher.

Radway, J. (1987) *Reading the Romance*, London: Verso.

Rubin, L. B. (1991) *Erotic Wars*, New York: Harper Perennial.

'Snuglet Puglet Loves to Snuggle with Snuglet Piglet': Alter Personalities in Heterosexual Love Relationships

Wendy Langford

What would it mean if it were to be revealed that large numbers of ordinary adults – your boss, your neighbours, your friends – lived secret lives, where they pretended not to be adult humans at all, but bunnies, babies, bears, or little mice? What would it tell us about love relationships if, in the guise of these 'alter personalities', they spent some, much or even all of their domestic lives talking in a coded language of 'baby talk' or 'pig and bear speak'? These questions intrigued me as I flicked through the annual display of Valentine messages in *The Guardian* wondering at the tantalizing glimpse they offered behind the public face of adult love. 14 February 1993 was the day when beside the human adult messages such as 'Celia, my heart is yours. Love Richard', Snuglet Puglet and Snuglet Piglet and hundreds of other cute, furry, and cuddly beings delighted in coming out of the closet and declaring at once publicly, yet anonymously, their feelings for one another.[1]

Notable amongst the sub-genres were 'baby names' which cried out for Freudian interpretation. Perhaps Booby, Booboo, Bigbooboo, Dumplings, Totties, Snuggle Lump, and Snoodle Boodle Bumps are suffering from oral fixation. Maybe Fluffy, Squinky Pinky, Fuzzy, Wriggler, Furry Patch, Widget Bulgy, and Zonker are stuck at the genital stage: while Poo Poo, Blossom Buttocks, Smelly, Whiffy, Bumcheeks and Murk had considerable problems with their potty training.

Being something of an animal lover however, I found myself drawn to attempting an analysis based on the very large number of cuddly and furry creatures that paraded across the pages of the newspaper. The most prevalent species were bears, including Baby Bear, Mrs Bear, Teddy Bear, Snooze Bear, Big Ted, Burglie Bear, Bear Major, Brown Bear, Teddy Edward, and three Poohs. Rabbits were second most common and included Bunnikins, Big Bad Rabbit, Flopsy Bunny, Peter Hopleaf Rabbit, Darlingest Bunny, Bestest Bunny, Bumbly Cuddle Bunny, and two Hunny Bunnies. In joint third place were cats, such as Mr Pussycat, Snugglepuss, Pussycat Princess, Pusskins, Kitten, and Kitty; and pigs including Wriggly Pig, Bulbous Piglet, Truffle Pig, Big Pig, Capability Pig, a vietnamese pot-bellied pig, Hogsy, Porcus, and two Piglets. Rodents, marsupials and dogs also contributed to the menagerie. Having completed a preliminary statistical survey, I set out to undertake some textual analysis in an attempt to understand something of the cultural significance of the 'fluffy bunny phenomenon'.

Of course cynics and sceptics might object that there is nothing more to all of this than a meaningless display of childish sentimentality, nothing more than an annual opportunity for grown up, sensible *Guardian* readers to snigger over breakfast: 'Darling, there's actually a couple here called Hubsy Fluffkin and Noggy Egg Fluffton; I can't believe that people would actually *call* each other things like that'. Well, it seems they do, and moreover, although such terms of endearment may often simply be nicknames, there are indications that for many they are much more than that. Some messages offer glimpses of safe, snug little shared worlds, with their own languages, customs, and special things to eat: 'Pigs are forever, always together, grunts, snorts, porkers'; 'Gridges loves Gruffles, radish to the radish power'; 'Ginger loves Tom very much. Meow, preow, purr'; 'This overweight cuckoo loves her fantastic nest builder'; 'Scamp wants to curl up in Beauty's basket'; 'Fresh Twigs, straw and a new cave. That's what bears like'. On occasion the cosy world is one recognisable to a wider audience: for example 'Mole seeks Toad for love in the Willows'; while the appearance in *The Guardian* of several Poohs and Piglets, as well as a Wol, a Kanga, three Tiggers, an Eeyore and a Heffalump testifies to the particular popularity of Hundred Acre Wood as a site of intimate communion.

Further cultural evidence of the fact that adult love relationships are often conducted through a discourse of cuddly animals can be found, for example, in the thriving card and gift industry. For weddings, birthdays, engagements, anniversaries and St Valentine's day itself, pairs of cooing, snuggling creatures act as bearers of sentiment between couples; their similarity to each other broken only in most cases by the fact that one has long eyelashes and a pink bow stuck on its head, as signifiers of the necessity of sexual difference in romantic love. Love across the species is also well represented, for instance by the Pooh and Piglet sector, where a whole range of cards and memorabilia, offering reconstructions and manipulations of the original children's story, evoke a lasting and meaningful relationship between a rather slow but well meaning bear and an excitable baby pig.

Heterosexual contradictions

Assuming that the majority of those engaging in this reassuring discourse are heterosexual couples, nothing could be in sharper contrast to what recent research tells us about these relationships.[2] Hite's (1987) study, for example, suggested that women most commonly feel lonely, frustrated and disillusioned in heterosexual love relationships, where they continually find themselves giving without reciprocity. Jack (1991) found heterosexual coupledom to be a major cause of depression in women, as in order to maintain relationships with men, they sacrificed their own needs, repressed their resultant anger and ended up losing a sense of self. Kelly (1988) found heterosexual relationships to be a common site of sexual violence towards women. My own current research (Langford, forthcoming) on love relationships confirms these findings, indicating that sexual coercion, humiliation, emotional withholding, overburdening with work, prohibition of conflict, sexual objectification and ridicule are common features of the way men behave towards the women they 'love'. The emotional atmosphere of heterosexual love relationships today is, it seems, often characterised by men who alternate between silent moody anguish and angry outbursts and women who alternate between frustration and despair, hardly the behaviour one would expect from Ollie Owl and Snugglepuss.

A second contradiction is suggested by the striking *asexuality* of the phenomenon. There are many cards, gifts and Valentine messages which bear the saucy statements and innuendo of dominant constructions of sexuality, but these are a contrasting discourse to the untainted innocence of 'Bunnikins I love you snugly in your Warren'. The latter exemplifies a quite different expression of sentiment from anything that could pertain directly to the eroticized relationship of dominance and subordination identified by some feminists as determinate of heterosexuality (MacKinnon, 1989). Furthermore, if in some cases this discourse is extensive, involving personalities, identities that go well beyond the exchange of superficial words of endearment, then it is also in sharp contrast to the public presentation of ourselves as mature, 'rational' adults.

The use of 'alter personalities' is one of many aspects of private lives and domestic space which have, as yet, escaped the attention of social science, seen perhaps as too trivial or mundane to be of academic interest. Yet this fact is in itself indicative for those of us interested in the workings of power in relationships. Feminist investigation has transformed our knowledge of the world through the process of making visible the private, the ordinary, the shameful, the hidden underside of life. Moreover, the invisibility of modern forms of power has been drawn to our attention by theorists such as Foucault, who has urged us to look to the mundane, the peripheral, the hidden areas of life to find the micropolitics which make possible the large dominations (Foucault, 1978: 94). Private worlds are every bit as socially constructed as public ones, constructed indeed to support the public, to make it possible. They contain the dirty laundry behind the ironed shirts, the emotional trauma behind the happy family. Moreover, 'the public' and 'the private' are not self explanatory categories, but ones which we continually reproduce and reconstruct through our daily decisions about what to show to the world, and what to keep hidden.

Viewed in this way, *The Guardian* valentine messages beg important questions about the hidden worlds they signify. Why do so many couples take refuge in these cosy domains? Why, and at what stage in relationships, do 'alter personalities' appear? How do couples use 'alter personalities' within their relationships, and what, if anything, can the interactions of 'alter couples' tell us about gendered power relations? In order to shed light on these questions, I shall analyse three literary representations of the use of alter personalities in heterosexual love relationships, and then two contemporary 'real life' accounts of their use, suggesting possible implications of this brief journey behind the public face of coupledom.

A Doll's House

Alter identities appear in Ibsen's feminist play *A Doll's House*, first published in 1879. The play concerns the middle-class marriage of the patriarchal Torvald Helmer who rules his household with stern supremacy, and his wife Nora who must work at flattering him and subduing herself – being as the title suggests a 'doll' in his house. Throughout the play Torvald refers to Nora in the diminutive – 'my stubborn little miss' (Ibsen, 1981: 43), 'helpless little thing' (57), 'the child' (60). One of the ways Torvald reinforces his authority is by making Nora into a pet – a skylark and a squirrel – and she responds by playing the part. For example in the opening scene, Torvald calls out to Nora as she returns home from Christmas shopping:

> TORVALD. Is that my little sky-lark chirrupping out there?
> NORA. Yes it is.
> TORVALD. Is that my little squirrel frisking about?
> NORA. Yes.
> TORVALD. When did my little squirrel get home?
> NORA. Come on out, Torvald, and see what I've bought. (pp1-2)

There follows a scene where Torvald reprimands Nora for her supposed extravagance at the shops. She is upset.

> TORVALD. There, there! My little singing bird mustn't go drooping her wings, eh? Has it got the sulks that little squirrel of mine? (p 3).

Later we learn that this presentation of Torvald as the benevolent provider and Nora as a scatty spendthrift is a sham. Torvald's worldly success was made possible by a huge loan, taken out illegally by Nora in the name of her dying father, in order to save her husband from ruin. To protect Torvald's pride and honour she lets him believe the money came from an inheritance and repays it through years of scrimping and saving from her housekeeping. Later in the plot however, when all is revealed and Torvald must risk his own honour to save Nora's, he declines to do so, interested only in saving himself. Realising the truth about the marriage, Nora leaves Torvald and their three children, an act so outrageous in its time that Ibsen was at the centre of a storm of public controversy (MacFarlane, 1981: vii–ix).

Within the marriage only Nora acts the parts of a squirrel and a skylark. She is Torvald's pet and he is her keeper, a pretence which makes her marriage bearable, while allowing her husband an affect of paternalism. It leaves her, however, unable to resist. We wonder was there *ever* a time in their marriage when Torvald too was a squirrel, a skylark, or another character. Was there ever any pretence of equality? Or was their unequal stature apparent from the start?

Lappin and Lapinova

A more fully developed 'alter relationship' is the subject of Virginia Woolf's 1938 short story *Lappin and Lapinova*. The story begins with the marriage of Rosalind to the upper middle class Ernest Thorburn. On the honeymoon, Rosalind wonders how she will bridge the obvious distance between herself and her stuffy and formal husband. As Ernest is eating his toast, Rosalind notices that his nose twitches slightly and she begins to warm to him as she imagines he is a rabbit. Ernest catches her looking and she has to explain.

> 'It's because you're like a rabbit, Ernest,' she said. 'Like a wild rabbit,' she added, looking at him. 'A hunting rabbit; a King Rabbit; a rabbit that makes laws for all the other rabbits.'
>
> Ernest had no objection to being that kind of rabbit, and since it amused her to see him twitch his nose – he had never known that his nose twitched – he twitched it on purpose (Woolf, 1989: 261).

Over the course of the honeymoon, Rosalind and Ernest develop a closeness through the creation of alter personalities. He became 'King Lappin', a bold and determined hunting Rabbit of the greatest character, she a shy and wary white hare – Queen Lapinova. On return from the honeymoon, Ernest and Rosalind possess a sophisticated secret world which enables marital intimacy. At dinner parties they look slyly at each other when people talk about rabbits and woods and traps and shooting. Rosalind wonders how she would have survived without this secret world, especially on their mandatory visits to the stiff and starchy Thorburn family.

Over the next two years Lappin and Lapinova happily spend their evenings together roaming in the woods. One day however it all ends.

> 'What do you think happened to me today?' she began as soon as he had settled himself down with his legs stretched to the blaze. 'I was crossing the stream when—'
>
> 'What stream?' Ernest interrupted her.
>
> 'The stream at the bottom, where our wood meets the black wood,' she explained.
>
> Ernest looked completely blank for a moment.
>
> 'What the deuce are you talking about?' he asked.
>
> 'My dear Ernest!' she cried in dismay. 'King Lappin,' she added, dangling her little front paws in the firelight. But his nose did not twitch.

Rosalind cannot sleep and is beset with panic as the realisation of her awful predicament dawns. The next evening, Rosalind tells Ernest that she has lost Lapinova. Ernest smiles grimly. 'Yes' he says. 'Poor Lapinova ... Caught in a trap ... Killed'. He sits down and reads the newspaper. 'So that was the end of that marriage' (p 268). Once again we see a relationship where intimacy is only possible through the discourse of a different world: a cosy, shared world where affection is possible. Once Ernest is secure in his domain however, he has no interest in maintaining the fantasy. Lapinova is killed off. Lappin disappears into the cold world of the Thorburns and Rosalind is trapped in a loveless marriage.

Look Back in Anger

A third account of the use of an alter relationship is found in John Osborne's play *Look Back in Anger* (1957) which is centred on the destructive relationship between Jimmy Porter, the 'angry young man' who is struggling with a crisis of masculine identity, and his wife Alison whom he subjects to misogynistic abuse. Jimmy is tortured by the paradox of his intense sexual desire for Alison, and his fear of being trapped in his relationship with her. The only respite that Alison and Jimmy have from this torturous relationship is escape into a secret world of bears and squirrels. One such episode begins with Jimmy, aware that his cruelty is hurting Alison once again, switches worlds to avoid yet more trauma:

JIMMY. (*Staring at her anxious face*). You're very beautiful. A beautiful, great-eyed squirrel.

She nods brightly, relieved.

Hoarding, nut-munching squirrel. (*She mimes this delightedly.*) With highly polished, gleaming fur, and an ostrich feather of a tail.

ALISON. Wheeeeeeeeee!

JIMMY. How I envy you!

He stands, her arms around his neck.

ALISON. Well, you're a jolly super bear, too. A really sooooooooooooooper, marvellous bear.

JIMMY. Bears and squirrels are marvellous.

ALISON. Marvellous and beautiful.

She jumps up and down excitedly, making little 'paw gestures'.

JIMMY. What the hell's that?

ALISON. That's a dance squirrels do when they're happy.

They embrace again.

Most of the dialogue is not so kindly however, and at the end of the play, having suffered the destruction of Jimmy's rage, Alison is broken. She collapses at Jimmy's feet, and he must face what he has done:

JIMMY. Don't. Please don't ... I can't—

She gasps for her breath against him.

You're all right. You're all right now. Please, I – I ... Not any more...

She relaxes suddenly. He looks down at her, full of fatigue, and says with a kind of mocking, tender irony:

We'll be together in our bear's cave, and our squirrel's drey, and we'll live on honey, and nuts – lots and lots of nuts. And we'll sing songs about ourselves – about warm trees and snug caves, and lying in the sun. And you'll keep those big eyes on my fur, and help me keep my claws in order, because I'm a bit of a soppy, scruffy sort of a bear. And I'll see that you keep that sleek, bushy tail glistening as it should, because you're a very beautiful squirrel, but you're none too bright either, so we've got to be careful. There are cruel steel traps lying about everywhere, just waiting for rather mad, slightly satanic, and very timid little animals. Right?

Alison nods.

(Pathetically). Poor squirrels!

ALISON. (*With the same comic emphasis*). Poor bears! *She laughs a little. Then looks at him very tenderly, and adds very, very softly.* Oh, poor, poor bears!

Slides her arms around him

CURTAIN

With the ultimate irony, Alison and Jimmy are left trapped in the very world they constructed as their escape.

Love, Power and Masculinity

All three stories address questions of power in heterosexual relationships, portraying the vulnerability of the female characters in the face of patriarchal authority, emotional distancing and misogynistic cruelty. All three stories use animal alter egos as part of their investigation of these issues. So what are the links between the representation of alter egos and the operations of patriarchal power?

All three alter relationships confirm the view of a safe and secure place, an unchanging place, a private space, a domestic space, a place which is above all a refuge. But what is it a refuge from? Overwhelmingly it seems, the alter relationship constitutes an escape from, or an attempted resolution of, the contradictions of heterosexual love in patriarchal society – the paradox of the romantic ideal of intimacy within a relationship which is one of structural and psychic inequality. The control enacted through the emotional construction of masculinity as distant, objectifying, ungiving, and emotionally expressive only in terms of aggression and cruelty, is subverted through the creation of alter identities. In the worlds of rabbits and hares, of squirrels and bears, Ernest and Jimmy are allowed to articulate friendship, care, fun and fantasy with their wives, in ways that are closed to them as adult men. Even Torvald, the patriarch, can show a softer side to a frolicking squirrel or a chirruping skylark than to an adult woman; although his particular brand of nineteenth century middle-class masculinity prevents him from going so far as to adopt a persona himself.

The female protagonists are seen to welcome entry into the animal world, where respite from the emotional distance and cruelty which otherwise characterises their marriages can be obtained. The ultimate unviability of giving without reciprocity is mitigated through the adoption of a persona that *can* be petted, and cared for, albeit by a bear or a rabbit rather than a man, thus rendering emotional survival possible. With varying degrees of success, the couple's joint creation of an alter relationship enables friendship, intimacy, mutual comfort, a greater degree of *equality* than is possible in the otherwise bleak emotional landscape of heterosexual coupledom.

Should we therefore celebrate the existence of these secret lives, welcoming them as subversive responses to the contradiction of the intimate power relation? To some extent maybe we should, for fantasy and escape are important coping mechanisms which sometimes enable our psychological and emotional survival. Over-reliance on alter personalities may, however, have a high price to pay, for although they can enable experiences of happiness, friendship, and intimacy, they do so at the risk of considerable denial.

Relationship Narratives

This double-edged character of alter relationships can be illustrated further by the following accounts of lived relationships taken from interviews with Claire regarding her previous relationship with Mark, and Katherine and Patrick regarding their ongoing relationship (all interviewees being self-confessed *Guardian* readers as it happens).

Claire and Mark as Furball and Monster

Claire's and Mark's alter personalities came into being when they were in their mid-twenties. They had already known each other for several years, but had started living together for the first time. Claire's alias, 'Furball', came into existence through some kind of word play on the word gerbil and referred to a kind of rodent-like creature. Mark's alias, 'Monster', was a big, furry, bear-like being. Monster and Furball's world was one of cosy domesticity, and included a 'surrogate family' of various pet animals they had at the time. For five years their whole life together was conducted in the roles of Monster and Furball, to the extent that Claire cannot remember whether they ever called each other by their human names at home. Bedtime was referred to for example as 'going up to the nest'. Looking back on her experience,

Claire now considers that the whole situation resulted from denial and a failure to address the considerable problems in their human relationship. Monster and Furball never argued. Neither did they have a sexual relationship. In retrospect, she sees the instigation of the Monster and Furball alter relationship as a desperate attempt to maintain intimacy at a time when it was disappearing.

Claire describes the human relationship as being one which was characterised by Mark's emotional dependency on her, and feels he used the Monster persona in an attempt to maintain a status quo which he found comfortable. Claire too gained something from the alter relationship, in that its development enabled a companionable, friendly relationship which was in many ways much more comfortable for her than their prior relationship which had been characterised by continual emotional trauma. However, Mark's heavy drinking and Claire's frustration and dissatisfaction could not be wholly compensated for by the Monster and Furball act, and after a particular crisis Claire eventually left him. One way Mark attempted to get Claire back was to write to her in the 'Monster' persona, saying that he realised he had been a 'bad monster', in an attempt to hold on to some sense of intimacy. Claire, however refused to be Furball and replied as Claire. Mark as Mark could do nothing and the relationship was at an end.

Katherine and Patrick as Pooh and Piglet

Katherine and Patrick are in their late thirties and have a current relationship of about eight years standing. Pooh and Piglet came into being within the first few weeks of the relationship. Katherine remembers the exact time when she first thought of Patrick as Pooh. They were at Patrick's parents' house for Sunday lunch. It was the first time she had met them and the association was one of awkward formality which Patrick, who had considerable difficulty in expressing emotion, did little to relieve. Although fond of Patrick, Katherine saw him very much as a 'stuffpot'. After lunch, Katherine was looking through the *Sunday Mail* supplement and was reading the cartoons, when she fancied she saw a likeness between the profiles of Pooh Bear and Patrick which amused her considerably under the stressful circumstances. 'I know who you really are!' she exclaimed, 'you're Pooh!' Over the next few weeks Katherine teased Patrick about being Pooh bear, and his character gradually became established as a sort of amalgam of things about him and his life and those of the character

Pooh. It wasn't long before Patrick named Katherine Piglet. Over the years their personalities have developed and changed and there is a well developed fantasy world with its own codes. The world of Pooh and Piglet is one of fun and play, safety, and security. There are lots of references to honey and acorns and shrunken red tee-shirts. The alter relationship is straightforward and innocent. There is no power, no sex, no emotional traumas or relationship crises in Hundred Acre Wood.

Patrick and Katherine recognise however that this fantasy world is not unproblematic. When asked when and why they adopted the alter personas, some interesting things are revealed. Katherine is aware that she uses the Piglet mode when she wants some care and affection from Patrick, or when she wants to have fun with him. Patrick confirms this, and accepts that expressing affection, and playfulness is something he often finds difficult. Sometimes it's much easier to pretend to be Pooh and say things like 'You're a really cute pig', than to be a grown up man who shows his feelings. One way in which Patrick admits using the Pooh mode is in an attempt to avoid conflict. For example at a time when their relationship was going through a very bad phase, Patrick withdrew from communicating. One way he would avoid confronting the problems was to go to bed early using tiredness as an excuse. Katherine would be angry and frustrated about this, wanting them to talk about the problems. Patrick would say for example 'Pooh's feeling snoozy. He thinks he'll go and warm the bed up', hoping that Katherine would respond as Piglet and not be angry with him. Pooh and Piglet never argue.

A denial of the considerable problems in Patrick and Katherine's relationship was also partly made possible by the pretence that the problems were not down to being a man and a woman, but due to being different species. Pigs and bears after all do not see the world in the same way. The relationship reached crisis point when the Pooh and Piglet game was no longer sufficient to maintain affection and cover up the problems. When it was finally admitted how bad the relationship was, Pooh and Piglet disappeared altogether. Since that time Patrick and Katherine's relationship has improved, but this has involved Pooh and Piglet becoming less important.

Conclusion

These personal accounts of alter relationships confirm the literary evidence that signifiers such as Wobbly Dog and Poochie are, at least in some cases, much more than superficial nicknames. They exemplify the processes of narrativization through which we construct our relational identities, becoming who we are partly through the stories we tell ourselves, and each other, about our relationships. Viewed in this way, the construction of alter identities can be seen as playing a crucial role in the maintenance of current forms of relationship. At the phenomenological level, the use of alter personalities in heterosexual love relationships may be pleasurable and rewarding for those involved, bringing comfort, security, harmony, and a feeling of intimacy. Secret codes and special worlds are reinforced by the exclusion of others. Yet this very secrecy, fortified by the anticipated shame and embarassment of public disclosure serves another purpose: it precludes change. This is, perhaps, the most problematic feature of alter relationships. Harmony, and a kind of non-threatening intimacy, are tempting solace for those frazzled by relationship trauma, but it is in conflict and contradiction that change originates. The escape, as in *Look Back in Anger*, can all too easily become the trap. It is also salutary to remember that, although the rewards of alter relationships are apparently mutual, it was Rosalind who was trapped when King Lappin ceased frolicking in the woods. Furthermore, the psychic division between any sexual relationship the human couple have, and the asexuality of the 'alter world', satisfies the paradoxical *masculine* desire for, and fear of, sexual intimacy. This separation whereby 'woman' can still be objectified as 'woman', while, as squirrel or hare, she can be petted and cared for, may not serve women's interests at all.[3]

The alter relationships I have looked at here clearly serve as an attempted resolution of the paradox of the contemporary liberal ideal of equality in heterosexual love, and the continuing existence of gender inequality in society. In mitigating the contradictions inherent in the idea of an intimate power relationship, they serve to hide the extent to which, at the level of the couple, male power is maintained and reproduced through the practices of emotional distancing and sexual objectification. Without such regulatory mechanisms to defuse conflict and compensate for the distressing effects of gendered power on women, the coupledom so central to the current social order may not be bearable enough to be maintained. Viewed in this way, Fluffy Bunny and Teddy Edward may not be quite so innocent as they appear.

Notes

[1] All pet names and messages are taken from *The Guardian*, 13/14 February 1993.
[2] Although I deal here with how alter personalities might function in heterosexual relationships, it is important to note that their use is by no means confined to that kind of relationship. I am aware of alter relationships involving lesbians and mothers and daughters, and would consider it likely that their analysis might similarly illuminate the particular conflicts and contradictions in those relationships.
[3] Women I have interviewed report distress at male partners' separation of sexuality from emotional intimacy. Examples include men being able to, and wanting women to be able to, 'perform' sexually, regardless of how they were feeling in the relationship generally.

Bibliography

Foucault, M. (1978) *The History of Sexuality: Volume 1*, London: Penguin.
Hite, S. (1987) *The Hite Report on Women and Love: A cultural revolution in progress*, London: Viking.
Ibsen, H. (1981) 'A Doll's House', in *Henrik Ibsen: Four Major Plays*, Oxford: Oxford University Press.
Jack, D.C. (1991) *Silencing the Self: Women and Depression*, Cambridge and London: Harvard University Press.
Kelly, L. (1988) *Surviving Sexual Violence*, Cambridge: Polity Press.
Langford, W. (forthcoming) 'The Power of Love: Domination and Resistance in Heterosexual Love Relationships', Lancaster University: unpublished Ph.D thesis.
MacFarlane, J. (1981) Introduction to *Henrik Ibsen: Four Major Plays*, *op. cit.*
MacKinnon, C. (1989) *Towards a Feminist Theory of the State*, Cambridge and London: Harvard University Press.
Osborne, J. (1957) *Look Back in Anger*, London: Faber and Faber.
Woolf, V. (1991) 'Lappin and Lapinova', in *Virginia Woolf:* 1957 *The Complete Shorter Fiction*, London: Triad Grafton Books.

'I never felt as though I fitted': Family Romances and the Mother-Daughter Relationship

Steph Lawler

> We all return to memories and dreams ... again and again; the story we tell of our own life is reshaped around them. But the point doesn't lie there, back in the past, back in the lost time at which they happened; the only point lies in interpretation. The past is re-used through the agency of social information, and that interpretation of it can only be made with what people know of a social world and their place within it. (Steedman, 1986: 5)

This chapter is concerned with the intersection of gender and class in mother-daughter relationships. It draws on the interviews I conducted with fourteen white women, all mothers of daughters. The chapter focuses specifically on the accounts of six of these women – those who defined themselves as having been born into the working class, and who now see themselves as middle-class. I want to explore these women's expressed sense of not 'fitting' with their birth families, and their desire to replace their mother with another mother.

I am particularly concerned here with the ways in which the women re-use the past 'through the agency of social information': my concern is with the women's *interpretation* of their relationships with their mothers.[1] I also want to draw attention to the absence which hovers on the edge of any account – that is, the absence of other accounts, other interpretations. In particular, I want to indicate the absent interpretation of the mother in the daughter's account. As Adrienne Rich points out, this interpretation would generate a different, if connected, story:

> Whatever I do write, it is my story I am telling, my version of the past. If [my mother] were to tell her own story other landscapes would be revealed. But in my landscape or hers, there would be old, smouldering patches of deep-burning anger. (Rich, 1986a: 221)

This chapter also represents my own account of the women's stories. This account is informed by my interpretation and re-interpretation of my own past as a working-class girl; an interpretation which, at least in part, derives from my present status as a middle-class woman, a status which I experience as both privileged and ambiguous.

Freudian Family Romance

Freud's 1909 essay, 'Family Romances', is an account of the reworking, in fantasy, of origins. In it, Freud describes and analyses the process through which young children come to feel that their parents are not, in fact, their parents; that they are really the children of more noble or more glamorous parents. Freud describes two stages in this fantasy reworking of origins: first, children come to feel that their parents do not love them as much as they would like – that they are not the unique focus of their parents' love. At the same time, they come to know other parents and realise that their own are not unique. At this stage, children, in fantasy, replace their parents with more noble parents – imagining themselves to be adopted, or step-children.

In the second stage, children learn something about the process of reproduction and come to realise, as Freud puts it, that 'pater semper incertus est' (the father is always uncertain) while the mother is 'certissima' (very certain). So at this stage, the child no longer doubts her/his maternal origins. Instead, it is the father – and only the father – who is replaced by another, more exalted, father. At this point, children's fantasies revolve around this replacement of the father – a process which Freud sees as being stronger in boys than in girls, because of the underlying conflict over authority between father and son. At the same time as the father's status is increased in this way, the mother's is diminished, as the child imagines her as conceiving her/him through an adulterous liaison.

Freud's essay is an account of the psychic mechanisms we use to deal with what he sees as the inevitable realisation that our insatiable desire for our parents' love cannot be met. Equally, it is an account of the child's identification with the parent of the same sex. Freud makes it clear that the displacement of the parent is an indication of the overwhelming importance of her/him. However, Freud's emphasis is on the conflict over authority between father and son; as Marianne Hirsch (1989) points out, the mother, for Freud, is ultimately no more than an instrument in the psychic drama played out between these two. The daughter, too, seems to be abandoned in Freud's account as he shifts his emphasis from the (sexually undifferentiated) child to the son, who must work out his Oedipal crisis.[2] Despite these absences, I want to suggest that Freud's analysis is a useful one, and one that is amenable to feminist appropriations.[3]

While I agree with critics of Freud that his theories are problematic for feminism, his account of the processes of family romances is nevertheless useful because it provides us with a way of looking at the *inevitability* of loss. In Freud's account, the parents *cannot* satisfy the child – cannot love her/him as s/he wants to be loved.[4] The *romance* of the Family Romance is the child's attempt to bridge the gap between the fantasied, desired parental love, and the love s/he feels her/himself to receive. I find this useful because it provides us with a different way of looking at the early mother-daughter relationship from that presented in many accounts. As Valerie Walkerdine and Helen Lucey (1989) argue, many of these analyses – both feminist and non-feminist – present this relationship as one in which the daughter *really was* inadequately mothered (Dinnerstein, 1976; Friday, 1979: Eichenbaum and Orbach, 1983). This inadequate mothering is seen as having profound implications for the daughter's adult life. There is frequently a suggestion that if only we had been more loved and more valued, or if only our mothers had allowed us to separate – in other words, if only we'd had better mothers – then we would be more liberated, have fewer hang-ups, be more able to achieve our potential. In this way, women's oppression is sometimes presented as the outcome of poor mothering, or, at least, of a kind of mothering stunted and distorted by patriarchy.

Of course, mothering and the mother-daughter relationship exist within, and are shaped by, patriarchal social arrangements, and these arrangements are certainly pernicious. However, our gender disadvantage cannot simply be reduced to inadequate mothering. Indeed, I would argue that the construction of 'good mothering' which underwrites many analyses – a construction which presents the good mother as one who is wholly available, wholly loving, but never imposing herself and never demanding – can itself be one of the features of our oppression (Chodorow and Contratto, 1982; Phoenix et al, 1991; Walkerdine and Lucey, 1989).

However, I also want to challenge some of the assumptions contained in Freud's original account. Firstly, Freud's lack of attention to the mother seems to be based, at least in part, on his assertion that the mother is 'certissima'. Since the child cannot manipulate her/his maternal origins, the mother is not the object of fantasy in the same way as the father is. However, I would challenge Freud's assertion that the mother *is* 'certissima'. Although the identity of the mother may be certain to those around her at the time she gives birth, for the child, there can be no absolute certainty. Most obviously, this occurs when children are adopted at birth or in early infancy, when they may or may not know of their origins, but there is always room for doubt.[5] Questioning the designation of the mother as 'certissima' has implications for the fantasy life of daughters: if the mother is uncertain, then she can, in fantasy, be replaced.

My second challenge to Freud's account centres on its universalism and reductionism. Carolyn Steedman (1986) argues that the exclusion of which Freud wrote in his original essay is not just the child's exclusion from the parents' love, but also mirrors a broader exclusion – an exclusion from material wealth and status. She suggests that it is no accident that the fantasied parents possess more material resources than the 'real' parents – although Freud himself seems hardly to have noticed this (Steedman, 1986; Chegdzoy, 1992).

Steedman places the child's sense of loss and exclusion within the context of the social and historical circumstances of the child's, and later the adult's, life:

> The first loss, the first exclusion, will be differently interpreted by the adult who used to be the child, according to the social circumstances she finds herself in, and the story she needs to relate. (Steedman, 1986: 111)

She suggests that the sense of exclusion which gives rise to the family romance is likely to be heightened in working-class children, who really are lacking in wealth and other valued resources, and who inhabit a world which is culturally constructed as 'other', as lacking, and as pathological.

I want to argue, then, that a woman's specific social circumstances, both in childhood and in adulthood, and the particular historical moment into which she is born, and in which she lives, will crucially mark out the shape of her psychic formations and, specifically, of her family romance.

Female Family Romances: Longing and Not Belonging

I want to turn now to consider the accounts of those women I spoke to who defined themselves as having been brought up in working-class families and as having moved, by dint of education or marriage to a middle-class man, into the middle classes. I am particularly concerned with the accounts of this group of women because their accounts contain the strongest elements of what I have characterised as a female family romance. That is, these women – and only these women – expressed a sense of not 'fitting' with their birth families, and a wish to replace their mothers, either now or in the past, with other women who displayed characteristics which they valued highly:

> Lynne: I always wanted to be somebody else's child. I thought they'd got mixed up in the nursery. I used to imagine I was some princess. I never felt as though I fitted.
>
> Hazel: I've always said I felt like a cuckoo in my family. Like, 'This isn't my nest! What am I doing here?'
>
> Lynne: But I'm still finding reasons why I'm not her child. I watch her now ... and I can see my mother getting more like her mother, and behaving the way her mother behaved when she got older, in this kind of petulant, demanding manner. And this kind of matriarchal 'do this, do that, do the other' kind of attitude. And I think, I am never, ever going to do that. You know, this is a reason not to be like her, that I do not want to continue this pattern, of how you get to be when you're sixty. I would do anything to avoid it.[6]

Lynne's account, above, illustrates a very common phenomenon in the narratives of this group of women, in that her family romance centres around the figure of the mother in a very specific way. Among all these women, the sense of not 'belonging' was almost always linked with the daughter's dread of becoming the mother. In this sense, then, I think Adrienne Rich's conceptualisation of 'matrophobia' can provide important clues about women's family romances.

Rich (1986a), following Lynn Sukenick, defines matrophobia, not as the fear of one's mother, or of motherhood itself, but as the fear of becoming one's mother. Rich ties in this process with the cultural devaluation of women, suggesting that the mother may come to represent, for the daughter, 'the restrictions and degradations of a female existence'. Rich comments, however, that matrophobia may be accompanied by 'a deep underlying pull toward [the mother], a dread that if one relaxes one's guard one will identify with her completely' (1986a: 235).

Rich, for me, encapsulates in this passage the ambivalence which seems to be characteristic of the mother-daughter relationship, and which I came across time and time again in the course of my research. Almost all the women I spoke to indicated an identification with their mothers, accompanied by an equally strong fear that they would become their mothers. But the women who had changed their class position spoke of this dual identification and dread most forcefully and most consistently. For example:

> Hazel: I'm very like my mother ...... I had an extremely difficult relationship with my mother. ... I had an extremely difficult relationship, and my goal in life for an awful long time was not to be like my mother. And you know there's still – I mean there's bits of me now that see that I'm like her and that's me and that's fine, you know. But there's still parts of me that – I will not be like my mother. You know, I *will not*. Erm, I guess I am very like her. ... I mean I think I've consciously tried to be not my mother in loads of ways.

I want to suggest, then, that women's family romances are intimately bound up with the figure of the mother; that they centre around the issues of the daughter's identification with her mother, and of her resistance to this identification. Indeed, the family romance may be a means of dealing with matrophobia; a way of putting a distance between ourselves and our mothers, and a way of constructing ourselves as women wholly unlike our mothers. If we are not our mother's daughters, then we cannot become them, however much we feel the 'underlying pull' toward them.

However, the cultural devaluation of women which Rich sees as the impetus for matrophobia takes place around a particular configuration of class and 'race', as well as gender. This is not to assume that working-class childhoods are uniform or monolithic, but rather, to argue that to grow up as a working-class girl is to be subject to the knowledge that you are excluded from a range of material and social resources which are highly culturally valued. Furthermore, working-class mothering practices are frequently pathologised within educational, medical and psychological discourses (Steedman, 1985; Walkerdine and Lucey, 1989; Phoenix *et al*, 1991): so to grow up the child of a working-class mother is to be subject to discourses which construct your mother's mothering as 'wrong', as 'inadequate'. Indeed, it could be argued that the pathologisation of working-class existence is crystallized in the body of the mother. For the daughter of the working-class mother, the fear of becoming one's mother may be bound up with a fear of coming to inhabit this position of pathology.

So, for working-class girls who have become middle-class women, matrophobia can take a specific form. We may fear, not just becoming our mothers, but, specifically, becoming our working-class mothers. We may dread re-entering that world which they inhabit and which is constructed as lacking, as 'other'. The family romance can remove us from our mothers, and create a distance between us. By constructing a 'self' which never fitted with our birth families we may feel that we are not part of the world which our mothers inhabit.

However, the accounts of the women who had left their mothers' class position contain many indications that this move, this distancing, is achieved only with pain, and is never achieved completely. They frequently spoke of the painful awareness of some lack in themselves – some lack which was linked with a sense of inhabiting two worlds, and of coming to belong more in the new, middle-class world, but of really belonging in neither. Very often, this lack was experienced as shame. Most of these women spoke with great pain about their own sense of lack and exclusion – less from the mother's or the father's love than from the wealth, the confidence or the knowledge which they saw as residing within, and belonging to, the middle classes. Those women who had been 'educated out of their class' described this process as most marked and most painful at school or university, but some women experienced it still:

> Frances: I noticed it acutely at university. Especially with a subject like French, 'cause the middle-class ones had been abroad and could speak French – well I hadn't and I couldn't. And I equated a facility with languages with intellectual ability, and I was so scared. And I was too scared to leave 'cause I thought I'd have to pay the money back.

> Barbara: I think socially, when you speak to people, they're tapping in to a wealth of knowledge that you haven't got, because they've had more money, more privilege. They've travelled more, maybe. They've done more. And you haven't had that.

As these extracts indicate, the women's portrayal of their sense of lack centres primarily not on money, but on *knowledge*. That is, their sense of being excluded from a middle-class world is a sense of being excluded from particular forms of knowledge. This knowledge is portrayed as the product of a materially privileged life, in which there is enough money to travel, to 'do more', but wealth and knowledge are intimately bound up, as the very phrase, 'a wealth of knowledge' indicates.[7]

The tenuous nature of their hold on knowledge may mean that women who have no history of being middle-class have to constantly construct and reconstruct themselves as the possessors of knowledge. One way of achieving this, I would suggest, is by reaffirming a sense of self which is in contradistinction to that of the (working-class) mother. I was struck by the number of times women described the gulf between their mothers and themselves in terms of their own intelligence, and their mothers' lack of it. I was shocked by this until I remembered the many occasions when I had labelled my own mother as 'stupid' – as just not understanding the knowledge I had learned at grammar school – how exams worked, for instance, or why I had to have exactly the right uniform.[8] 'Cleverness' or 'intelligence', then, may be a metaphor for a form of knowledge which is highly class-specific – for a world of knowledge which the daughter has entered and from which the mother is excluded. Yet the designation of this knowledge as 'intelligence' naturalises it, constructing it as an innate characteristic. In this way, not only does the possession of this kind of knowledge act as a signifier of distinction between daughter and mother; it also marks out that distinction as located within the 'selves' of each of them.

I have suggested that the family romance may be a way for the daughter to remove herself from her mother; a way of dealing with the fear of *becoming* her mother. I have further suggested that the pathologisation of working-class existence and, particularly, of the figure of the working-class mother may make this process especially marked for girls or women who leave their mothers' class position. The question remains, however, if we are not our mothers' daughters, whose daughters are we? A feature of the family romance, I have argued, is the desire to *replace* the mother, and this desire for another mother was expressed by all those women who had changed their class position. This desire is also implicit in some feminist celebrations of the mother-daughter relationship as the model for relations between women. However, it seems to me that both the celebration and the denigration of the mother-daughter relationship obscure the ambivalence of the relationship: both rest on a 'splitting' of its positive and negative features (Klein, 1962, 1963; Sayers, 1984; Benjamin, 1988).[9] The denigration of mothering can become a denigration of mothers; its celebration obscures the rage which the daughter may feel towards her (actual) mother, and displaces her longings for connection onto other women, who are more 'suitable' role models (Davis, 1992).[10] The messy contradictions of the mother-daughter relationship become resolved in mother-blaming, or in an idealisation of 'motherly' behaviour, neither of which offers scope for a radical critique of the material and discursive conditions of mothers' lives.

Moreover, the search for replacement mothers can be the search for the mother of fantasy – for the mother who will love and accept us, and demand nothing in return (Chodorow and Contratto, 1982). Such a conceptualisation of mothering, and of the mother-daughter relationship, dislocates the practice of mothering from the person of 'mother'; it obscures the material conditions of the mother's life and erases the desires of the mother, effacing them in favour of the daughter's desires.

Indeed, there is little discursive space within which women can formulate *both* their desires for connection, for nurture and for acceptance, *and* their rage at their mothers. There is also little discursive space in which mothers can be given a subjectivity;[11] still less within which mothers can voice *their* ambivalence towards their children. Within psychoanalytic accounts, as elsewhere, the mother's subjectivity is literally wiped out in the face of the daughter's desires.[12] We need, then, to acknowledge the daughter's desires, but to acknowledge them as the products of fantasies which themselves arise out of a specific set of social and historical relations.

I want to end by suggesting that we also need a language of desire for the privilege of the middle class. Carolyn Steedman (1986) has argued that there exists no language which can express the desire for material goods and for class privilege as anything other than trivial. What we do have, however, is a language in which to castigate the mother for her failure to help us achieve. It is small wonder, then, when working-class desire is constructed as trivial, as petty, as the 'politics of envy' that working-class girls and women may express their desires as the desire for a different kind of mother.

I would like to express my thanks to the women who participated in the interviews, without whose generosity and commitment this work would not have been possible. Earlier versions of this chapter were given as papers at the *Romance Revisited* conference, the Motherhood, Maturation and Kinship seminar (both at Lancaster University) and at the 1993 Women's History Network conference. I would like to thank participants for their comments. Thanks, too, to Kate Chegdzoy for letting me read extracts from her unpublished Ph.D. thesis, and to Jackie Stacey for her helpful and encouraging comments on earlier drafts of this chapter.

The research on which this chapter is based is supported by E.S.R.C. grant no. R00429024828.

Notes

[1] Although I also spoke to the women about their relationships with their daughters, it is their relationships with their mothers which is the focus of this chapter.

[2] It is worth noting that Freud wrote 'Family Romances' several years before he outlined his revised theory of the psychic development of girls, in which he acknowledged a fundamental asymmetry in the development of male and female children (see Freud, 1924, 1925, 1931, 1933). Before the 1924 essay, Freud was arguing that the girl's development roughly parallels that of the boy.

[3] For interesting feminist analyses of the family romance in literature see Hirsch, 1989 and Chegdzoy, 1992. Both Hirsch and Chegdzoy analyse a female family romance which centres around the figure of the mother. Both,

too, avoid the essentialism of Freud's account by examining the family romance in the light of material conditions.

[4] Freud seems to see the processes of the family romance and the inevitability of this loss as universal. Certainly, in his paper on 'Female Sexuality' (1931) he argues that the daughter's (albeit incomplete) turning from her mother is likely to be a universal psychic phenomenon. I see this loss as inevitable only under certain historical and social conditions. In contemporary and recent Western culture, the figure of the mother is constructed as 'everything' vis à vis her children, and 'failure' is therefore inevitable. See Chodorow and Contratto, 1982; Doane and Hodges, 1992; MacPherson, 1991.

[5] Recent media stories of infants in Britain and the U.S. apparently swapped at birth and sent home from hospital with the 'wrong' parents (see, for example, Reed, 1993) are one indication that the certainty of the mother's identity is not so complete as Freud asserts. The advent of assisted procreation also shifts the meaning of motherhood and undermines the certainty attached to the mother, in ways Freud could not have anticipated (Stanworth, 1987). More intriguingly, and as Marianne Hirsch (1989) comments, Freud seems to have overlooked the peculiar circumstances of Oedipus here.

[6] The names used are pseudonyms. This extract was taken from a group discussion; all other extracts are from interviews at which only myself and one woman were present. In all quotations from interviews, three dots (...) indicate that the text has been edited; six dots (......) indicate a pause.

[7] Bourdieu (1984) analyses this accumulated knowledge as a constituent of 'cultural capital', which Johnson (1993: 7) glosses as: 'a form of knowledge, an internalized code or a cognitive acquisition which equips the social agent with empathy towards, appreciation for or competence in deciphering cultural relations and cultural artefacts'. Cultural capital is accumulated over a lifetime through the agency of the family, formal and informal education, etc. While it is not reducible to economic capital (or wealth), it is, like wealth, unequally distributed between social classes.

[8] Steedman relates a similar sentiment (and, in the case of school uniform, over the same issue) in relation to her father. Her point is that her father, as a working-class man, did not represent authority so clearly nor so totally as the father of Freud's Oedipal account: 'He knew some rules, but he didn't embody them: they were framed by some distant authority outside himself' (1986: 57).

My point here is a somewhat different one; I am arguing that the mother may not *know* the same rules as the daughter because she may, in belonging to a different class, inhabit a different 'social space' (Bourdieu, 1984, 1990). As Bourdieu argues, not all social spaces are equally legitimate; moreover, the social spaces inhabited by the dominant classes are culturally constructed as *inherently* legitimate.

[9] I am aware that, in counterposing the Kleinian model to the Freudian one, I am in danger of imposing another universal on psychic development. Ambivalence, and its resolution through 'splitting', do seem to me to be characteristics of the mother-daughter relationships I studied (including my own). However, I am not suggesting that these characteristics are universal or inherent: I see them as products of social practices and social relations.

[10] The celebration of mothering and the search for mother-figures among other women might itself be seen as a feminist family romance. Hirsch argues that feminist family romances (in literature) centre on connections between women, but that the daughter's, rather than the mother's, perspective remains at centre-stage: 'The woman as *mother* remains in the position of *other*, and the emergence of feminine-daughterly subjectivity rests on the continued and repeated process of *othering* the mother' (1989: 136).

Hirsch also argues that matrophobia may be the underside of this feminist family romance: she suggests that women writers' 'othering' of the mother stems from a fear of becoming her.

[11] Hirsch (1989) suggests that one of the few literary 'spaces' within which mothers are given a subjectivity (and are able to express ambivalence) is within recent texts by African-American women writers (Toni Morrison's *Sula*; Alice Walker's 'One Child of One's Own', for example). Chegdzoy (1992) analyses Angela Carter's *Wise Children* as an example of a literary text in which both the maternal body and maternal subjectivity are reinstated within the family romance.

[12] Object-relations theory, with its emphasis on the mother, is sometimes regarded as a more appropriate basis for feminist theorising (Chodorow, 1978). However, object-relations theory continues the psychoanalytic tradition of focusing on the child; it thus presents us with an account of the child's relation to the mother, rather than the father. The subjectivity of the mother continues to be effaced. The figure of the mother is also highly problematic within object-relations theory. Even 'good enough' mothers (Winnicott, 1965, 1968) seem to exist only in order to be devoted to their children. For feminist critiques of object-relations theory, see Hirsch, 1989; Walkerdine and Lucey, 1989; Barrett, 1992; Doane and Hodges, 1992. For a feminist object-relations approach which acknowledges this problem and aims to position the mother as a subject (rather than as merely the object of children's fantasies), see Benjamin, 1988.

Bibliography

Barrett, Michele (1992) 'Psychoanalysis and Feminism: A British Sociologist's View', *Signs* 17(2) pp 455–466.

Benjamin, Jessica (1988) *The Bonds of Love: Psychoanalysis, Feminism, and the Problem of Domination*, New York: Pantheon.

Bourdieu, Pierre (1984) *Distinction* (trans. Richard Nice), London: Routledge.

Bourdieu, Pierre (1990) 'Social Space and Symbolic Power', in *In Other Words: Essays Towards a Reflexive Sociology* (trans. Matthew Adamson), Cambridge: Polity.

Bourdieu, Pierre (1993) *The Field of Cultural Production: Essays on Art and Literature*, Cambridge: Polity.

Chegdzoy, Kate (1992) 'Family Romances in Angela Carter's *Wise Children*', paper given at Lancaster University's Centre for Women's Studies.

Chodorow, Nancy (1978) *The Reproduction of Mothering: Psychoanalysis and the Sociology of Gender*, Berkeley: University of California Press.

Chodorow, Nancy and Susan Contratto (1982) 'The Fantasy of the Perfect Mother', in B. Thorne and M. Yalom (eds), *Rethinking the Family*, New York: Longman. Reprinted in Chodorow, 1989.

Chodorow, Nancy (1989) *Feminism and Psychoanalytic Theory*, New Haven: Yale University Press.

Davis, Deanna L. (1992) 'Feminist Critics and Literary Mothers: Daughters Reading Elizabeth Gaskell', *Signs* 17(3) pp 507–532.

Dinnerstein, Dorothy (1976) *The Mermaid and the Minotaur: Sexual Arrangements and Human Malaise*, New York: Harper.

Doane, Janice, and Devon Hodges (1992) *From Klein to Kristeva: Psychoanalytic Feminism and the Search for the 'Good Enough' Mother*, Ann Arbor: University of Michigan Press.

Eichenbaum, Louise and Susie Orbach (1983) *Understanding Women: A Feminist Psychoanalytic Approach*, New York: Basic Books.

Freud, Sigmund (1953) *The Standard Edition of the Complete Works of Sigmund Freud (S.E.)* ed. J. Strachey, London: Hogarth Press and the Institute of Psychoanalysis.

Freud, Sigmund (1909) 'Family Romances' *S.E.* 9, pp 235–41.

Freud, Sigmund (1924) 'The Dissolution of the Oedipus Complex', *S.E.* 19, pp 171–79.

Freud, Sigmund (1925) 'Some Psychological Consequences of the Anatomical Distinction Between the Sexes', *S.E.* 19, pp 241–58.

Freud, Sigmund (1931) 'Female Sexuality', *S.E.* 21, pp 221–43.

Freud, Sigmund (1933) 'Femininity', *S.E.* 22, pp 112–35.

Friday, Nancy (1979) *My Mother My Self: The Daughter's Search for Identity*, London: Fontana.
Hirsch, Marianne (1989) *The Mother/Daughter Plot: Narrative, Psychoanalysis, Feminism*, Bloomington: Indiana University Press.
Johnson, Randal (1993) 'Editor's Introduction', in Bourdieu, 1993.
Klein, Melanie (1932) *The Psycho-Analysis of Children*, London: Hogarth Press and the Institute of Psychoanalysis.
Klein, Melanie (1962) *Envy and Gratitude*, London: Tavistock.
Klein, Melanie (1963) *Our Adult World and Other Essays*, London: Heinemann.
Macpherson, Pat (1991) *Reflecting on The Bell Jar*, London: Routledge.
Phoenix, Ann, Anne Woollett and Eva Lloyd (1991) *Motherhood: Meanings, Practices and Ideologies*, London: Sage.
Reed, Christopher (1993) 'U.S. girl "divorces" parents', in *The Guardian*, 19 August.
Rich, Adrienne (1986a) *Of Woman Born: Motherhood as Experience and Institution*, London: Virago.
Rich, Adrienne (1986b) 'Toward a Woman-Centred University', in A. Rich, *On Lies, Secrets and Silence*, London: Virago, pp 125–55.
Sayers, Janet (1984) 'Feminism and Mothering: A Kleinian Perspective', in *Women's Studies International Forum* 7 (4) pp 237–41.
Stanworth, Michelle (1987) 'Reproductive Technologies and the Deconstruction of Motherhood' in M. Stanworth (ed), *Reproductive Technologies: Gender, Motherhood and Medicine*, Cambridge: Polity Press, pp 10–35.
Steedman, Carolyn (1982) *The Tidy House: Little Girls Writing*, London: Virago.
Steedman, Carolyn (1985) ' "The Mother-Made-Conscious": The Historical Development of a Primary School Pedagogy', in *History Workshop Journal* 20, pp 149–163.
Steedman, Carolyn (1986) *Landscape for a Good Woman*, London: Virago.
Walkerdine, Valerie and Helen Lucey (1989) *Democracy in the Kitchen: Regulating Mothers and Socializing Daughters*, London: Virago.
Winnicott, D.W. (1965) *The Family and Individual Development*, London: Tavistock.
Winnicott, D.W. (1968) *The Child, the Family, and the Outside World*, Harmondsworth: Penguin.

'You Meet 'Em and That's It': Working Class Women's Refusal of Romance Between the Wars in Britain

Judy Giles

Feminist debates in the 1980s confirmed the continuing significance of romance as an important aspect of women's lives. Women, it seemed, would keep buying the myth of romantic love, and no-one more than working-class women who appeared particularly susceptible to its seductions. The early feminist impulse of the 1960s and 70s to wish away romance as 'false consciousness' seemed doomed; instead there was a need to study the ways in which romance functioned in women's lives more carefully, and the result was a considerable re-assessment of romance (of which this book is part) (Modleski, 1982; Snitow *et al*, 1984; Radway, 1984: Fowler, 1991). This chapter contributes to this debate by raising questions about the universal application of such claims, and asks whether the trajectory of romantic love is always represented as a significant characteristic of all women's lives? Does the historical moment in which a woman lived, her class and her need to represent herself in different ways at different times, shape her response to, and her understanding of, herself in relation to romance? Are there times when a woman might resist, refuse or deny the pleasures of romance as not serving her best interests? And if so, can such a refusal always be understood as progressive and radical?

To explore these questions I have drawn upon a series of recorded interviews I conducted in 1987 and 1988 in which working-class women who grew up in Britain before the Second World War talked to me about their childhoods, their courtships, their marriages and their children.[1] Recent work on language and subjectivity makes it impossible to read off recorded life stories as simple reflections of an external reality in which common patterns of biography can be identified (Benstock, 1988, Steedman, 1992). Nonetheless, oral testimonies can offer us access to the ways in which women made, and make, sense of their lives, from a nexus of specific social, historical, cultural and psychological factors at play in any one woman's life at any given moment, one feature of which might be her understanding and experience of romance. Feminist historiography needs to focus not only on the public aspects of women's roles in the past but also on the private and the domestic where feminine subjectivities are constructed, sustained and reproduced. In order to do this it is necessary to listen not only to what women say about the past but how they tell it and why they tell it in particular ways: the quest for love and intimacy articulated in the narrative of romance has often been chosen by women as a way of framing their lives.[2]

Historiography and Oral Narratives

Marie-Francoise Chanfrault-Duchet has suggested that the life story produced from an oral dialogue represents 'a meaning system complete unto itself' and as such can be seen as a text and opened to the methods of textual as well as content analysis (Chanfrault-Duchet, 1991: 77). Hence the use of repeated refrains, key phrases and the use of pronouns may express the relationship between speaker, history and her social world. For example in the interviews I recorded the recurrent use of the phrase 'In those days you had to ...' suggested a distancing of self by the speaker from the impositions of her social world and a distancing from the past ('those days') in which such impositions occurred. Equally important was the way in which the narrator positioned herself in her own story. She might present herself as victim, as stoic, or as rebel, as excluded or as belonging. Although all these positions were variously adopted, not one of the women interviewed chose to represent herself as romantic heroine, despite widespread reading and enjoyment of romantic fiction and autobiography.[3] In constructing the stories which made sense of their lives the women also used cultural myths and archetypes, the most powerful of which were the good, nurturing mother and the demonised 'gold-digging whore'. For example the phrase 'she was a bad lot' signified certain sexual behaviours rather than criminal behaviours and its usage was based on a tacit understanding of this. Hence close analysis of the textual details of these women's stories made it possible to understand the self-definitions, imbricated in dominant definitions of class and gender, which the narrator wished to offer within the social event of the interview.

Significantly, the oral history interview was understood by interviewees as a public event rather than the private conversation I had hoped to construct it as. Social markers such as the researcher's professional position and the switching on of the tape recorder signalled that this was a public performance for an unseen audience. As Kristina Minster has observed, the 'objective' interviewer waits expectantly for the interviewee's story which will then be disseminated to a wider readership, often in a more privileged social position than those being researched (Minster, 1991: 28). The working-class women I interviewed, unused themselves to such public performance, but conversant with its conventions via television and the media, were anxious about speaking. 'Will I have enough to tell you?'; 'it won't be very interesting'; and 'you'd do better to ask my husband' were common responses; and I was initially surprised to be met by interviewees who had quite obviously dressed for the occasion, as well as having cleaned the room, and providing tea in the best china. Women have always relied on oralcy as a means of representing ourselves, our romances, our social world and our past, but this has conventionally been in the context of a personal relationship, an intimate conversation or, where written, in the form of letters or diaries. The life stories of the women I interviewed were produced from a social context which, to its working-class participants, signified performance and public speaking, and, as the women felt it, required a *public* image and hence self-censorship. Their stories emphasised prudence and restraint and denied or 'forgot' romance, desire and intimacy. The frequent use of the pronoun 'You' signalled this need to split the self 'I', who might have desired, from the public 'You' who related and existed in a social and communal world. If romance was significant in these women's lives, it had been erased from the self they wished to construct for public consumption. Moreover, as I shall argue, denying romance was not simply a psychological defence against the insistent intrusions of middle-class observers, both then and now, but also materially expedient at a specific historical moment when working-class aspirations were changing.

The Social and Economic Context

Although Britain witnessed massive unemployment and economic slump in areas of industrial stagnation in the period between the wars, certain sectors of the economy expanded and, for those in regular work, wages were rising. This fact, in addition to state provision of working-class housing and an increase in the number of cheap houses for purchase by mortgage, made it possible for an increasing number of working-class families to escape the poverty and deprivation that had characterised the lives of the previous generation. Girls growing up in the early years of this century experienced a widening of their social horizons which had not been available to their mothers. The upheavals of the First World War, the cinema, the dance hall, the raising of the school leaving age to 14, cheap transport and expanding job opportunities provided a welter of experiences and images, presenting a world beyond the family, domestic service and the immediate locality. Yet if girls were no longer willing to enter domestic service they did not display the same reluctance with regard to marriage. They might reject the tyranny of service and the back-breaking drudgery of their mothers' daily lives, but they did so via the material aspirations of marriage and a commitment to domesticity rather than the equal pay/job opportunities route advocated by one strand of inter-war feminism (Banks, 1986; Giles, 1989; Glucksmann, 1990).[4] For this generation of young working-class women marriage offered very real material advantages. The move towards smaller families, the advent of labour-saving technologies and the possibility of a house of one's own rendered attractive the role of full-time housewife: a role further elaborated by the quasi-scientific discourses of 'housewifery' and 'domestic science', and sentimentally celebrated in the coy addresses of women's magazines to 'the little wife in her little home' (*Home Chat*, 1925: August/September).

Discourses of Romance Between the Wars

It is hardly surprising, therefore, that working class girls aspired to the financial and material security of domesticity and that they perceived romance as a 'silliness' liable to jeopardise such aspirations. The anti-heroic, anti-romantic mood of post First World War England with its refusal of sentiment and its retreat into the private worlds of suburban domesticity – 'a nation of gardeners and housewives' – celebrated precisely those attributes so long valued and practised by 'respectable' working-class women – restraint, cheerful stoicism and prudence (Light, 1991: 211). The 'modern' young woman was expected to be robust, sensible and free from the constraints of Victorian 'sentimentality'. Romantic fiction rewarded common-sense, unselfishness and above all cheerfulness – heroines get their men because they have not made 'a fuss'. 'The mysterious, fragile femininity of the 19th century imagination was a historical legacy to be blown away with the cobwebs of Victorian prudery' (Giles, 1993: 244).

The disavowal of sentiment and intensity characteristic of these years relegated its cultural expression to the marginal and much criticised arena of working-class 'glamour' and 'pulp' fiction. *The Oracle, Red Star Weekly, Silver Star* and *Lucky Star* offered stories with titles like 'Scandal Ruined Her Life', 'Branded by Satan'; and 'Three Years of Stolen Love', in which intensity of emotion and sexual desire are roads to ruin and misery, or the prerogative of the villainous 'other' woman (Fowler, 1991: pp 51–71; Jephcott, 1943: 98–111; Melman, 1988: Pt.3). Educationalists and youth workers were anxious about the influence of such fiction on the ideals and behaviour of working-class girls, seeing it as offering them spurious fantasies of romance and adventure outside the parameters of their gender and class. Pearl Jephcott, for example, writes,

> Only very *immature* people or girls whose tastes have begun to be *perverted* could endure the constant repetition of this kind of description: 'Glyn Curtis was the only man who could make her heart throb with longing – the longing to be taken into his arms, to feel his lips upon hers. Not lightly, caressingly as he had kissed her before but –!' (Jephcott, 1943: 110) (my emphasis).

The point I want to make is that in the 1920s and 30s the acceptable response to the longing expressed in romantic fiction was to read these as 'silly', 'perverted' and 'immature', marginal and potentially threatening to the 'real' experiences of a woman's life which consisted of prudential marriage and the provision of a comfortable, hygienic home in which to sustain a male breadwinner and rear healthy children. This dominant discourse offered the women I interviewed an acceptable narrative in which to define themselves in the present, in what appeared to them a performative context, calling for a public account of their lives. Equally, in the past, it may well have provided a self-dignifying and expedient rationalisation for what must have appeared frighteningly dangerous to young women brought up with little knowledge of their bodies. Such cultural ideals offered a space in which working-class women might appropriate dignifying self-definitions which could enable them to achieve certain material aspirations. Yet, of course, the refusal to recognise or present a narrative centred around passion and romance does not mean these did not exist or were not longed for. The stories which follow show both the deployment of an anti-romantic discourse *and* the forms in which those expediently suppressed desires could be articulated both then and now.

Refusing Romance – Women's Stories

> You go to the pictures and you meet 'em and that's it. (Mary MacDonald)

> Neither me nor my sister would ever get married in the war. Didn't want to be widows. (Ivy Brown)

> We just sort of plodded along. We knew we couldn't afford to get married or anything. (Doris Arthurs)

> I was with a friend, we'd been to the pictures and Ted was coming down the road with a friend and we knew him and we stopped and talked to him. And he's been there ever since. (Mary Porter)

In the above accounts there is a deliberate rendering of courtship as a prosaic and pragmatic event: an almost defiant need to challenge the prevailing narratives of romantic fiction by presenting 'boy meets girl' as a singularly unimportant and insignificant life event. The problems of sexual desire or the excitement of romance and passion have been elided or denied in these accounts which focus instead on the importance of presenting the narrator as in complete control of the relationship (Giles, 1992: 252). In the rest of this section I want to examine in detail two narratives and consider how the interpretive framework established above can explain these stories.

Nancy Fellows and Gertie Harris were born in York in 1916 and 1905 respectively. Both women came from large families and faced difficult childhoods characterised by poverty and hard work. Nancy's father died when she was still a young child and her mother eked out a living, taking in lodgers and working casually where she could. Gertie's father was physically violent, was often drunk and rarely earned enough to keep her and her four siblings. Her mother took in washing and Gertie herself undertook a variety of casual jobs for neighbours once she was old enough. Both women worked in the factory at Rowntrees, the chocolate manufacturers, until they married in 1942 and neither returned to work until their children were grown-up. Gertie and Nancy experienced a significantly improved material life from their mothers: both had fewer children, Nancy and Harold bought their own home and Gertie and Bernard rented one of the new council houses on the outskirts of York. The lives of both women were shaped by the historical and social circumstances in which they found themselves, yet the way in which these circumstances were experienced and understood differed. This difference is articulated in their accounts in the ways they positioned themselves with regard to romance and 'reality', private desires and social necessities.

Nancy sees her life as having given her what she calls 'peace of mind'. Her narrative constantly returns to the theme of moral standards – 'doing what was right', 'doing her duty'. Nancy tells her story as that of the exemplary daughter, girlfriend, wife and mother – for example she recounts with pride how she had been headgirl at her elementary school and how in later life she took daily care of her mother until her mother's death. She feels very strongly that moral standards have declined and presents herself as an enduring example of duty incarnate. In telling her story thus she denies romance or pleasure, representing her life as one of endurance and constant disappointment. Yet Harold and Nancy had spent nearly forty years together when I interviewed her and it is unlikely that there have not been *any* moments of romance and intimacy during that time.

Harold and Nancy met when she was 18 and married 8 years later. Their long courtship was made particularly difficult by Harold's illness,

> You see he had a lot of illness and while we were saving up to get married he was off work with his leg and all our savings went ... So we had a hard time then and anyway it was one of them things. They were terrible days really, I mean this day and age it's absolutely marvellous.

As a woman Nancy was dependent on Harold's earning power. Working, as she did, for low pay on a factory conveyor belt her opportunities for social mobility even via marriage were few; furthermore her need for and commitment to 'respectability' rendered any such fantasies ultimately unrealisable. Nancy reveals a strong sense of the role of class in structuring what was possible. She speaks throughout of 'people like us' and recalls that 'others were lucky ... but we never really got off the ground' and 'you have got to be either born into it or you have got to have a bit of luck'. 'Luck' in Nancy's moral scheme had little to do with falling in love and rather more to do with financial security and good health. Pleasure, romance and sexual flirtation were in Nancy's account the prerogative of other classes and implicit in her comment is the recognition that 'goings-on' require a degree of economic stability,

> ... in the upper class there was goings on but the working class, if somebody had to get married it was, you know, thought terrible and you were the talk of the place. I said I wouldn't have brought that on my mother ... and we never did what was wrong before we got married ... we never ever and it was something I was proud of in my lifetime.

The idea of sexual relations as potentially hazardous co-existed with and contradicted the equally powerful belief that heterosexuality was natural and compulsory (Rich, 1983; Jeffreys, 1985: 165–185). The accounts of women, like Nancy, in which prudence and stability are opposed to, and irreconcilable with, romance reveal the importance of those material factors in working-class marriage which the myths of romantic love seek to deny. In the accounts of Nancy and Gertie opposing terms such as self control/lack of control, common sense/silliness, maturity/immaturity are all linked and related to material security. The mature woman is restrained, down-to-earth and sensible: her reward is the material and moral status of 'good' wife and mother (Giles, 1992: 249). This is not to deny romance or sexual desire between Nancy and Harold but to suggest how in the retrospective *public* narrative of Nancy's life there is a need to 'forget' those aspects of their partnership and to foreground those which define her as mature, responsible and respectable. Yet, of course, such denials can never be complete, and throughout Nancy's account there is a barely suppressed resentment at a world which failed to reward her virtue. The nostalgia she frequently expresses for 'the good old days' sits unhappily with her memories of how hard it was and how much she and Harold have endured. The romantic myth of a golden past is striated by the knowledge, which can only be expressed obliquely, that as a working-class woman at a specific moment in time she was ultimately to be excluded from virtue's reward of affluence *and* from the sexual/romantic pleasures which the circumstances of history made more readily available to her daughters,

> I mean it is a terrible day and age that we live in and I am glad I am on this end of life ... they seem to get things on a plate so much to what we did and yet it is not appreciated. I don't think it is.

In contrast, Gertie's story is expressed in terms of rebellion and defiance. She consistently positions herself as struggling against social injustice whether it be in the act of defying her father, her work as a shop steward or in securing social justice and welfare for her three children. Gertie's narrative refuses the romantic refuge of the past: her story articulates a vision of history which believes in the possibility of change and battles against resignation and stoicism, whilst simultaneously being a story of endurance and bravery. Gertie loved dancing and became an expert ballroom dancer, entering county championships. However, her father forbade her to dance and Gertie would slip out when he was asleep to attend the dances she loved. Her willingness to take such risks was motivated by her enjoyment of exercising a skill ('I was the main Charlestoner in York'), the pleasures of potential romance and the glamour of the dance hall,

> I was having a marvellous time and the men after you and you get to dance if you was a good dancer, and I was rather a pretty girl in them days, a lovely figure and everything, a lovely bust, and you could get dance band leaders (to dance with you) and I remember once Victor Sylvester's brother ... and there was Sid Fay, the trumpeter, and Bobby Martin on the drums. You could go out with any of them!

When the Second World War broke out Gertie's regular boyfriend of fifteen years was sent abroad and Gertie continued her dancing, meeting Bernard, ten years younger and, according to Gertie's account, a marvellous dancer, good looking and charming. Within three weeks Gertie had finished her previous relationship and married Bernard. Gertie's parents disapproved of Bernard: they refused to attend the wedding and she was estranged from them for many years. The marriage after the initial romance was not a happy one: Bernard continued to go dancing after the birth of the children and proved to be an unreliable provider. Gertie continues to castigate herself for her 'silliness',

> Well he (the steady boyfriend) would have made a good husband but I somehow didn't want to settle down. I was a fool when I look back, but as long as I could dance it didn't matter, all that mattered was going dancing and being dressed up and folk saying 'you look lovely tonight'. This is all that my life was, it was silly, it was a silly life, it was living in a cloud because you have to come down to earth ... and I did – with a bang ... We stayed together but things didn't ...

Gertie presents her story as exemplifying her lack of caution and control. Whatever pleasure she may have received from her brief transgression is censored out of the consciousness she now presents as her adult (and public) self – it was all 'silliness'.

By the 1930s dancing had become one of the recognised ways, particularly with the decline of churchgoing and church activities, whereby young women might expect to find a husband. Dances could range from the locally organised social to the considerably more expensive functions at the large dance halls which burgeoned after the First World War (Stevenson, 1984: 397–8). Commentators often expressed anxiety at the 'overwhelming passion' for dancing amongst working-class girls, seeing the dance hall as stunting mental development and developing an 'over-stimulated' sexuality.

> There is nothing that is creative here, nothing that puts any responsibility on young people or makes any demands on them as members of society. Thoughts are nowhere directed to anything

> apart from the bodily movements of the moment and the person with whom one is in contact. The syncopated music ..., the lowered lights and the excitement of all the new contacts mean that for many young adolescents, the sex instinct is being over-stimulated at precisely the age when this should be avoided. (Jephcott, 1943: 124, 125)

Certainly, Gertie's story can be read as illustrating the dangers of dance hall romances and she consciously tells it as a cautionary tale against herself. Nevertheless, the dance hall offered a space in which dreams of romance might be entertained whilst allowing women the possibility of controlling the extent to which they involved themselves with men. It was very common for women to partner women, preferring a skilled female partner to an inept male. Moreover, as Gertie recognised, a good dancer could have her pick of partners,

> You could choose who you wanted to dance with, anybody scruffy and you would think 'no'!

Conclusion

Gertie and Nancy's stories should warn us against applying a single understanding of women's relation to romance to all women regardless of social, cultural and historical difference. Both women found themselves inhabiting a historical moment when the discourses of an anti-romantic consciousness, allied to the potential for a better material future, produced a cultural space in which it became expedient for working class women to construct themselves as prudent, realistic and restrained. In doing so they might also contest the subjectivities offered by middle-class observers which interpellated working class women as over-burdened victims, sexual predators or peculiarly susceptible to the seductions of romance. Indeed, it is interesting to speculate how far this charge of romantic susceptibility is a means by which middle-class women have distanced themselves, both then and now, from the irrationality implicit in romance and from those who, it is believed, succumb more easily to such forces. Paradoxically, of course, the role of women in romantic love has conventionally been a bourgeois representation, involving the 'ladylike' behaviours of waiting and passivity. Such behaviours have never been useful for working-class women for whom active choice of a future partner was perhaps even more essential than it was for bourgeois women. The women interviewed refused romance, not because of a lesser sensibility, but because 'being swept off your feet' was a fate too dangerous, however seductive, to even contemplate, for a consciousness formed from poverty and exclusion.

In their recounting of their stories in the present both Nancy and Gertie, as we have seen, were at pains to distance themselves from romance: Nancy in her insistence on duty; Gertie via her condemnation of her younger self. Thus both women were able to represent a self-dignifying, as they saw it, self-definition within the performative context of the life story interview. This is not to suggest that in another, 'private', context Nancy and Gertie would necessarily tell their stories differently, though they might, but rather to make the point that the context in which stories are told is as much a part of the meaning of those stories as the explicit subject matter. We need to understand the ways in which the stories of working-class women are not simply articulations of a one-dimensional and empirical reality but function to express the complex layers of meaning from which selfhood may be produced. For example, the insistence so often articulated amongst the women I interviewed on 'keeping yourself to yourself' cannot be understood simply as signifying a spurious respectability, but may well be a more complex way in which psychological needs and social imperatives were experienced and expressed. Women of all classes have faced difficulties in entering public discourse: for working-class women who have traditionally been the object and rarely the speaking subject of public discourses, concepts of a 'private identity', an inner and private self, privileged around sexuality, have necessarily been felt and articulated differently (Walkowitz, 1992: 1–15, 45–80).

Finally, we should remember that whilst feminists in the 1960s and 70s resisted and denied romance in order to liberate women into more progressive and equal relationships, the women I interviewed refused romance not in order to reform, but essentially to maintain, the status quo. This should remind us that refusing romance may not always be in the service of a progressive sexual politics but may, as here, stem from 'conservative' impulses and imaginings. Any 're-thinking' of romance requires a recognition that it may be understood and experienced differently by different women at different times and in different places. This will involve a questioning of when, how, and why women have not only affirmed and celebrated, but also resisted, romance.

I would like to thank Jackie Stacey, whose comments and suggestions on earlier drafts of this chapter were very productive in stimulating my own thoughts.

Notes

[1] The oral accounts on which this paper is based were collected as part of my unpublished doctoral thesis. There is a fuller account in this of the criteria by which respondents were selected and biographical details of the women interviewed. Briefly, the thesis argues that the improved living conditions of the inter-war period were particularly available to those who committed themselves to the values of 'respectability' and concludes that the price for women may have been to reinforce their commitment to a single sphere – domesticity (Giles, 1989). This chapter also draws on and contributes to my more recent re-thinking about women and domesticity in the period (Giles, 1992, 1993).

[2] In this context it is worth noting Vera Brittain's autobiography, *Testament of Youth: An autobiographical study of the years 1900–1925*, which represents Vera's recovery from the bereavements and psychic traumas of the First World War in terms of a new romantic attachment. The trajectory of the narrative (romantic, private) and the expectations (academic, public) raised by the title suggest a blurring of the distinctions between public and private discourses in Brittain's re-presentation of herself.

[3] Women's magazines of the period often carried 'autobiographical' accounts of 'true life romances'. For example, 'the true story of Janine who has an educated heart' and wins her man by silence and self-denial, *Home Chat*, 5 September 1925.

[4] Out of 64 young women interviewed by The Pilgrim Trust in 1938, 62 said their ambition was to get married, and fantasised, according to the interviewers, about marrying someone wealthy (Pilgrim Trust 1938: 254).

Bibliography

Banks, O.(1986) *Becoming a Feminist: The Social Origins of 'First Wave' Feminism*, Brighton: Wheatsheaf.

Benstock, S. (ed) (1988) *The Private Self: Theory and Practice of Women's Autobiographical Writings*, London: Routledge.

Brittain, V. (1933) *Testament of Youth: An autobiographical study of the years 1900–1925*, London: Gollancz.

Chanfrault-Duchet, M-F. (1991) 'Narrative Structures, Social Models and Symbolic Representation in the Life Story', in S. B. Gluck and D. Patai (eds)

Women's Words: The Feminist Practice of Oral History, New York: Routledge.
Fowler, B. (1991) *The Alienated Reader: Women and Popular Romantic Literature in the Twentieth Century*, London: Harvester Wheatsheaf.
Giles, M. J. (1989) 'Something that bit better. Working class women, domesticity and respectability, 1919–1939', unpublished D.Phil. thesis, University of York.
Giles, J. (1992) 'Playing Hard to Get: Working class women, sexuality and respectability in Britain, 1918–40', *Women's History Review* 1, 2: 239–255.
Giles, J. (1993) 'A Home of One's Own: Women and domesticity in England 1918–1950', *Women's Studies International Forum* 16, 3: 239–253.
Glucksmann, M. (1990) *Women Assemble: Women Workers and the New Industries in Inter-War Britain*, London: Routledge.
Home Chat, (1925), London: Amalgamated Press.
Jeffreys, S. (1985) *The Spinster and Her Enemies: Feminism and Sexuality 1880–1930*, London: Pandora.
Jephcott, P. (1943) *Girls Growing Up*, London: Faber and Faber.
Light, A. (1991) *Forever England. Femininity, Literature and Conservatism Between the Wars*, London: Routledge.
Melman, B. (1988) *Women and the Popular Imagination in the Twenties*, London: Macmillan.
Minster, K. (1991) 'A Feminist Frame for the Oral History Interview', in S. B. Gluck and D. Patai (eds), *Women's Words: The Feminist Practice of Oral History*.
Modleski, T. (1982) *Loving with a Vengeance: Mass-produced fantasies for women*, London: Methuen.
Pilgrim Trust, The (1938) *Men Without Work*, Cambridge: Cambridge University Press.
Radway, J. (1984) *Reading the Romance: Women, Patriarchy and Popular Literature*, London: Verso.
Rich, A. (1983) 'Compulsory Heterosexuality and Lesbian Existence' in E. Abel and E. K. Abel (eds) *The Signs Reader: Women, Gender and Scholarship*, Chicago: University of Chicago Press.
Snitow, A. B., Stansell, C., and Thompson, S. (eds) (1984) *Desire: The Politics of Sexuality*, London: Virago.
Steedman, C. (1992) *Past Tenses: Essays on Writing, Autobiography and History*, London: Rivers Oram.
Stevenson, J. (1984) *British Society 1914–45*, Harmondsworth: Penguin.
Walkowitz, J. (1992) *City of Dreadful Delight: Narratives of Sexual Danger in Late-Victorian London*, London: Virago.

Anti-Romantic Discourse as Resistance: Women's Fiction 1775–1820

Joan Forbes

How do women resist oppressive ideologies? What happens when women are denied outright challenge? How have women resisted the ideologies of romance in such circumstances? These are important questions for feminist theory and literary criticism that are often overlooked in critiques of romance and courtship fiction. In exposing the patriarchal conventions of this fiction, feminist criticism has tended to focus on the ways in which these conventions demand the submission and subordination of women – of both its heroines and authors – to a patriarchal authority. While this kind of critique has been both necessary and influential within feminist literary criticism, it has often led to a marginalisation of women's resistance against patriarchy and patriarchal literary conventions.

In this chapter, I want to consider how women were able to resist the oppressive sway of romance when such resistance could not be made explicit. I have chosen to locate this study at the end of the eighteenth century, a period often hailed as the beginning of the Romantic age, when a new primacy was given within literature and social philosophy to ideas about romance and romantic love. In the literary, philosophical and political discourses of gender relations, at the end of the eighteenth century and since that time, women were firmly and oppressively placed within a romantic paradigm. However, during this period, women were denied outright challenge in social and political struggle. Excluded from the dominant discourses of this period, how were women able to resist the ideologies and scripts of romance? My analysis suggests that women's resistance at this time was often 'hidden' within the cultural arena. Increasing opportunities available to women to write and publish novels provided them with an important social voice and subversive possibilities (see Moers, 1978; Olsen, 1980; Spender, 1986, 1992; Lovell, 1987).

My reading of the courtship fiction of female authors at this time reveals a 'hidden' and oppositional discourse which is covertly woven into the text. This discourse is comprised of several inter-related themes, such as women resisting romance and rejecting romantic love, and I will be exploring these themes in two popular texts, written towards the end of the eighteenth century; *Evelina* (Burney, 1778) and *Emmeline* (Smith, 1788). Such a discourse can be understood as fundamentally anti-romantic, challenging the dominant discourses of romance and the male Romantic aesthetic. In this chapter, the meaning and significance of anti-romantic discourse will be related to an analysis of women's oppression and their resistance of patriarchal ideologies of romance and romantic love. Within this analysis, the normalising ideology of a patriarchal, heterosexual romance is seen as pivotal not only in securing women's subordination, but in influencing possible strategies of resistance.

Much of women's subordination to men can be understood as mediated through ideologies of romance and romantic love. Women are not only oppressed but their oppression is also concealed, rendered 'private' and powerfully normalised through such ideologies. Although disadvantage is pervasive in women's lives, what is less obvious is how this disadvantage is 'hidden' within an almost 'forced' integration with men – as wives, girlfriends, mothers, sisters. Women's subjugation can be seen, therefore, as transacted through this 'enforced' intimacy and integration with men, creating affectional bonds and 'ties that bind' within an institutionalised heterosexuality which, in itself, is not generally viewed as oppressive. Women's compliance within heterosexuality, although very often presented and understood as 'natural', is demanded within femininity and reinforced through coercive ideologies and practices, such as those of romance (Rich, 1989; Cameron, 1990: Bartky, 1990).

This analysis of women's oppression has important implications for conceptualising women's resistance and the kind of strategies that are available to women. Affectional bonds and close emotional attachments to men, through which much of women's oppression is transacted, makes polarised opposition to men untenable for many women. Outright challenge as a strategy may be both unattainable and experienced as inappropriate by most women. When denied such an explicitly oppositional position, women's resistance will consist of more 'hidden' strategies of subversion and tactical manoeuvring. This also relates to women's position within a patriarchal aesthetics; the 'ties' that bind women are also literary. Denied an oppositional voice, the only available position for women, in life and writing, may be one of subversive resistance from within patriarchy and patriarchal aesthetics, as political position and literary strategy.

Subverting the Conventions

One of the ways in which women developed an anti-romantic discourse was to subvert the literary conventions that were available to them. Samuel Richardson's best-selling novels of the mid-eighteenth century developed the tradition of courtship fiction already established by women writers like Eliza Haywood, and to a great extent, provided the 'template' for women writing later in the century. Women writers, constrained to work within the available conventions, appear to have subverted them in weaving into the text an anti-romantic discourse. This can be illustrated by first looking at the conventions of the courtship novel, developed by Richardson in his popular texts of *Pamela* (1740) and *Clarissa* (1747), before considering how women writers reworked them. Texts like *Pamela* and *Clarissa* helped to establish a romantic paradigm within which women were draped with the model of romance. Within a romantic paradigm, as exemplified in these texts, women occupied a special place in relation to the romantic in which their subjectivity was defined, femininity celebrated, and through which their compliance within an oppressive heterosexuality was achieved.

In *Pamela*, the poor servant heroine provides an 'exemplum' for all women. She not only retains her sexual innocence, virtue and honour, but overcomes all the obstacles and finds 'true love' in the arms of her master. Her virtuous behaviour in response to the social-sexual machinations of Mr B, her master, the oppressor and would-be-seducer, is rewarded with marriage. In this text, female subordination is implicitly announced and celebrated, although now no longer dependent on either male force or command. Mr B promises to blot out the words 'command' and 'obey' from his vocabulary, but female compliance is still ensured by the construction of romantic desire for 'woman'. A 'Pamela' does not require male force, command or even persuasion; she 'wants' to fulfil the subordinate position which romantic desire requires. The language of power and woman's subordination becomes hidden and normalised through the patriarchal romantic dream. Within this romantic dream, women are tied to the 'silken fetters of desire' (Fowler, 1991) and their coercion is achieved through the construction of a gendered and romantic subjectivity.

In *Pamela*, the romantic paradigm is reinforced by the presence of a 'true love' which conquers all. In contrast, such love is absent in the tragic tale of *Clarissa*, where the heroine provides more of a 'warning' than an 'exemplum' for women. Unlike Pamela, Clarissa's test is not for mere mortal women, of sexual innocence, virtue or honour, but is designed by Lovelace's 'plotting genius' to see 'whether she be woman or angel'. More than a woman, but not quite an angel, Clarissa's fate in this world is to become another 'entangled girl' caught in the 'snares' of Lovelace's 'amorous see-saw'. Guilty of taking the 'fatal steps' which place her outside the moral jurisdiction of the patriarchal family, and thus at the mercy of Lovelace, Clarissa experiences the worst that patriarchy metes out to its fallen daughters. In the war of the sexes, the heroine may resist Lovelace's 'imperial will' but she cannot survive in this world. Without true love, there is no future for either a Clarissa or Lovelace. Here, the romantic paradigm is asserted through the *absence* of a 'true love' which can save and redeem the two 'fatally attracted lovers'.

It was literary conventions like these, comprising a textual tyranny for women, that were available to women writers and which they subverted in creating an anti-romantic discourse. Women writers re-inscribed the conventional plot of the vulnerable woman seeking to maintain her moral virtue and sexual innocence during courtship, but in these texts women learn to act and regain control. This can be illustrated if we look at how the conventions are subverted in *Evelina* and *Emmeline*, written thirty years later. In both texts, the narrative follows an orphaned/rejected young woman making her entry into the public world, through the 'trials' of courtship until narrative closure at marriage. They can be read as a form of female Quest, in that both Evelina and Emmeline have to negotiate their way through courtship in a hostile world, where they are transformed into sexual prey and reduced to merchandise within the marriage market. Unlike Pamela or

Clarissa, these heroines are not seduced or raped against their will and there is no ultimate submission or ruin. On the 'discovery' that she is vulnerable to male predatory designs, the heroine secures her social survival by learning to act and protect herself. When the heroine marries, as marry she must, she does not, as did Pamela, marry the man who has romantically harassed her across the pages of the narrative. In these tales it is female resistance and survival that are celebrated, rather than romance or romantic love.

Resisting Romantic Love

If the 'surface' story told by texts like *Evelina* and *Emmeline* is about love and courtship through to marriage, there is a destabilising sub-text in which the heroine struggles not for the right to love or against the obstacles to her love, but struggles against the social and sexual machinations of men. The conditions associated with the orphan status in which we first find the heroines, of poverty, exclusion and marginality, serve to highlight the essential vulnerability of woman. As Mrs Selwyn, a self-declared 'anti-romantic' in *Evelina*, comments, 'Young ladies are ... *nowhere*' (p275). Evelina, herself, is described as sitting 'like a cypher, whom to nobody belonging, by nobody noticed' (p340). There is no social place, recognition or secure positioning for women in this patriarchal world. Evelina and Emmeline have to be constantly on their guard against the sexual and social ploys of men with whom they come into contact. In love or life, there is little collaboration here with men, who are frequently portrayed as acting against the interests of women. As Evelina poignantly records in her letters: 'I cannot but lament to find myself in a world so deceitful, where we must suspect what we see, distrust what we hear, and doubt even what we feel!' (p259). Romantic love for women, in these texts, is given a firm social context within a patriarchal system which renders women vulnerable and demands the necessity of suspicion and alertness. To be young, female and 'alone' is to be open to 'offers', 'rude questions and free compliments' and here, romantic encounters are presented at best as sexual harassment, and at worst, which is more frequently, as sexual and psychic violation. Within the text, romantic love is presented as a dangerous luxury which women can't afford. In fact, the romantic position in these narratives can only be safely occupied by men.

Within these courtship narratives, as in the Female Gothic, the threat to women comes from men, and there is much in *Emmeline*, appropriately sub-titled *Orphan of the Castle*, that is reminiscent of the Female Gothic; men scheme and plot against the heroine, Emmeline, who is virtually imprisoned in the castle, later pursued around the country and eventually abducted. Within this text, however, the man who instigates Emmeline's flight and eventual abduction is not the 'Mad Monk' or 'Evil Count' of the conventional Female Gothic narrative from whom the heroine is eventually rescued by the 'hero'. In *Emmeline*, the heroine is harassed, pursued and abducted by none other than her dashing, adoring and passionate suitor, Lord Delamere. The narrative constantly seeks to remind Emmeline (and the reader) that Delamere conforms to the familiar conventions of the romantic suitor and hero of the romantic narrative. He, too, offers Emmeline the fairy tale dream encoded by romance, whereby the heroine achieves social and economic power through courtship and marriage with the handsome, rich and aristocratic suitor. The heroine's task, within the romantic narrative, has thus been described by one feminist critic as 'working to make the hero fall in love with her' (Cohn, 1988). Within this conventional narrative, Emmeline – poor, orphaned, rejected and homeless – would be only too pleased eventually to accept such an eminent suitor, and would be rewarded by marriage and wealth, following the hero's 'discovery' of her virtue and 'difference' from other women. This romantic convention is underlined by Augusta, Delamere's sister, who dreams 'romantically' that Delamere and Emmeline 'were born for each other' (p78).

Pulling back the surface story in *Emmeline* reveals a sub-textual narrative which breaches the romantic conventions, although on the surface much appears the same. Here, a young, beautiful woman, poor and without means, is wooed passionately by her suitor, Delamere, who appears to have all the conventional characteristics to equip him in his role as romantic suitor and hero. As his father, Lord Montreville, points out to Emmeline, should she agree to marry Delamere:

> You will possess the most unbounded affluence, and a husband who adores you ... an immense fortune [which] is every day increasing. You will be considered by me, and by Lady Montreville, as a daughter of the house of Mowbray. The blemish of your birth will be wiped off and forgotten (p135).

But this is an offer that Emmeline does refuse. She is prepared to resist the romantic possibilities and forego such rewards, in order to preserve her fragile sense of autonomy and self. So that when Emmeline cries, it is not for the rewards that could be hers, but because the romantic binds and constraints, placed upon her against her will, are fundamentally compromising. She rejects Delamere precisely because he *is* the romantic hero and Emmeline experiences romance as coercion.

The problem posed in *Emmeline* is that the 'boyish and romantic' Delamere and his relationship to Emmeline are constructed upon a romantic paradigm which she finds compromising and threatening. In contrast to Emmeline's thoughtful reasoning, Delamere is only too susceptible to romantic ideas and passion, boasting that, since the age of ten, he has been 'dying for some nymph or other' (p33). Such romantic passion for Emmeline causes her considerable difficulties. Frightened by Delamere's romantic sensibility, his overwhelming moods and 'deep' feelings, she is continually forced to 'abandon her little home' and change her existence to escape from his seductive manoeuvres (p77). Emmeline may feel 'pity and regard' for Delamere, but she is not 'in love'. So when Emmeline agrees reluctantly to an engagement with him, it is a short-term strategy to protect herself from any further romantic harassment. In this way, the narrative is driven not by love or a struggle by the hero and heroine against the impediments to their love, but by Emmeline's active resistance and attempts to escape from romantic passion.

Similarly, in *Evelina*, the heroine is confronted with a series of romantic/seductive encounters which are experienced as personal violation and sexual harassment. These encounters are initiated by seducer-rakes who, despite the charms and riches they offer, are presented within the narrative as acting against the interests of the heroine. The passionate, romantic man is dangerous in that he psychically and sexually violates the autonomy of women. In these texts, it is the adoring, passionate suitors or would-be suitors who plot, scheme and sexually intimidate the heroine, the 'enemy' from whom she escapes.

If heroines are denied outright challenge within the available conventions of the courtship novel, both Evelina and Emmeline resist a coercive romance through subversive strategies. The heroine may blush, her eyes may fill with tears, she may become ill (for illness is one of the few strategies available to women to preserve their personal space and autonomy) but it is she who remains in control in contrast to the uncontrolled behaviour of her enamoured and passionate suitor. Emmeline thinks and reasons her way out of predicaments, while Delamere is overcome by his feelings. Unlike Clarissa, Emmeline has made no fatal 'slip' which precipitates her on a path leading to further loss of control and eventual social ruin. When Emmeline flees from and is eventually abducted by Delamere, her abduction would, within the courtship convention, follow an initial 'slip' and signal her ultimate sexual and moral fall, through seduction and ruin. Within this familiar scenario, women are made into victims and rendered out of control over what happens to them. In *Emmeline*, however, this convention is inverted. When this heroine is abducted, she persuades her captor to take her back and to leave her. In this instance, abduction provides an opportunity for Emmeline to develop and exercise skills of control.

In the same way, Emmeline takes on her guardian, Lord Montreville, and the lawyers that have disinherited her by using reason, force of argument and persistence. Emmeline's sensibility may be conventional within feminine decorum, but it does not deprive her of words, reason, and challenge. Montreville, her guardian, is obliged to recognise her intellectual and moral superiority when Emmeline questions his sense of honour. He is 'angry that she should be in the right when he wished to have found something to blame in her conduct', and resentful that 'a little weak girl should pretend to a sense of rectitude and a force of understanding greater than his own' (p134). Here, feminine decorum and moral correctness, together with reason and tenacity, become weapons in Emmeline's armoury of resisting strategies. She may appear 'a little weak girl' but she learns to effectively subvert the plans of those more powerful and regain her rightful position. Evelina, also described as a 'poor, weak, ignorant girl' (p36), could be speaking for Emmeline and her women friends when she asks 'Why do I have to be humbled by a man?' (p267).

Emmeline stands in a triadic relationship of three women, with Mrs Stafford and Lady Adelina, all of whom are resisting or combating the actions of men by whom they have been romantically 'tied'. Mrs Stafford uses all her resources and skills to protect herself and her children against a husband who gambles, drinks, squanders their money and keeps mistresses. Lady Adelina has been abandoned by her husband, seduced by his best friend and has given birth to his child. Adelina struggles to secure her physical and social survival. Both Mrs Stafford and Emmeline, and of course ultimately the female author, court social disapproval and a ruined reputation to support and help the socially outcast Adelina, and provide the means by which she can re-enter society. The relationship between these women characters provides the narrative drive and moral force of the book. By the use of subversive tactics, reasoning, resisting, supporting, and secretly scheming, they are shown to win on their own terms.

Romantic Love Displaced

Within the conventions available to women writers of the courtship novel, the heroine must marry, and certainly in these texts, as in life, living outside of marriage was a choice available to few women. However, anti-romantic discourse within the narrative sub-text has served to problematize romance for women and the conventional narrative closure of marriage based on romantic love. The message conveyed is that within a patriarchal society romance and romantic love further threaten women's fragile autonomy and control. For women, already disadvantaged in a male dominated world, marriage is too important a life decision to be made on the basis of romance. If the lie of romantic possibilities, of a transcendant passion and romantic love, is rejected by the female author for her heroines, what can be constructed within the available narrative conventions as a suitable ending and appropriate reward for the heroine?

Constrained within patriarchal conventions which deny the heroine (and female author) outright challenge and an explicitly oppositional voice, the only available position is one of subversive resistance, from 'within'. Against the rich and complex panoply of seductive suitors/predators presented as the 'enemy', the hero must necessarily be constructed as an exception to this patriarchal 'rule'. Within anti-romantic discourse and outside of the conventional romantic paradigm, the relationship provided for the heroine at narrative closure suggests an alternative model – not so much of romantic or courtly love, but more brotherly protection offering her respect, safety and affection. Here, romantic love is displaced by an alternative wish: for the brother-protector.

In *Emmeline*, for example, the heroine marries Godolphin, 'God-like' and the brother of her closest female friend. In the final chapter of *Emmeline*, in keeping with the conventions of courtship fiction, the heroine is rewarded and has a dream come true. However, within this narrative, Emmeline's dream, of returning to her rightful property and living there in peace with her friends, is certainly unconventional by romantic standards and most consistent with the anti-romantic discourse covertly interwoven into the text. At the end, the reader is not presented with a picture of romantic fulfilment and conjugal union but, for the period in which it was written, a rather unusual household consisting of 'Godolphin, his Emmeline, his sister and her little boy' (p552), later to be joined by a second close female friend, Mrs Stafford.

Similarly, Evelina marries Orville whom she also loves 'as a sister' (p261). As the narrative progresses, this relationship is increasingly described in terms of brother-sister. This is made explicit in an exchange between Orville and Evelina who, after being sexually intimidated and compromised by a drunken Lord Merton, cries out: 'Would to Heaven ... that I, too, had a brother! and then I would not be exposed to such treatment!' (p314). Whereupon, Orville asks for the honour of taking that title, and promises Evelina: 'think of me as if I were indeed your brother, and let me entreat you to accept my best services ... my respect for you ... as your brother I can advise you against my own interest' (p315). This is more than a romantic ploy or communication between coy lovers. The theme of brother/sisterly protection and affection is further elaborated in the narrative as Evelina also discovers and is reunited with her 'real' brother, and Orville's 'real' sister is shown straying from her brother's guidance, at her peril. For women in these texts, access to a 'brother' becomes a prized and cherished means of obtaining respect and affection as well as protection from sexual advances. In many ways, the brother-protector is presented as 'ideal' and rather two dimensional compared to the more 'real', seductive and dangerous male characters, and to some extent, they can be read as the ultimate fiction of the narrative.

Within the conventions of the courtship narrative, this displacement of romantic love by brotherly protection is not achieved without difficulty or contradiction. In *Emmeline*, Godolphin provides the more consistent alternative to the romantic and passionate Delamere, who is rejected by Emmeline and dies a suitably romantic death, brought about by his extreme and uncontrolled passion. However, in *Evelina*, the displacement of romantic by brotherly love is not so consistent or complete and the contradictions contained within the narrative closure on marriage suggest the darker, problematic ending of Jane Austen's novels. The problem here is that Orville is not always able to fulfil his promise of 'disinterested' brotherly affection and protection, and to the extent that he 'lapses' into a more romantic and passionate mode, Evelina is again subjected to jealous doubts and questioning. Particularly in the final volume of the novel, when Evelina and Orville see each other daily under the same roof, the reader experiences a sense of foreboding that this 'brother' will go the way of other male characters in the novel, and prove to be equally encroaching. Towards the end, we watch Evelina struggle not only against the seducer-rakes, Sir Clement and Lord Merton, who would sexually compromise her, but now, on occasion, with Orville, her 'protector', whose suspicions and insinuations are emotionally compromising and threatening.

Earlier in the narrative, Burney cleverly uses the device of a 'misunderstanding' to introduce and sustain the doubt that the hero, Orville, is not fundamentally different from other men. When Evelina reads Sir Clement's seductive and compromising letter, believing it mistakenly to be from Orville, the reader, although allowed into the 'trick', is invited through the epistolary form, to share the conclusion Evelina herself reaches: that Orville, too, is a seducer who will compromise and betray her, and as such, he is like all the others. Not only does this letter awaken Evelina to the possibility that Orville loves her romantically, thus framing Orville's feelings within the dominant romantic-seductive model of the narrative, but it also presents her and the reader with a picture of seemingly relentless seduction, compromise and betrayal by men. Within the literary conventions of the time, this could not be made explicit. Since conventions demand that Evelina will marry, Orville must be later rehabilitated as 'hero' and the seduction and betrayal must be illusory. But through the device of a fiction within a fiction, the reader is confronted with Evelina's experience of the world as insistently hostile to women, of men as sexual predators, and an inconstant and shadowy hero in Orville.

Disrupting the 'Happy Ending'

There are particular tensions created within the narrative when the conventions of the courtship novel demand a happy union between the heroine and romantic hero. Within both the texts that have been discussed here, the narrative energy has been driven by the heroine resisting romance and romantic seductions. It is these tensions created by the convergence of an anti-romantic discourse with courtship conventions that give rise to disjunctions of form, particularly on closure. These textual disruptions, resulting from the contradictions generated by the co-existence of an anti-romantic discourse within a courtship narrative, are most apparent at narrative closure, in the form of an ending which is too 'pat' or inconsistent and underlying doubts or questions which are not fully resolved.

Within the narrative ending, we see, for example, a similar foreshortening effect to that developed later by Austen to such ironic effect. In *Evelina* and *Emmeline*, as in Austen's novels, the narrative ends almost abruptly upon the announcement of the heroine's marriage. Further events, relating for example to the marriage plans and wedding ceremony, are summarised briefly to produce a foreshortening effect in the time scale of the narrative. When the heroine accepts marriage, she marries quickly and the narrative resolutely closes. We do not know, as we do in *Pamela*, for example, what follows after their wedding. Here, Richardson presents the reader with the social trials that Pamela undergoes to be accepted as Mr B's wife, but all doubts threatening a romantic ending are finally dispelled. Mr B's oppressive behaviour is, as in so many contemporary romance fictions, ultimately forgiven and justified in retrospect as true love and passionate desire. If *Evelina* and *Emmeline* are driven by a sub-textual narrative of women's resistance to romance, there is no continuing narrative possible after marriage. The story of woman's resistance and survival within marriage prefigures another narrative.

A 'happy' narrative resolution in these texts, which conforms to the required romantic convention of love and marriage, depends on the construction of an alternative model of love and a hero who is an exception/alternative to the patriarchal norm. The co-existence of contradictory discourses throughout the narrative has rendered a conventional 'happy' romantic ending unlikely. When closure is investigated, the repressed elements of the sub-text are still present in shadowy form as unanswered questions: does a Godolphin 'exist'? Will Orville be 'different'? Within anti-romantic discourse, the doubts and contradictions contained within the ending further problematize romance and romantic love as inimical to woman's interests.

Bibliography

Bartky, S. (1990) *Femininity and Domination – Studies in the Phenomenology of Oppression*, London: Routledge.

Burney, F. (1982) *Evelina*, Oxford: O.U.P. World's Classics.

Cameron, D. (1990) 'Ten Years On: Compulsory Heterosexuality and Lesbian Existence', in *Women, A Cultural Review*, vol. 1, no. 1, April.

Cohn, J. (1988) *Romance and The Erotics of Property*, North Carolina: Duke University Press.

Fowler, B. (1991) *The Alienated Reader*, Hemel Hempstead: Harvester Wheatsheaf.

Lovell, T. (1987) *Consuming Fiction*, London: Verso.

Moers, E. (1978) *Literary Women*, London: The Women's Press.

Olsen, T. (1980) *Silences*, London: Virago.

Rich, A. (1989) 'Compulsory Heterosexuality and Lesbian Existence', in Richardson, L. and Taylor, V. *Feminist Frontiers 11: Rethinking Sex, Gender and Society*, London: Random House.

Richardson, S. (1985) *Pamela: Or, Virtue Rewarded*, Harmondsworth: Penguin Classics.

Richardson, S. (1985) *Clarissa*, Harmondsworth: Penguin Classics.

Smith, C. (1988) *Emmeline – The Orphan of the Castle*, London: Pandora Press.

Spender, D. (1986) *Mothers of the Novel*, London: Pandora Press.

Spender, D. (1992) *Living by the Pen – Early British Women Writers*, New York: Teachers College Press.

Notes on Contributors

Lynne Pearce is a Lecturer in English and Women's Studies at Lancaster University. She is co-author of *Feminist Readings/Feminists Reading* (Harvester Wheatsheaf, 1989) and author of *Woman/Image/Text: Readings in Pre-Raphaelite Art and Literature* (Harvester Wheatsheaf, 1991) and *Reading Dialogics* (Edward Arnold, 1994). She has also published several essays on the 'gendering' of readers which she is now aiming to combine with new work in this area in a book entitled *Feminism and the Politics of Reading* (Edward Arnold, forthcoming). Her work on contemporary women writers and romance is cited in the bibliography to the Introduction.

Jackie Stacey is author of *Star Gazing: Hollywood Cinema and Female Spectatorship* (Routledge, 1994) and co-editor (with Sarah Franklin and Celia Lury) of *Off-Centre: Feminism and Cultural Studies* (Routledge/Harper Collins, 1991) and (with Hilary Hinds and Ann Phoenix) of *Working Out: New Directions for Women's Studies* (Falmer, 1992). She has taught women's studies and film studies in the Department of Sociology since 1988, and in the autumn of 1994 at Lancaster University took up a new appointment in the Centre for the Study of Women and Gender at the University of Warwick.

Inge Blackman has directed a short film for Carlton Television *Ragga Gyal D'bout!* on women who are fans of ragga music. She is currently directing *Work It!* for Carlton Television about people who use their bodies for work. She co-authored with Kathryn Perry 'Skirting the Issue – Lesbian Fashion for the 1990s' for *Feminist Review* 34, *Perverse Politics: Lesbian issue* Spring 1990. Inge has written 'Queer as Fuck! But What the Fuck is Queer?' a critique of queer activism to be included in a collection of lesbian and gay sexuality and visual culture published by Routledge in 1995. She has written a short story 'Me and Verbena, We is Family', published in *Critical Quarterly* Spring 1994.

Helen (charles) likes the shape of her sur-name to be respected. The fact that the 'family' names of many Black people originate in the nomenclature of slave-owners means that naming has not been a matter of free choice for centuries. She is currently based at Sussex University, researching Black, lesbian, and 'white' identities in Britain.

Diana Collecott teaches in the Department of English Studies at Durham University, where she also co-directs the Basil Bunting Poetry Centre. Her courses include Modern Poetry, African-American Literature and 'Love Stories: Plots and Counterplots in Women's Fiction'. Her research interests include writing by British and American women (especially H.D.) and gay and gender studies. She has held several fellowships at Yale University, and contributed essays to such collections as: *Women Reading Women's Writing* (Roe (ed), 1987), *Denise Levertov: Critical Essays* Wagner-Martin (ed), 1990), *Signets: Reading H.D.* (Friedman and DuPlessis (ed) 1990) and *Sexual Sameness: Textual Differences in Lesbian and Gay Writing* (Bristow (ed) 1992).

Jean Duncombe is Senior Research Officer at Essex University on the ESRC-funded project (with Dennis Marsden) on 'The Role of Ideologies of Love in the Social Construction of Coupledom'. She studied sociology at Cardiff, where her undergraduate project was on extra-marital relationships. Subsequently her M.A. at Essex University was on 'Alexandra Kollontai and the crisis of heterosexual feminism'. She has also published work on attitudes to women's work and on YTS.

Joan Forbes is a lecturer in the School of Social Work at the University of Leicester. She is currently working on a study of anti-romantic discourse in women's fiction.

Bridget Fowler is a lecturer in Sociology at the University of Glasgow, with research interests in the area of cultural theory and the sociology of literature. She is author of *The Alienated Reader: Women and Popular Romantic Literature in the Twentieth Century* (Harvester Wheatsheaf, 1991).

Sarah Franklin is a lecturer in anthropology and women's studies at Lancaster University. She is co-author of *Technologies of Procreation: Kinship in the age of assisted conception* (MUP, 1993) and numerous articles addressing the cultural dimensions of new reproductive and genetic technologies.

Judy Giles teaches English and Women's Studies at the University College of Ripon and York St. John in York. She also teaches for the Open University and is currently tutoring a fourth level course in oral history. She has published articles in *Women's History Review* and *Women's Studies International Forum*. Her chapter is part of a wider project on women, identity and 'private' life in the inter-war years to be published next year.

Gabriele Griffin is a Reader in Women's Studies at Nene College, Northampton where she teaches on the MA in Women's Studies and, together with Lesley Holly, runs the newly established Centre for Research in Women's Studies. In 1993 she published *Heavenly Love? Lesbian Images in 20th Century Women's Writing* (Manchester UP). She has also edited *Difference in View: Women and Modernism* (Falmer, 1994) and *Outwrite: Lesbianism and Popular Culture* (Pluto, 1993), and co-edited *Stirring It: Challenges for Feminism* (Falmer, 1994). She is currently working on issues of AIDS and representation, and on gender issues in elder abuse.

Stevi Jackson is lecturer in sociology and women's studies at the University of Strathclyde. She is the author of *Childhood and Sexuality* (Blackwell 1982), co-editor of *Women's Studies: A Reader* (Harvester Wheatsheaf 1993), has written a number of articles on sexuality, romance and marriage, and has just completed a book on Christine Delphy soon to be published by Sage. She is now compiling a reader on domestic consumption in collaboration with Shaun Moores and is co-authoring a collection of essays on women and popular fiction with Pauline Young and Deirdre Beddoe, both to be published by Harvester Wheatsheaf.

Wendy Langford is based in the Sociology Department at Lancaster

University, where she is currently writing her PhD thesis on the subject of power dynamics in heterosexual love relationships. Her previous publications include 'The Sexual Politics of Loving Too Much: Discourses of Popular Advice on Heterosexual Relationships' (1993), Centre for Women's Studies: Lancaster University (occasional paper); and 'The Sociology of Sexual Violence' (1994), in N. Abercrombie and A. Warde, *Studies in British Society* Vol. 1.

Steph Lawler is a postgraduate student in the Department of Sociology, Lancaster University. She is currently completing her Ph.D. thesis, an examination of constructions of the self within the mother-daughter relationship.

Celia Lury is a lecturer in Women's Studies and Cultural Studies in the Sociology Department at Lancaster University. She is co-editor (with Sarah Franklin and Jackie Stacey) of *Off-Centre: Feminism and Cultural Studies* (Routledge/Harper Collins, 1991) and author of *Cultural Rights: Technology, Legality and Personality* (Routledge, 1993).

Dennis Marsden is Professor of Sociology at the University of Essex. He has worked for the Institute of Community Studies where (with Brian Jackson) he wrote *Education and the Working Class*. After research on overspill and labour migration at Salford Royal CAT, he moved to the University of Essex to work with Peter Townsend on *Poverty in the United Kingdom*, which led to the publication of *Mothers Alone*. He has researched and written on comprehensive schools and examinations; the impact of unemployment on family life, published as *Workless*; family violence; the emotional costs for married daughters of caring for their elderly mothers; and (with David Lee *et al*) on YTS, published as *Scheming for Youth*.

Kathryn Perry works for the publisher Zed Books and is co-author with Inge Blackman of 'Skirting the Issue: Lesbian Fashion for the 1990s', in *Feminist Review* 34, *Perverse Politics: Lesbian Issues*, Spring 1990.

Felly Nkweto Simmonds is senior lecturer in Sociology at the University of Northumbria, Newcastle Upon Tyne. She has worked as a development education worker for Oxfam's education department, and as a teacher and freelance Women and Development consultant in Zambia, Tanzania and Sierra Leone. Her previous publications include: 'She's Gotta Have It: The Representation of Black Female Sexuality on Film', in Lovell (ed), *British Feminist Thought* (Basil Blackwell, 1990); 'Difference, Power and Knowledge: Black Women in Academia', in Hinds, Phoenix, and Stacey, (eds), *Working Out: New Directions for Women's Studies* (The Falmer Press, 1992). She is currently doing an MA in Creative Writing at Sheffield Hallam University and has written on her recent experience of breast cancer. She has a daughter and two sons.

Lizzie Thynne is a freelance film-maker and writer. She has worked on several drama and documentary productions including *Out* for Channel Four. She teaches part-time at the University of Northumbria and edited *Studying Film* for the British Film Institute.

Sue Vice is a lecturer in the Department of English Literature at the University of Sheffield. Her edited volume, *Literature and Addiction* (1994), with Matthew Campbell and Tim Armstrong, is published by Sheffield Academic Press.

Rosalynn Voaden is a D. Phil. candidate in the Centre for Medieval Studies and the Department of English at the University of York. Her principal research interests are medieval women visionaries, and the gendered construction of mysticism in the Middle Ages. She is also interested in the literary construction of women in various genres of popular fiction.

Jenny Wolmark teaches Cultural Studies in the School of Art, Architecture and Design at the University of Humberside; she has published articles on science fiction and feminism and is the author of *Aliens and Others: Science fiction, feminism and postmodernism* (Harvester Wheatsheaf 1993).